T0301378

Institutional Case Studies on Necessity Entrepreneurship

Institutional Case Studies on Necessity Entrepreneurship

Edited by

Jeremi Brewer

Co-Founder and CEO of Elevate and Ballard Fellow, Brigham Young University, USA

Stephen W. Gibson

The Academy for Creating Enterprise, USA

Cheltenham, UK • Northampton, MA, USA

Published by
Edward Elgar Publishing Limited
The Lypiatts
15 Lansdown Road
Cheltenham
Glos GL50 2JA
UK

Edward Elgar Publishing, Inc.
William Pratt House
9 Dewey Court
Northampton
Massachusetts 01060
USA

A catalogue record for this book
is available from the British Library

Library of Congress Control Number: 2016931525

This book is available electronically in the **Elgar**online
Business subject collection
DOI 10.4337/9781783472338

ISBN 978 1 78347 232 1 (cased)
ISBN 978 1 78347 233 8 (eBook)

Typeset by Servis Filmsetting Ltd, Stockport, Cheshire
Printed and bound in Great Britain by TJ International Ltd, Padstow

Contents

List of contributors   vii
Foreword by Alejandro Poiré   xiii
Acknowledgements   xvi
Introduction by Jeremi Brewer   xvii

PART I   GOVERNMENT FUNDED PROGRAMS

1. Supporting the transition from unemployment to
    self-employment—a comparative analysis of governmental
    support programs across Europe   3
    Melvin Haas and Peter Vogel

2. From unemployment to self-employment: government
    support programs in Greece   39
    Argyro Nikiforou

3. Pete Suazo Business Center   50
    Gladys Gonzalez, Robert Heyn and Jessica Pino

PART II   PRIVATE/NON-GOVERNMENTAL PROGRAMS

4. Bharatiya Yuva Shakti Trust   57
    Raj K. Shankar

5. Hanhua Guarantee   75
    Lingzhi Zhang and Spencer Brown

6. Prospera: a case for microenterprise among necessity
    entrepreneurs   91
    Macarena Hernández, Gabriela Enrigue and Justin Oldroyd

7. The Academy for Creating Enterprise   104
    Jeremi Brewer and Stephen W. Gibson

PART III   PROMISING HIGH-IMPACT PROGRAMS

8.   Entrepreneurship Finance Lab   121
     Asim Khwaja, Bailey Klinger and Colin Casey

9.   Building a scalable training solution for necessity
     entrepreneurs in the missing middle   144
     Jeff Brownlow

10. SEBRAE: Serviço Brasileiro de Apoio às Micro e Pequenas
     Empresas   160
     Jeff Roberts and Nathalia Myrrha

11. Self-reliance through self-employment: an approach by The
     Church of Jesus Christ of Latter-day Saints   179
     Geoffrey K. Davis and Andrew Maxfield

12. Microfranchising: a solution to necessity entrepreneurship   195
     Philip Webb and Jason Fairbourne

PART IV   THE NEXT STEP

Conclusion   227

Index   231

Contributors

Jeremi Brewer is the Co-Founder and CEO of Elevate Global, a for-profit company that teaches Entrepreneurship and English. Jeremi resides in Asunción, Paraguay with his wife and two daughters. He received his PhD from the HISP Department at Texas A&M University with an emphasis in Culture, Poverty, and Necessity Entrepreneurship. Jeremi conducted his postdoctoral research at Brigham Young University where he led the Micro-Enterprise Education Initiative at the Ballard Center for Economic Self-Reliance in the Marriott School of Management. He previously served as the Executive Director of the Academy for Creating Enterprise, a multinational NGO operating in the Philippines, Mexico, Brazil, and Zimbabwe. He is co-editor of the first volume in this series on necessity entrepreneurship.

Spencer Brown is an undergraduate student at Brigham Young University, majoring in International Relations with a minor in Business Management. He currently serves as a navigator for entrepreneurial student ventures through the Ballard Center for Economic Self-Reliance. Spencer is gaining professional fluency in Mandarin Chinese in preparation for a career in international business, and recently completed an internship with Schouten Global in Beijing, China. He plans to pursue a Masters of Business Administration upon graduation.

Jeff Brownlow received his MBA at Stanford Graduate School of Business, and graduated *cum laude* from Brigham Young University. He worked at Bain & Company, Bain Capital, and Peterson Advisors as an analyst, investor, and a consultant. He also worked in the Treasury Department of the United States Government during the financial crisis. Jeff is married, and is the father of four young sons.

Colin Casey lives in Nairobi, Kenya and manages East Africa operations for EFL Global. He has led engagements with a wide variety of financial institutions to leverage alternative data analytics to expand financial inclusion among micro, small and medium enterprises. Colin has also worked on EFL's business development and R&D efforts in Southeast Asia and Latin America, and worked in microfinance in Cape Town, South Africa prior to joining EFL. Colin graduated at Stanford University with

Interdisciplinary Honors from the Center on Democracy, Development and the Rule of Law. Colin was born and raised in Annapolis, Maryland.

Geoffrey K. Davis is the director of the Perpetual Education Fund, a program of The Church of Jesus Christ of Latter-day Saints whose mission is to educate church members living in poverty, empowering them to become self-reliant and successful. He has served as chairman, board member and CEO of many companies beginning in 1994, including Unitus Equity Fund. Geoff received his bachelor's from Brigham Young University in International Relations and an MPP in Economics from Harvard Kennedy School of Government.

Joseph S. Demple is a dean's list junior at the University of Utah double majoring in Linguistics and English, and currently preparing for graduate school. He was featured in the national award winning short film "Dominus" in 2013.

Gabriela Enrigue is the founder of Prospera, a social enterprise designed to help microentrepreneurs lower supply costs. In 2008, she co-founded CREA, a non-profit organization training women entrepreneurs in Mexico. Gabriela is the investment climate advisor (IFC) to the World Bank Group in Washington, DC. She received her MPA from the Goldman School of Public Policy at UC-Berkeley, where she assisted in the creating of business models at the Base of the Pyramid, Competitive Strategy, Social Entrepreneurship and Supply Chain Optimization.

Jason Fairbourne is CEO at Fairbourne Consulting, a firm specializing on designing business models in developing markets. He is also CEO of Bamba Water, a Kenyan company that provides safe and affordable water using innovative marketing strategies. He received his MSc in Development Management from the London School of Economics and Political Science. Jason served as Director of MicroFranchise Development Initiative and of Business Solutions for Development. Jason spoke at TEDx on "Designing Business Models for the Poor" in 2011.

Stephen W. Gibson is an entrepreneur, author, social-innovator and the Founder of the Academy for Creating Enterprise—a 501(c)3 organization that provides the poor with culture-centered business and entrepreneurial curriculum. He is also the Senior Entrepreneur-in-Residence at Brigham Young University.

Gladys Gonzalez is on the board of directors for The Pete Suazo Business Center in Salt Lake City, Utah, a business educational resource for minority business owners. She is also the co-founder and president of HMC, an advertising firm that focuses on diversity in advertising. Gladys is from

Bogota, Colombia where she worked with multinational corporation BASF Quimica Colombiana. She has received a bachelor's degree in business, minoring in Foreign Trade.

Melvin Haas is doctoral researcher at the Chair of Entrepreneurship and Technology Commercialization (ENTC). He holds a PhD from École Polytechnique Fédérale de Lausanne (EPFL). His thesis "Necessity Entrepreneurship: Individual, Environmental and Public Policy-Related Factors Influencing the Process of Opportunity Exploitation under Unfavorable Circumstances" concentrates on critical research questions dealing with necessity entrepreneurship. Melvin has contributed to several academic conferences, including the Academy of Management (AOM) and the International Council for Small Business (ICSB).

Macarena Hernández received her Bachelors of Science from Instituto Tecnológico de Estudios Superiores de Occidente (ITESO). She is the Managing Director of *Prospera*, a 501(c)3 aimed at fostering development among necessity entrepreneurs in Mexico.

Robert Heyn is currently the CEO of the Academy for Creating Enterprise (ACE). Before working at ACE, Robert served as Director of Education and Mentoring at The Pete Suazo Business Center for eleven years. Robert holds an MBA in Marketing and Finance and a Bachelor's of Science in Information Systems from Brigham Young University.

Asim Khwaja received his PhD in Economics from Harvard where he is currently Associate Professor of Public Policy. As an undergraduate, he studied at MIT, earning Bachelor of Science degrees in Economics and Mathematics with Computer Science. Asim is a Carnegie scholar, and his work can be found in numerous economics journals. Asim leads the Entrepreneurial Finance Lab Research Initiative (EFL), an Evidence for Policy Design (EPoD) research project.

Bailey Klinger is CEO and co-founder of the Entrepreneurial Finance Lab (EFL). The technology used at Bailey's EFL is designed to help lenders assess risk when lending to individuals with little to no credit history. His research centers on providing funding for necessity entrepreneurs, structural formation, and private sector growth in developing countries. Bailey holds an MPA in International Development from the Kennedy School of Government, and earned his PhD in Public Policy at Harvard.

Andrew Maxfield is the Executive Director of the Influence Institute, a private operating foundation that maintains a portfolio of strategic consulting projects focused on alleviating poverty and improving educational outcomes for at-risk youth. He is also the owner-operator of the music and arts publishing company Yalecrest LLC. Andrew graduated as Valedictorian of his 2006 class at Brigham Young University, and received an MBA from The University of Wisconsin-Madison where he was awarded the James J. Weinert Outstanding Graduate Entrepreneurship Student Award.

Nathalia Myrrha is a junior at Brigham Young University, majoring in Economics and minoring in International Development. She works collecting and coding data for WomanStats, the most comprehensive database on women in the world. Besides work and school Nathalia has been involved in projects with the Perpetual Education Fund. These include finding and recommending microfinance institutions in Brazil and Ghana, and helping to create an online library in Portuguese and English with topics in education, employment, and self-employment. After graduation she plans to go to graduate school in Economic Development.

Argyro Nikiforou is currently conducting postdoctoral research at École Polytechnique Fédérale de Lausanne (EPFL). She earned her PhD in Entrepreneurship from Athens University of Economics and Business. Argyro holds an MPhil from the University of Cambridge and an MSc from the London School of Economics and Political Science. The focus of her research is on necessity entrepreneurship, specifically on unemployment and entrepreneurship.

Justin Oldroyd is currently an Associate Consultant at Bain & Company in Dallas, Texas. He also serves as the Executive Director of the Cambodian Job Foundation, a Phnom Penh-based organization focused on fostering economic self-reliance in individuals and families. He graduated *Magna Cum Laude* from Brigham Young University with degrees in Economics, Business Strategy, and International Development.

Jessica Pino is an MPA student at the Marriott School of Management in Brigham Young University minoring in Social Innovation. She currently works as a research assistant developing M&E for non-profit organizations in Paraguay. Jessica is also involved with the Ballard Center for Economic Self-Reliance as an Internship Director for the Y-Prize competition, a contest that encourages students to create a social enterprise to solve distribution challenges in the developing world. After graduation, she plans to work in international development.

Jeff Roberts is passionate about finding innovative solutions to the world's most pressing social issues. Jeff is a Master in Public Administration (MPA) candidate at Brigham Young University (BYU) with a Global Management certificate and minors in Social Innovation and Information Systems. He also works part-time for the Perpetual Education Fund, a global humanitarian organization focused on teaching self-reliance through employment, self-employment, and education. Jeff received a bachelor's degree in Finance with a minor in Nonprofit Management from BYU and is a Certified Nonprofit Professional (CNP). He loves sports, outdoors, traveling, and spending time with his wife and little boy.

Raj K. Shankar is a national award winning entrepreneurship educator, and the author of three books on entrepreneurship. His book *Entrepreneurship: Theory and Practice* is a widely used postgraduate course book in India. Raj has designed and delivered management development programs for CxO level executives. His programs have been hosted by institutions such as UNIDO, STPI, APIN, ISBA, EDI, and NEN. Raj has taught courses on entrepreneurship at IIT Madras, Symbiosis International University, GLIM, VIT, PSG Tech, among others. He is a highly sought after mentor at forums like BYST, supporting aspiring need driven entrepreneurs. Raj is currently a doctoral student at Entrepreneurship Development Institute of India, Ahmedabad. You can read Raj's thoughts on entrepreneurship at: http://rajshankar.wordpress.com.

Peter Vogel is a renowned serial entrepreneur, writer and researcher. He received his PhD from the EPFL (Switzerland) where he investigated government programs that help unemployed transition to self-employment. He is the Head of the Competence Center Technology Ventures at the University of St. Gallen. His organization Peter Vogel Strategy Consulting advises governments and universities on their labor market-, innovation- and entrepreneurship strategies. He is a think tank member of the World Entrepreneurship Forum and a World Economic Forum Global Shaper. He spoke at TEDx, the Global Economic Symposium, and the OECD among others. Find him on www.petervogel.org.

Philip Webb manages an impact investment fund and is the Executive Director of Operation Kids Foundation. He received his bachelor's degree from Brigham Young University and an MPA from The George Washington University, where he studied non-profit management and international development. His experience in the development space spans almost 15 years, from the capital side with a large foundation in Washington DC, to on-the-ground management with start-ups and small enterprises. He is fluent in Spanish and Portuguese and focuses his fund's portfolio on Latin America.

Lingzhi Zhang is a Master of Public Administration student at Brigham Young University. Currently, she is a vice president of SIMBA (Social Impact Masters at BYU Association) in the Ballard Center for Economic Self-Reliance. In 2014, she worked as a research intern for Reason

Foundation in California. She received her bachelor's degree at Hengyang Normal University in China. In 2013, Lingzhi worked as an Energy-Saving Specialist for TCL, one of the largest consumer electronics enterprises in China. Lingzhi recently started her research on Hanhua Guarantee under the mentorship of Dr. Jeremi Brewer.

Foreword

My career in government—as an academic researching democracy and politics, and as a civil servant implementing public policy in Mexico—has granted me certain privileges that few others have experienced. I am cognizant of this privilege and humbled by the assignments I have been asked to lead.

During my tenure as Mexico's Secretary of the Interior, I was aware of the multiple interdependencies that exist between the private and public sectors at the national and international levels. Additionally, in many of the positions I held in the ministry, I was not only charged with the task of engineering and increasing the accountability of policy solutions for national security, but I was also tasked with organizing policies to address many of Mexico's most pervasive and chronic social challenges. These challenges included healthcare, education, corruption and economic development.

My position in government also provided me with the opportunity to meet with Dr. Jeremi Brewer. At the time, Dr. Brewer was conducting his postdoctoral research at Brigham Young University on necessity entrepreneurs from the missing middle around the globe. More specifically, he was searching for programs and institutions that were focused on training microenterprise operators how to start and/or improve their small businesses. Thanks to other social entrepreneurs in Mexico, I also learned about "La Academia"—the non-governmental organization Dr. Brewer had started with Stephen W. Gibson in Mexico City in late 2010. I was immediately interested in helping him with his efforts. I have since been inspired by his efforts as he and his business partner, Jeff Brownlow, have incubated "Elevate Business Academy" (a promising high-impact entrepreneurship and leadership company) at the Graduate School of Business at Stanford University and Brigham Young University. As an academic, social entrepreneur and policymaker, I have high hopes for their program.

Eventually, Dr. Brewer arrived at my office in Mexico City, and we had a chance to spend several hours together discussing his work. I inquired more about the mission and vision of "La Academia" and the "Microenterprise Education Initiative" he had started at BYU. I was pleased to know that my country was benefiting from a social entrepreneur whose heart and mind were properly aligned behind solid scholarly research.

Our conversation centered primarily on the following three questions Dr. Brewer posed, and that were particularly germane to contemporary public policy in Mexico:

1. Why is the process for registering a non-profit/non-governmental entity in Mexico so cumbersome and 'impossible' to navigate?
2. Did I believe in the argument that Mexico was inundated with "necessity entrepreneurs"?
3. Would I be willing to contribute to this book?

The first question merits much more than what I am able to write in this foreword. However, I will mention here that the process for registering social-entrepreneurship ventures, not-for-profit ventures, and/or non-governmental ventures in Mexico is indeed cumbersome. In some sense, this derives from the fact that Mexico is still a very statist political system. Its history is less one of citizens organizing together to create a certain form of government, and much more one of elites (foreign and domestic) using the state apparatus to further their individual interests—most of the time limiting access to power and competition for it. Despite the alternation in power that came after the years 1997–2000, Mexico's political elites still believe that it is the State's (with a capital "S") responsibility to regulate social, economic and social life—that the State embodies some kind of common and superior good, and social actors must abide by the rules set forth by those running the polity—from government and Congress. And as much as in government we tried to change these views, old habits die hard, and registration of not-for-profits remained burdened by this perspective.

My answer to Dr. Brewer's second question was that Mexico was, in fact, inundated with what he has defined as "necessity entrepreneurs." Granted, I was not familiar with the term, but I was familiar with the description. In Mexico, I knew that the majority of small business owners did not have a registered entity, did not pay taxes, had employees without healthcare, and had almost no formal business training. Additionally, the vast majority of Mexicans who started college would not complete their university studies and that only about one in ten would actually find a job in the industry they studied.

This foreword is in a sense an answer to Dr. Brewer's third question. Over time, he and I grew closer, as I have learned more about his work both in Mexico and abroad, and have been inspired by his life story and his many accomplishments. I have founded a social start-up myself, *México*

Crece, and currently contribute to an institution that firmly believes in the power of education to transform oneself.

Thus I am grateful for Brewer's insistence that I can add value to the discourse on necessity entrepreneurship and economic development among the missing middle. And, while I am not familiar with each of the organizations or initiatives covered in this work, I am aware that there remains a significant need to train necessity entrepreneurs around the world. I am convinced that Mexico is not the exception and that hundreds of millions of people around the globe would benefit from receiving business management training in addition to receiving capital through microfinance loans, while they rethink of themselves as masters of their own destiny.

I wish to challenge all of those who will read this book, as well as Volume I of this series, to continue searching for scalable solutions that address some of the greatest social challenges around the world. In his own way, Dr. Brewer has found a niche and will surely be successful at training tens of thousands of people in Mexico (and other nations) each year. From one who has seen the spectrum of social trends, I am thoroughly convinced that by training necessity entrepreneurs how to start and/or grow their small businesses will inevitably lead to bottom-line economic development in each country.

I also urge all of those who read these works to get involved in the work that Dr. Brewer and others are conducting around the world; these are good and inspiring people, with good ideas, and with a solid understanding of how to impact at scale.

In closing, I leave you with this thought: governments will never solve the problems of their countries in isolation, and neither will NGOs or private enterprises. Together, however, our reach will be much greater and the positive impact will be longer lasting. But in order to work together, we must have the courage to take risks and move forward. This is the only way we will ever achieve that which we deeply desire: bottom-line economic development.

Alejandro Poiré, PhD
Dean
Graduate School of Government and Public Policy
Tecnológico de Monterrey

Acknowledgements

This book is the second volume of the two-volume series on the growing literature regarding necessity entrepreneurs and necessity entrepreneurship around the world. Without question, this volume would not have been possible without the patience, support, and collaboration of Joey Demple—who, having never worked in the capacity as a research assistant, has performed his duties with excellence spending countless months working with each collaborator cited in this volume. Mr. Demple—we wish you the best in your pursuit of your PhD and we are forever grateful for your efforts. Thank you.

We also wish to thank Alan Sturmer at Edward Elgar Publishing who has worked tirelessly to help this volume become a reality. Finally, we send our admiration and respect to each contributor of this volume for the time spent on preparing meaningful content that will surely shape the discourse of economic development throughout the world—your programs and initiatives featured in this volume are making a significant difference.

Introduction

Jeremi Brewer

This volume features the top programs and initiatives that focus on training necessity entrepreneurs around the world. Several of the programs in this volume (from both the private and public sectors) have been operating for decades, while other programs and initiatives are only a few years old.

This book is dedicated to every single individual who is searching for answers to complex problems. You may be a student of social entrepreneurship, international relations, economics, law, or education; or, you may be a professor, policymaker, entrepreneur, or some type of NGO practitioner. Whatever your trade and/or focus is, it is my sincere hope that you will find answers, ideas, and hope as you reading through the in-depth overviews of the programs mentioned in this book.

This volume is separated into three main parts. In Part I: Government Funded Programs, you will read through several of the largest government funded programs around the world. In Chapter 1, Melvin Haas and Peter Vogel provide empirical findings regarding how effective Europe has been in helping individuals transition from unemployment to self-employment. In Chapter 2, Argyro Nikiforou—a native of Greece—overviews the government funded programs to help Greek citizens shift from unemployment to self-employment. In Chapter 3, Gladys Gonzalez, Robert Heyn, and Jessica Pino—three Latinos who have successfully immigrated to the United States—discuss the history, mission, and purpose of the Pete Suazo Business Center in Salt Lake City, Utah—a government funded project helping Latinos in the US start and grow small businesses.

Part II is entitled: Private/Non-Governmental Programs. This section centers primarily on private programs that are currently operating and/or directly interacting with necessity entrepreneurs. We begin with Chapter 4, where Raj K. Shankar explains in detail the mission, reach, and vision of the India-based Bharatiya Yuva Shakti Trust—one of India's premier kick-starting entrepreneurship programs dedicated to mentoring necessity entrepreneurs. Chapter 5 is written by BYU graduate student and Chinese-native Lingzhi Zhang, along with her American classmate Spencer Brown, and offers a detailed description of Hanhua Guarantee, a subsidiary of

Hanhua Financial Holding—one of the largest guarantee companies in China which helps microcredit borrowers establish small businesses. In Chapter 6, Macarena Hernández, Gabriela Enrigue and Justin Oldroyd, highlight *Prospera*—a social enterprise working in urban areas throughout Mexico that empowers female-led micro businesses and connects them with citizens/consumers looking to create a more equal and engaged society. In Chapter 7, Jeremi Brewer and Stephen W. Gibson highlight the Academy for Creating Enterprise (ACE), which is modeled after Gibson's Philippines-based program with the same name.

Part III is entitled Promising High-Impact Programs and focuses solely on programs that have high-impact and/or have promise to reach the masses of necessity entrepreneurs around the globe. In Chapter 8, Asim Khwaja, Bailey Klinger, and Colin Casey provide an in-depth review of their Harvard-based Entrepreneurship Finance Lab (EFL)—a program with a mission to tackle the 2.5 trillion dollar financing gap for micro, small and medium enterprises (MSMEs) around the world through their digital psychometric credit assessment tool that evaluates small business owners on key elements of entrepreneurship in a scalable and automated manner. In Chapter 9, Jeff Brownlow, co-founder of and chairman of Elevate Global, provides a detailed account of his interviews with students at the Academy for Creating Enterprise (ACE) in Mexico. These interviews reveal how desperately students at ACE, and other necessity entrepreneurs, are in need of business training. Chapter 10, written by Jeff Roberts and native-Brazilian Nathalia Myrrha, outlines Brazil's long-lasting history of SEBRAE—one of the largest necessity-entrepreneurship-training programs in the world. In Chapter 11, Geoffrey K. Davis and Andrew Maxfield expound on the history and mission of the Perpetual Education Fund and explain the promising future of this worldwide program aimed at training hundreds of thousands of the poorest of the poor around the world. In Chapter 12, social entrepreneur and investor Philip Webb and microfranchising pioneer Jason Fairbourne outline the practical framework and implementation of microfranchising as a promising high-impact solution for training necessity entrepreneurs.

PART I

Government funded programs

1. Supporting the transition from unemployment to self-employment—a comparative analysis of governmental support programs across Europe

Melvin Haas and Peter Vogel

INTRODUCTION

Governments around the world are facing increasing pressure to reduce unemployment. A deficit of 50 million jobs as compared to the situation before the 2008 financial crisis prevails (ILO, 2002). This not only represents a significant amount of unused economic potential but also threatens to undermine the social stability of entire societies through a marginalization of large groups of people from the working population. One mechanism to help reduce unemployment is to support those who want to become self-employed. For this purpose, several active labor market programs (ALMPs) have been developed across Europe, providing support to those seeking to start a business after a period of unemployment. Despite constituting a relatively small portion of national active labor market expenses (1–6 percent of ALMP spending; OECD, 2000), firms established by the previously unemployed make up a large proportion of all new firms as indicated by the 30 percent in Sweden (Statistics Sweden, 1998), and more than 25 percent in France (Désiage, Duhautois, and Redor, 2010). The political and economic importance of these programs has led to an increased scholarly attention over the past years (Benus, 1994; Block and Sandner, 2006; Corral, Isusi, and Stack, 2006; Bosma et al., 2008; Caliendo and Kritikos, 2009; Block and Wagner, 2010) and it is likely that their political importance will further rise due to ongoing labor market instabilities (ILO, 2002).

Despite the enhanced awareness of these programs that have been widely adopted in a number of countries across Europe, most prior research has restricted its scope to analyzing only one specific country, rather than engaging in an international comparative study. A few notable, however outdated, exceptions have employed an internal lens to compare alternative policy schemes and share experiences—both positive and negative—across borders (Staber and Bögenhold, 1993; Meager, 1996; OECD, 2000). While some countries have gained considerable knowledge about how to structure their policy initiatives based on experiences from past revisions, other countries have only recently introduced such policy schemes. An international comparative analysis that is able to offer an encompassing yet also detailed an overview of existing self-employment support programs could therefore serve as a basis for policymakers trying to improve existing—and implementing new—support programs.

The purpose of this chapter is to provide an overview and analysis of such policy schemes from several European countries. The selection of countries seeks to reflect the diversity with regards to economic importance, political orientation, history and culture, as well as the variety of program structures that have been implemented. It includes the large economies of France, Germany and Great Britain; their smaller, centrally located neighbors of Austria, Belgium, the Netherlands and Switzerland; the northern, Scandinavian country of Sweden; the eastern European countries of Poland and the Czech Republic; and the southern European countries of Greece and Spain.

Similarities and differences between the programs are investigated in order to contribute to increasing their effectiveness (for example, pointing out suitable policy instruments) and their efficiency (for example, by employing limited public funds with maximum positive impact). The program structure, the eligibility requirements, the different forms of financial support, as well as the availability of nonfinancial business support services are presented. Subsequently, a number of differing policy approaches are identified and analyzed in greater detail. The chapter concludes with a discussion of our findings, including suggestions for policymakers and employment agencies that are responsible for the implementation and operation of such programs.

EVOLUTION OF SELF-EMPLOYMENT SUPPORT PROGRAMS

Over the past three decades, many European countries have established dedicated programs designed to help unemployed individuals transition into self-employment. Research about the nature and processes of firm creation by formerly unemployed individuals has identified two fundamental reasons advocating the implementation of such policy schemes, namely

(1) market failures in the allocation of capital and entrepreneurial talent, and (2) a number of positive economic—and externalities—social resulting from the creation of new businesses (ILO, 2002; Nolan, 2003).

Market failures can be addressed by governmental interventions to improve access to entrepreneurial resources, such as financing and business support services. Formerly unemployed entrepreneurs often lack financial resources to set up and grow their businesses and may be refused bank loans (typically due to their lack of income, because the amounts are too small, or because of missing collateral). For these reasons, formerly unemployed firm founders are experiencing disproportionate difficulties in starting a business. Without self-employment support programs, they are thus more likely to be establishing under-resourced businesses with poor survival chances from the onset (ILO, 2002). Support programs can additionally help mitigate the lack of entrepreneurial skills that concerns some of these people through the provision of different types of business support services and entrepreneurial training.

Positive economic and social effects resulting from the creation of new businesses represent the second reason promoting the implementation of self-employment support schemes. Supporting unemployed people in their transition to self-employment is supposed to relieve the welfare system, promote efficient markets and ultimately lead to economic stability and economic growth (Storey, 1994; Fritsch, 2008). Furthermore, the programs stimulate the labor market as many of the supported firms have been shown to create additional jobs (Parker 1994; Nolan, 2003; Dencker, Gruber, and Shah, 2009a). Even in case the self-employment experience finally proves unsuccessful, prior studies have reported a favorable impact on the chances of becoming re-employed (for example, Kellard and Middleton, 1998; OECD, 2000; Caliendo and Künn, 2011). In contrast to other active labor market programs—such as vocational training or job creation through established companies' schemes—empirical evidence on the efficiency and effectiveness of such policy schemes is still scarce, yet mainly indicates positive results. However, as the majority of prior studies have focused on a single country, including Germany (Caliendo and Künn, 2011; Dencker, Gruber, and Shah, 2009a; Dencker, Gruber, and Shah, 2009b), Poland and Hungary (O'Leary, 1999), Romania (Rodríguez-Planas, 2008), Spain (Cueto and Mato, 2006), Sweden (Carling and Gustafson, 1999), and the United Kingdom (UK) (Meager, Bates, and Cowling, 2003), these studies can not be generalized and do not allow for an international comparison.

Policy schemes designed to support formerly unemployed individuals in their transition to self-employment have evolved from fairly simple structures through a number of revisions until their current, more refined state of development. These modifications have typically occurred based on

experiences made within the respective nation, yet international coordination attempts are gaining more importance in parallel with the European
Union integration efforts throughout the last decade. While each country
has its own program development history, three stages of maturity can be
differentiated. These evolutionary stages of development will be detailed
in the following paragraphs in order to provide a better understanding
of the origins of the current generation of public policy support schemes
discussed in this chapter.

Early Policy-development Initiatives

The development of the earliest programs took place as a response to the
increasing rates of unemployment in the 1970s, particularly within the
larger OECD economies. France launched their "Aide au chômeur créant
ou reprenant une enterprise" (Assistance to those starting a business out
of unemployment) program (ACCRE) in 1977, pioneering the concept
of a one-time, lump sum payment as a financial contribution equal to the
respective unemployment benefit allocation of the applicant. Germany's
"Überbrückungsgeld" (bridging allowance) initiative was introduced in
1986 to cover entrepreneurs' subsistence during the start-up phase. At
the time, the self-employment contributions consisted of the respective
unemployment allowance plus an additional social security insurance contribution for the duration of up to six months. Other examples for these
"early-experimenters" include the UK, which introduced their "business
startup scheme" in 1983, and Spain with the "Prestaciones por desempleo
Capitalización" (Unemployment Capitalization Benefit) in 1985. These
early initiatives were all based on a rather simple structure with the main
focus being the financial contribution.

Universal Adoption and Expansion of the Policy

Rising levels of unemployment in the beginning of the 1990s amplified the
pressure on policymakers to identify those ALMPs that had the capability
of reversing this trend. As a result, policies designed to support the creation of new businesses by the unemployed were gaining momentum in a
number of national initiatives during this period (OECD, 1992). Several
smaller countries such as Belgium (program introduced in 1992), the
Netherlands (1996), Austria (1998) and Switzerland (1998) subsequently
adopted the programs that the pioneering countries had created. In
France, the initially devised program was changed by legislators in 1987,
both revoking the originally granted legal right to the contribution and
also requiring a basic economic feasibility assessment from its applicants.

In 1993, Sweden reviewed their previously created policy scheme, removing a major obstacle, suddenly making the program accessible to a wider audience, resulting in a surge of participants shortly after being launched (Carling and Gustafson, 1999). Due to the policy initiative, an evidently large, latent demand for opportunities to become self-employed suddenly became feasible. Subsequent evaluation of the program has been largely positive (Carling and Gustafson, 1999). Similarly, Germany revised their "Bridging Allowance" policy in 1994, which resulted in a considerable increase in the number of new firms created. This policy scheme consequently became established as a promising instrument within the existing national ALMP landscape.[1] The Czech Republic established their self-employment support program as early as 1989, however, it consisted primarily of an indirect backing through a self-employment-friendly tax system. In subsequent years, the initial policy was supplemented by the facilitated access to bank loans. Starting in 2004, additional forms of support including direct financial contributions were introduced using capital provided by the EU Structural Funds (Veverková, 2012). Likewise, Poland (2004) and Greece (2008) have given more political attention to their support schemes to help unemployed people start businesses. During this stage, many countries additionally began administering dedicated programs restricted to certain demographic groups such as for women, younger people and older generations that might otherwise have difficulties re-entering the job market. Additionally, some programs are specifically directed at disadvantaged regions or target only certain subsets of new firms such as social businesses. This stage is thus characterized by an increase in complexity and diversity of the programs.

Continued Refinement and Recent Developments of the Policy Schemes

Resulting from their increased popularity and visibility, several countries went through additional revisions of their policy schemes based not only on their own past experiences, but also shaped by political debates and societal trends. As a result, the policy schemes have sometimes been altered repeatedly. For example, in France, the initially drafted loan was transformed in 2001 into a grant, only to be transformed back to a loan in 2004. Since 2009, an interest-free loan is available in addition to a partial exoneration from a number of social charges such as health insurance and a companionship-program lasting for three years designed to support those in transition to self-employment through the provision of various business support services. In addition to the existing "Überbrückungsgeld" (bridging allowance) program, Germany launched a policy program termed "Existenzgründungszuschuss" (also known as

"Ich-AG," "Me-Corporation") in 2003 in order to better cater to those unemployed for extended periods. The total number of supported founders in the country increased to roughly one million people in the following years (IAB, 2007). Although these two programs were replaced by the "Gründungszuschuss" (start-up grant) in 2006, several studies appraised the scheme's effectiveness (for example, Baumgartner and Caliendo, 2008). Furthermore, the survival—and employment-growth rates of previously unemployed founders have been found to be largely comparable to those of companies created by founders without previous unemployment (Pfeiffer and Reize, 2000), the participant income was found to be significantly higher than that of non-participants, and the support schemes were furthermore regarded as comparatively cost-effective labor market policies (IAB, 2007). The new start-up grant offered an extension of the duration for financial support of up to nine months, but simultaneously increased the eligibility requirements for the proposed business concept. In 2012, budget restrictions rendered the previously practiced, comprehensive evaluation of the proposed business idea unfeasible, altering the nature of support from being a legal entitlement to a merely discretionary offer made to those deemed well-prepared. The self-employment support programs in the UK underwent a number of revisions in the 1990s (Duggan, 1998) indicating only limited effectiveness (Storey, 1994), specifically for formerly unemployed individuals (Metcalf, 1998). Current revisions of the program in the UK are also more targeted towards specific groups, such as the "Start-up Loans" program, launched in 2012, dedicated to promoting youth entrepreneurship.

On the one hand, these examples demonstrate how the current stage of development is characterized by an increased professionalism with regards to the administration and implementation of the public policy programs. Many current reforms are rooted in scientific evaluations and a number of countries have established dedicated labor market research institutions charged with the task of monitoring and controlling the effectiveness and efficiency of the national policies. On the other hand, today's popularity and visibility makes the programs increasingly the subject of political discussions, and as a consequence, policies are sometimes repeatedly altered depending on the current political climate and the country's economic situation.

Over the last decades, international bodies such as the OECD or the European Social Fund have begun to recognize the benefits of—and demands for—these types of policy schemes. As a result, coordination efforts in Europe are shifting away from predominantly domestic initiatives towards trans-national coordination efforts, such as the formation of the "European Employment Strategy" (European Commission, 1997) and the "OECD Employment Outlook" (OECD, 2000). In recent years, governmental agencies responsible for these policy schemes have organized international conferences aiming at facilitating the exchange of best practices among researchers and practitioners. Moreover, the current "Europe 2020 Strategy" contains entrepreneurship as a key policy priority, not just with regards to economic growth and as an instrument for addressing youth unemployment, but also in relation to the creation of employment in general following the global recession (European Commission, 2010).

While the motivation behind these policy schemes and the evolution of the programs has been illustrated in this section, it also has become apparent that the large diversity of approaches cannot be readily analyzed without the prior identification of meaningful dimensions of comparison. The following section thus identifies a list of criteria facilitating a structured comparative analysis of the current programs in Europe. Existing policy differences are subsequently analyzed based on these dimensions, leading to the examination of three contrasting policy approaches of supporting formerly unemployed individuals in becoming self-employed.

OVERVIEW OF CURRENT SELF-EMPLOYMENT SUPPORT PROGRAMS

In order to derive meaningful criteria of differentiation between the respective policy initiatives, an overview of the approaches and objectives of the current generation of policy initiatives in selected European countries is given. Following this overview, the program structure, the eligibility criteria for participation, the provision of financial support and the availability of business support services are discussed in more detail. In order to facilitate the design of policies in this realm, we also provide an overview of the key policy dimensions.

Table 1.1 details the programs currently implemented in Austria, Belgium, the Czech Republic, France, Germany, Greece, the Netherlands, Poland, Spain, Sweden, Switzerland, and the UK. As revealed in the introduction, these countries have been selected in order to reflect the cultural, economic and geographic variety in Europe as well as to show the diversity of existing programs. The policy in each country is described by the program name, the governmental agency responsible for its implementation and the date of the initial program (column 1), the program's objectives as well as the forms of aid that are being offered (column 2), as well as the eligibility criteria, the admission procedure, the presence of a potential fallback-solution and requirements regarding the repayment of funds, if applicable (column 3).

Table 1.1 Self-employment assistance for the unemployed across Europe

Title / Agency / Date of Enactment	Objectives and Forms of Aid	Eligibility / Procedure / Fallback / Return of Funds
Austria Title: Gründerprogramm = Agency: Arbeitsmarktservice (AMS) Initial Enactment: 1998	Objectives: Offering support and advice for founders, providing incentives to unemployed people to create their own company and job, training programs and, under specific conditions, a monetary contribution. Forms of Aid: The support consists of financial aid of up to six months (exceptional extensions) through continued unemployment payments or emergency-state payments (Arbeitslosen- und Notstandshilfegeld), training (accounting, marketing etc.) and financial support (Gründungsbeihilfe) during the first two months after firm creation.	Eligibility and Procedure: Unemployed persons with intentions of starting a company based on an idea that matches their previous professional experience can apply for the program. Once these prerequisites are fulfilled, external advisors assess the business plan, assessing its eligibility for funding. Fallback and Return of Funds: Allocated funds are in the form of subsidies and therefore do not have to be returned. In case the self-employment project is abandoned, the person can return into the unemployment insurance.
Belgium Title: Prêt Lancement Agency: Office National de l'Emploi (ONEM) Initial Enactment: 1992	Objectives: Financing the working capital requirement accompanying the launching of a business or the implementation of the investment project concerned. Forms of Aid: Unemployment insurance can be extended for another six months in order to prepare the administrative tasks necessary for setting up the company prior to generating sales. Eligible persons can also receive favorable starter loans. Professional support from a coaching and mentoring program is	Eligibility and Procedure: Unemployed, jobseekers (more than three months registration with the regional employment office), and beneficiaries of waiting allowances. Assessment criteria include the project's chances of success, the person's business competence and the outlook for repayment capacity. Repayment of the loan takes place in monthly increments starting from the 2nd (optionally 3rd or 4th) year. Fallback and Return of Funds: If the company fails during the first five years (bankruptcy, demise of

Czech Republic
Title: Překlenovací příspěvek
Agency: Ministerstvo práce a sociálních věcí České republiky
Initial Enactment: 1989, significantly expanded in 2004

furthermore offered for a maximum duration of 18 months. In addition, there are special support programs for younger as well as older persons, including special funding and coaching support.

Objectives: The program covers operating costs at the start of self-employment. However, the Czech Republic has a strong focus on re-employment in their active labor market policies and somewhat less on self-employment.

Forms of Aid: The program constitutes a bridging contribution for three months that amounts to the average monthly wage.

the person or extraordinary circumstances), the Participation Fund will not claim the remaining balance of the loan. The person can again register as unemployed if the company closes during the first 15 years.

Eligibility and Procedure: Registered unemployed that have had a previous employment of at least 12 months in the last three years.

Fallback and Return of Funds: There exists only a limited fallback solution, as the general unemployment benefits only last for six months except for older employees. The subsidies do not have to be repaid unless the business survives less than two years. If the training programs provided are abandoned prior to completion, the costs for these need to be repaid.

France
Title: ACCRE / NACRE
Agency: Pôle Emploi
Initial Enactment: 1977

Objectives: To provide support to unemployed and social security claimants in order to set up a business.

Forms of Aid: ACCRE ("Aide au chômeur créant ou reprenant une entreprise" / "Assistance to those starting a business out of unemployment" in English) offers exonerations from some social security contributions (maximum for three years), monetary support paid in two tranches of 50% of the remaining credit in the unemployment insurance each.

Eligibility and Procedure: Registered unemployment including the right for monetary support (exceptions: young people under 30, people with disabilities or those whose employer has declared bankruptcy). The applicant has to (1) create a new company or take over a company, (2) apply no later than 45 days after business registration, and (3) cover more than 50% of the start capital.

Fallback and Return of Funds: In case of cessation, the applicant can return into the unemployment insurance to receive any remaining support.

Table 1.1 (continued)

Title / Agency / Date of Enactment	Objectives and Forms of Aid	Eligibility / Procedure / Fallback / Return of Funds
	In some cases, applicants can also get a loan bonus if a bank approved their application. NACRE: coaching / training program for three years after company creation.	Exonerations and contributions that have been granted do not have to be returned.
Germany Title: Gründungszuschuss Agency: Bundesministerium für Arbeit und Soziales Initial Enactment: 2006 (previously "bridging allowance" and "Me Inc" since 1986)	Objectives: Support formerly unemployed company founders. Forms of Aid: Founding subsidies offer financial support (six months continuation of last unemployment benefits + 300€, with a possibility of a nine-month extension if the business performs well), the allocation of industrial real-estate space and founding-related coaching (in cooperation with the KfW Bank). The "Einstiegsgeld" (start-up grant) is a monetary support mechanism for those people that are not eligible for unemployment benefits but still want to start a business.	Eligibility and Procedure: Subsidies are granted to those entitled to unemployment payments (ALG II) having at least 150 days of unemployment benefits remaining. Sufficient knowledge and the viability of the idea need to be proven. Fallback and Return of Funds: Generally, the person has the possibility of returning to the unemployment insurance, if sufficient funds remain. Subsidies do not have to be repaid.
Greece Title: Πρόγραμμα Νέων Ελεύθερον Επαγγελματιών (New Freelancers) Agency: Greek Manpower	Objectives: This program offers monetary support and counseling to firm founders from the unemployment. Forms of Aid: It consists of counseling and funding of varying duration and amounts (18,000–24,000 € in multiple installments throughout the funding period, depending on	Eligibility and Procedure: Granted to registered unemployed (Greek or EU citizens) that have attended OAED entrepreneurship courses, have at least 30 days of unemployment support remaining and have registered with the tax office. Fallback and Return of Funds: If the company fails, the person can return to the unemployment

the age and pre-conditions). In addition, the government offers specific programs for young people and unemployed women. If the firm survives for more than 12 months, a monetary bonus can be requested.

Employment Organisation (OAED)
Initial Enactment: Early version: 1980s (larger program: 2008)

Netherlands
Title: Besluit Bijstandsverlening Zelfstandigen (BBZ)
Agency: Dutch Public Employment Service (UWV)
Initial Enactment: 1996

insurance if there are sufficient benefits remaining. The funds do not require repayment unless the firm fails within the funding period, in which case a proportion of the subsidies need to be repaid.

Objectives: Provide monetary and non-monetary assistance to self-employed and unemployed wanting to start a business. Forms of Aid: Income support (maximum of 18 months), loans (maximum of 26 weeks with 70% of prior income), tax-incentive programs for private investors (Aunt Agatha Scheme), microfinancing (loans of less than 35,000 € and coaching).

Eligibility and Procedure: People receiving unemployment benefits (WW) whose business plans are approved by the "Werkbedrijf" ("work-coach") of the Dutch Public Employment Service (UWV).
Fallback and Return of Funds: After two years, the UWV Werkbedrijf will calculate the amount of money that should be paid back.

Poland
Title: Ustawa o Promocji Zatrudnienia i Instytucjach Rynku Pracy
Agency: Ministerstwo Pracy i Polityki Społecznej
Initial Enactment: 2004

Objectives: The act explicitly states its objective to promote employment and to reduce unemployment. Forms of Aid: One of the mechanisms is to support self-employment, but also re-employment, with grants provided consisting of a loan of up to 20 times the national average wage from the Labor Fund. Immediate repayment is required if the business is not started. According to our sources, the loans are rather uncommon.

Eligibility and Procedure: Unemployed are eligible if (1) they did not reject a valid job offer during the previous 12 months of unemployment and (2) they did not receive any public funds for starting a new business during the last five years. Strict criteria are applied, limiting the program to a small number of applicants. The business has to be started at latest two months after signing the contract.
Fallback and Return of Funds: The unemployed person has to return the funds if the business ceases within 12 months or if specific provisions from the contract were infringed. After 24 months, the principal for the loan is reduced to 50%.

Table 1.1 (continued)

Title / Agency / Date of Enactment	Objectives and Forms of Aid	Eligibility / Procedure / Fallback / Return of Funds
Spain Title: Prestaciones por desempleo Capitalización (Unemployment Capitalization benefit) Agency: Servicio Público de Empleo Initial Enactment: 1985	Objectives: Unemployment capitalization aims at boosting employment, supports those starting companies and those taking over companies. Forms of Aid: One-time payment of parts or the full amount of the remaining unemployment allocations as well as a coaching component. The Institute of Employment (Instituto Publico de Empleo) promotes different courses for unemployed people, allowing them to develop specific skills that may help in setting up a business.	Eligibility and Procedure: Registered unemployed (with more than three months of unemployment benefits remaining) who have not received unemployment capitalization during the previous four years and start business not later than one month after receiving the money. A detailed viability check is made prior to the funding. Fallback and Return of Funds: There are three conditions that need to be fulfilled to be eligible to return into the unemployment insurance: (1) some of the benefits are still available, (2) The business ceased in the first two years after start, (3) the person has a proof of his/her prior unemployment. Funds do not have to be repaid in case the business ceases for economic reasons.

Sweden
Title: Start-up Grants Program
Agency: Arbetsförmedlingen (Swedish Public Employment Service)
Initial Enactment: 1985

Objectives: The program targets the general population, disadvantaged minorities and the unemployed.

Forms of Aid: The "Startup Grants" are equivalent to the remaining unemployment allocations and are paid for a maximum period of six months; less generous grants are also available to those without unemployment insurance. There is also a microfinancing program in place (Almi mikrolån) and special programs for young people under the age of 26.

Eligibility and Procedure: Registered unemployed or those at risk of becoming unemployed. The Public Employment Service decides whether to grant financial assistance based on external consultants who rate the potential of the business and the candidate's abilities. Registration is required prior to producing the first revenues. Candidates must not have received a prior bank loan.

Fallback and Return of Funds: It is possible to come back into the unemployment insurance in the case of failure. Grants do not have to be returned.

Switzerland
Title: Taggelder
Agency: Swiss federal secretary of economy (SECO)
Initial Enactment: 1996

Objectives: Supporting unemployed transitioning to self-employment.

Forms of Aid: Unemployed individuals can receive maximum of 90 days of their unemployment benefits (Taggelder) and work on their business ideas without having to actively look for jobs. At the end of this period, they decide to proceed or not. Tax reductions exist for investors. Special support programs exist for disadvantages regions (e.g., Valais, Jura, etc.). Other forms of support include an online information portal, further monetary bonds as well as a coaching program.

Eligibility and Procedure: An individual is eligible for the support program if they became unemployed without actual fault, is 20 years of age or older and has a project proposal for the business endeavor. The business must be related to prior professional experience and no revenues may be produced during the period of support.

Fallback and Return of Funds: An extended period of support can be granted in case the business is not started or if for some reason self-employment is ended.

Table 1.1 (continued)

Title / Agency / Date of Enactment	Objectives and Forms of Aid	Eligibility / Procedure / Fallback / Return of Funds
United Kingdom Title: New Enterprise Allowance (NEA) Agency: Department of Work and Pensions Initial Enactment: 2012 (earlier programs since 1983)	Objectives: Helping Jobseeker's Allowance (JSA) claimants aged 18 and over who want to start their own business. Forms of Aid: The New Enterprise Allowance (NEA) consists of a weekly allowance worth £1,274 over 26 weeks, paid at £65 a week for the first 13 weeks and £33 a week for a further 13 weeks and a facility to access a loan of up to £1,000 to help with start-up costs.	Eligibility and Procedure: Jobseeker's Allowance (JSA) claimants aged 18 and over who want to start their own business can get extra help though the New Enterprise Allowance (NEA). After submission of a business plan, experts will evaluate the eligibility. Fallback and Return of Funds: In case the business ceases, the individual needs to re-apply to the Jobseeker's Allowance and there is no short cut as compared to other people registering. Funds do not have to be returned in case the business ceased.

Program Structures

Differing political landscapes, economic conditions, as well as distinct strategic goals of the various national ALMP instruments have led to several structural differences between the support initiatives. In particular, these programs differ along two main dimensions: (1) whether the programs are administered by centralized or decentralized entities; and (2) whether the initiatives are fully dedicated to those transitioning into self-employment out of unemployment, or whether the participants are channeled into generic support programs also open to firm founders without a prior unemployment experience.

Centralized versus decentralized structure

As Table 1.1 shows, there is heterogeneity with regards to whether the support programs are centrally—or de-centrally—organized. While the majority of countries in this study offer financial subsidies through a nationwide, centralized support program (for example, Germany—see case study below), other countries feature a range of more decentralized programs (for example, UK). However, due to a large variety of regional programs, the UK underwent a major consolidation effort in 2009 within their Business Support Simplification Programme (BSSP) to reduce the more than 3000 existing programs to less than 100, thus equally shifting towards a more centralized policy administration structure.

Case Study, Germany: Hierarchical Organization of Program Administration
The organizational structure for the administration of the German public-policy landscape revolves around the "Zentrale der Bundesagentur für Arbeit," a statutory body that acts as the central managing institution for all labor-market related statement of affairs currently in action as defined by the legislative system. These headquarters are well connected to other public institutions concerned with the implementation of policy instruments, as well as to an in-house research and intelligence department for internal controlling purposes. As direct subordinates to the central office, ten regional units across the country govern the implementation of labor-market policies at the intermediate level. These entities coordinate their duties of implementing national policies with other regional initiatives as well as with regional politics. The regional centers furthermore act as a link to the roughly 175 employment agencies ("Agentur für Arbeit") and 600 branch offices ("Geschäftsstellen") throughout the country that are responsible for operationally implementing the strategies defined at the higher levels within their local areas. (Bundesagentur für Arbeit, 2012)

Specific versus general self-employment promotion programs

While most countries have established dedicated programs to help unemployed individuals transition into self-employment (for example,

Austria, France, Germany, Spain and Switzerland), others are less focused on this group and combine those starting businesses out of unemployment into generic self-employment support initiatives that are open to anyone interested in starting a firm (for example, in Sweden, Poland and the Czech Republic). Specialized support programs to financially assist unemployed individuals aim at offsetting disadvantages they face with regards to accessing capital, as compared to founders without an unemployment background. We are unaware of any international studies comparing dedicated to generic programs in terms of effectiveness or efficiency.

Program Eligibility and Admission Criteria

Another key dimension differentiating the national policy schemes represents the eligibility requirements and admission criteria, thus limiting the program's access to a pre-defined group of individuals. This dimension directly reflects the country's strategy of following a more inclusive (for example, Belgium, France, the Netherlands and Sweden), or a more selective (for example, Austria, Germany, Greece, Spain and Switzerland) active labor market strategy. Furthermore, while the general framework of the programs is being defined on a national level, regional actors are responsible for the implementation and execution, partially resulting in a significant variance not only across countries, but also between different regions within the same country. While the majority of countries studied in this chapter have established formal viability checks of new business concepts (1), subjective assessments often play a significant role in determining who is admitted into a program (2). In the following, these two key practices related to the program eligibility and admission criteria are discussed in greater detail.

Viability-check of new business concepts
Today, the majority of the national programs require the unemployed to provide a business plan when applying for financial support. In order to be eligible for the financial contribution, the proposal typically needs to be assessed and approved by a qualified institution. This trend has likely been fueled by past experiences from overly permissive policy schemes (for example, "Existenzgründungszuschuss" program in Germany), which lead to increased cases of abuse. Some people enrolled in the program for continued monetary support shortly before losing eligibility for unemployment benefits, while others registered as unemployed just to receive the monetary support while starting a company they would likely have started even without the contribution (the "free-rider" phenomenon).

While permissive programs have the advantage of allowing many people to discover whether self-employment is a viable career path for them, excessively elevated restrictions on the other hand limit the support to people who have increased chances of success, potentially constraining other positive externalities resulting from self-employment. The profound impact of this parameter will be discussed in greater detail in "An Examination of Contrasting Policy Approaches."

The influence of subjective assessments
Although the eligibility requirements for receiving the support are typically stated in the form of legal decrees referring to clearly defined factors such as a minimum or maximum length of unemployment or the applicant's age, a subjective assessment through the employees of the regional employment agencies is a common practice. In Germany for example, local program coordinators are given authority to decide who is eligible for starting a business and who is denied the financial support. In Switzerland, the cantonal authorities are given autonomy about how strictly the admittance criteria for their policy scheme are applied. As a result, the policy implementations may differ significantly between regions. Comparable project proposals accepted in one region may thus be rejected somewhere else. Although a detailed analysis of such regional differences is beyond the scope of this chapter, it is likely that similar discrepancies exist in countries other than the ones just mentioned.

Practices Related to the Provision of Financial Support

Capital constraints represent a major barrier for becoming self-employed (for example, Blanchflower and Oswald, 1990). Having access to adequate amounts of financial capital helps founders respond to adverse circumstances, overcome liquidity constraints and influence external stakeholders' perception of the new venture (Shane, 2003). While some basic financial investment is required to start any type of business, the amount varies strongly depending on the type of business opportunity exploited by the founder. Evidence from prior research suggests that unemployed individuals are more likely to become self-employed in manual—and labor-intensive—businesses with a low capital investment (Kellard and Middleton, 1998), likely in part due to financial constraints.

This reality is reflected in the structure of all investigated programs as they offer at least some basic financial support to help bridge the funding gap before the founder can draw a steady income from the new business. However, the specific conditions differ widely across the countries studied in this chapter. In the following, three central factors differentiating the examined programs are discussed, namely: (1) whether the financial support is provided in the form of a grant or as a loan; (2) whether it is paid as a single, lump sum payment or as regularly recurring allowances; and (3) whether there exists a fallback solution for the program participant in case the self-employment project is abandoned.

Grants versus loans

Monetary support is provided in different forms within the analyzed countries. Although there is a general trend of offering grants (funds that are distributed by one party to a recipient that do not have to be repaid) from the unemployment insurances (for example, Austria, Czech Republic, France, Germany, Greece, Spain, Sweden, Switzerland and the UK), some countries have implemented loan schemes that require repayment (for example, Belgium and the Netherlands, as well as France through its NACRE program). In one case, the repayment is only required if the business ceases to operate within a certain timeframe (Poland).

Single payment versus recurring payments

The above-described monetary support is either provided as a single, lump sum payment (Poland and Spain), or through recurring monthly payments (Austria, Belgium, Czech Republic, France, Germany, Greece, Netherlands, Sweden and Switzerland) or weekly (UK) allowances. Nascent self-employed often need to cover up-front investments, which can vary in magnitude depending on the industry and the activity. The possibility of receiving subsidies in form of a single, lump sum payment can be helpful to cover such expenses. Yet, in order to cover the cost of living, recurring payments (similar to the reception of a regular salary) seem to be advantageous.

Provision of a fallback solution

A fallback solution allows the participants to re-enter the national welfare system in case the self-employment activity is abandoned, for example due to economic reasons. Offering a fallback solution into the general welfare system in case the business remains unsuccessful appears to be a well-received practice. While all countries in this section have some sort of fallback scenario, the specific approaches are different. Some countries offer general fallback solutions with the only criteria being the availability of remaining individual allocations in the unemployment insurance scheme (for example, Austria, France, Germany and Switzerland). Other countries have fallback solutions that are linked to specific requirements such as how long the firm needs to be operating and the mode of failure (for example, the Czech Republic and Poland).

Nonfinancial Business Support Services

In addition to an appropriate level of funding, the founder's prior knowledge and professional experience have been shown to influence the long-term success of a new business concept (for example, Shane, 2003; Dencker, Gruber, and Shah, 2009a). Research suggests that nonfinancial business support services can positively influence the success of formerly unemployed firm founders through two central mechanisms.

First, instead of imposing strict eligibility criteria that exclude insufficiently refined business concepts, evidence suggests that supporting individuals to improve unrefined business concepts can potentially increase the supply of promising business concepts (Guérin and Vallat, 2000; Nolan, 2003; Jakobsen and Ellegaard, 2012). Second, once a refined business concept has been developed, there is ample evidence that the establishment and growth of the new businesses can be positively influenced through the provision of appropriate business support services (for example, Brüderl and Preisendörfer, 1998; Sheikh et al., 2002).

While coaching and training programs have long been a central element of the active labor market programs implemented in many countries, initiatives designed to support individuals transitioning into self-employment through the provision for education and business support services represent a comparatively new element of these systems. As a result, the available nonfinancial support varies widely across regions and is often restricted to metropolitan areas; those located in more rural areas are thus occasionally disadvantaged.

However, the educational, nonfinancial component of the governmental support schemes is regarded as being one of their most valued aspects (Kellard and Middleton, 1998). Scientific studies that have been conducted on this matter indicate generally positive outcomes of the self-employed assistance components (OECD, 2000; Martin and Grubb, 2001; Van Es and Van Vuuren, 2011). Even in case the self-employment experience ultimately proves unsuccessful, positive spillover effects with regards to re-employment chances have been discovered (Kellard and Middleton, 1998; OECD, 2000). The comparison of the business support services conducted for this chapter revealed a number of differences with regards to (1) the types of business support available to the program participants; (2) the encouragement of participation in these offerings; and (3) the provision of support through government—or private-sector—organizations.

Type of business support service
The evidence we collected shows that the business support services that are relevant to firms founded by the unemployed can be divided into

three main types: *Professional training* initiatives offer vocational or technical training typically aimed at individuals seeking to work in skill and labor-intensive professions; *general education programs* focus on the transfer of theoretical knowledge in a classroom or lecture hall setting, while *personalized coaching and consulting support* is targeted at individuals in need of advice regarding specific topics arising during the creation of their businesses. Analogous distinctions between the different forms of business support services have been made in the past (for example, Sheikh et al., 2002), yet with a broader focus on micro, small and sole proprietor businesses in general. Table 1.2 provides an overview of the key types of nonfinancial support available to formerly unemployed founders.

Most countries have offerings related to all three types of business support, yet the respective programs receive differing degrees of emphasis and their availability can vary widely not just across different countries, but also across different regions within the same country. Belgium can be seen as an example of a country putting special emphasis on *professional training* as a viable path to help formerly unemployed individuals transition into self-employment, sporting several institutions with high national visibility (for example, SYNTRA, IFAPME, EFPME). The Czech Republic similarly puts strong emphasis on this type of nonfinancial support within their national ALMP. A focus on providing *general education* can be observed within the "public university" ("Volkshochschule"; VHS) concept in Germany, but similar institutions can also be found in Austria, the Scandinavian countries, and others. Despite its relatively high costs, some countries such as France explicitly focus on the *consulting/coaching* components within their unemployment support policies. In this case, the business support is integrated within the national policy scheme and participants are supported for a maximum duration of up to three years. As each type of business support service is important for a specific type of business, it is still unknown to date which approach is the most cost-effective from a governmental perspective.

Mandatory versus voluntary participation

Participation in the nonfinancial support offerings is typically voluntary; however an exception to this rule could be identified in Slovakia, a country outside of our sample, where the completion of preparatory courses organized by the Labor Office is required in order to receive the financial contribution. Nevertheless, most countries have installed mechanisms as incentives for their participants to profit from the nonfinancial support that is being offered, for example by distributing coaching vouchers or contributing financially to consulting services that have been used. An example of this practice can be found in France, which has implemented

Table 1.2   Professional training versus education programs versus consulting/coaching

Type	Professional Training	General Education	Consulting/Coaching
Primary Audience	Skill- and labor-intensive professions such as the freelance professions and crafts; focuses on teaching practical skills	Applicable to broad audiences; focuses on the transfer of theoretical knowledge	More unique business concepts requiring personalized strategy development and idiosyncratic solutions
Group Size	Smaller groups	Larger groups possible	Individuals / small groups
Example Content and Details	• Food preparation license training; computer skills • Includes a wide range of professions such as journalists, graphic designers, hairdressers, electricians, accountants, cabinetmakers and others • Collaboration between participants is encouraged • Duration of courses: from a few sessions to several years	• Provision of basic information, education about procedures for setting up a company and facilities • Writing a business plan • Financial management or general business courses • Lower cost but longer time investment needed	• Coaching, experimental market-study; development of an advertising strategy • Consulting for strategy and supplier-related issues • Psychological counseling • High added values, very effective • Expensive due to personalization

a consulting-voucher system within its ACCRE program. Participants receive a number of tickets that can be spent on counseling services at the beginning of the creation of the firm and during the following year (OECD, 2000). Authorities in the Netherlands offer to refund costs for coaching, courses or market surveys relating to the new business (Bekker, 2010). In Sweden, consultants who have been hired for business support services (for example, the evaluation of a business idea) can be paid by the authorities. The UK follows an indirect approach, granting an increase in the financial allowance in case the unemployed participates in some form of training. A number of prior studies have found that the publicity and visibility of support services appear to be strongly limited for the small and medium-sized companies (Thomas, 1994; Das Dores Guerreiro et al., 2000). This suggests that, in addition to the aforementioned incentives that have been put in place, policymakers may want to concentrate on making information about the various types of support more available to those seeking to start businesses.

Governmental versus privatized provision of support

While historically the majority of educational programs have been operated by governmental institutions, private contractors and Internet-based training programs have become more prominent in recent years (Nolan, 2003). For example, websites on the topic of business creation are being operated by government agencies in Germany, providing basic information about the most common questions surrounding new business creation. The regional employment offices supplement this central knowledge database as a provider of more personalized information available in the region, and by acting as hubs for connecting entrepreneurs with local contacts. Similar arrangements have been implemented by the Czech Republic, the Netherlands and Switzerland. The shift towards Internet-based support services is further strengthened through remote e-learning solutions to educate the unemployed on how to start and operate a business (for example, in the Czech Republic).

Several countries have partly or fully outsourced the business support of their program participants to private contractors (for example, Austria, Belgium and the Netherlands). This strategic move appears promising, as prior research indicates that the provision of business support services through private organizations will lead to greater success of the participating companies than services provided by government bodies (Kluve and Schmidt, 2002; Wössmann and Schütz, 2006) and that government-supported advisory services are less proficient at supporting firm growth, but rather at rescuing ailing firms (Bennett and Robson, 1999). Some of these services are offered free of charge for the participants, the duration is projected to last between six (Austria) to 18 months (Belgium).

Since positive outcomes of these services might not be immediately visible, it is especially vital to have a longer-term focus when evaluating the costs and benefits of business support services (Card, Kluve, and Weber, 2010); one source is citing a timeframe of three to four years as reasonable (Nolan, 2003).

Table 1.3   Key program dimensions

Program Structure	Program Eligibility	Financial Support	Nonfinancial Support
Centralized vs. Decentralized Structure	Viability-check of New Business Concepts	Grants vs. Loans	Training, Consulting and General Education
Specific vs. General Self-Employment Promotion Programs	Influence of Subjective Assessment	Single Payment vs. Recurring Payments	Mandatory vs. Voluntary Participation
		Provision of a Fallback Solution	Government vs. Privatized Organization

Summary of Key Program Dimensions

Building on these findings, Table 1.3 summarizes the key dimensions differentiating the policy schemes within the countries in this study: the program structure (centralized versus decentralized organization; specific versus general self-employment promotion programs), the program's eligibility requirements (objective versus subjective assessment; viability-check of the new business concept), practices related to the provision of financial support (grants versus loans; single versus recurring payments; provision of a fallback solution) as well as differences in the offering of nonfinancial business support services (types of business support, mandatory versus voluntary participation, public versus privatized provision of support services).

These dimensions reflect the major cornerstones of self-employment promotion programs for formerly unemployed individuals. Policymakers aiming at modifying existing programs or implementing new programs and those seeking to understand these policy initiatives can use these dimensions as a reference. Clearly, some factors are more important than others from both a governmental and a participant's perspective. Considerations regarding the program structure have a profound impact on the governmental resources that need to be devoted for the administration of the policy schemes. The choice of a centralized versus a decentralized structure needs to carefully balance specific advantages and disadvantages of the two approaches, and also needs to take into account a range of country-specific factors (for example, country size, population and existing policy infrastructure). The choice of operating a dedicated self-employment program for unemployed individuals as opposed to grouping them with others into a general self-employment promotion program needs to account for the difference between the unemployed and the non-unemployed founders with regards to the average level of education, skills and experience, which varies from country to country.

The nonfinancial support, on the other hand, is of greatest concern for those who create new businesses and need this type of support. Because business support services are characterized by a variety of private actors at the regional or local levels, they are oftentimes dissociated from centralized policymaking efforts, resulting in the apparent large heterogeneity across regions.

Other policy dimensions such as the strictness of eligibility and the level of financial support available to the program participants have a profound impact on both governments as well as participants. Choices related to these factors are much more flexible in the short and medium term compared to the structure and nonfinancial support, making these factors suitable levers for adapting active labor market strategies to changing political, economic and labor market circumstances. The impact and implications from the eligibility requirements and the available level of financial support from both a governmental as well as a participant perspective will be discussed in greater detail in the next section in order to shed light on the implications arising from these parameters.

AN EXAMINATION OF CONTRASTING POLICY APPROACHES

The previous section reveals how the policy schemes differ based on several criteria. While some practices are hardly comparable across the countries studied in this chapter and difficult to influence within policy revisions, two central parameters—the available level of financial support and the strictness of eligibility—are indicative of the general strategy followed by the government. These two dimensions not only define who is receiving how much financial support but also for how long. As both parameters are of particular interest to those affected by unemployment and wishing to become self-employed, these dimensions merit an in-depth discussion.

The first dimension describes the level of financial support, relating to both the amount and the duration of financial support that is being offered, as well as the type of financial support (grant versus loan). Several parameters that have been discussed in the section "Practices Related to the Provision of Financial Support" are grouped together in this dimension. The countries have been classified into low, medium or high levels of financial support. A "low level of financial support" corresponds to a period of less than six months of monetary support. Available support for a maximum duration between six to twelve months of financial support or a non-refundable single payment of an equal amount has been classified as "medium level of financial support," whereas any support lasting longer than one year or a one-time grant of similar size has been classified as "high levels of financial support." The second dimension indicates the strictness of eligibility for program participants. The countries have been classified as having either low or high eligibility requirements where countries classified as "low strictness" only demand the registration as unemployed in order to be eligible for funding, and countries listed as "high strictness" are imposing extended viability proofs (for example, assessing the business plan by a qualified institution, limiting the choice of industrial sector to those cases in which the applicant can document prior experience).

The classification of each country was made based on publicly available information about the programs, whereas unclear cases have been verified through interviews with employees of the national policy administration agencies. Figure 1.1 illustrates this categorization.

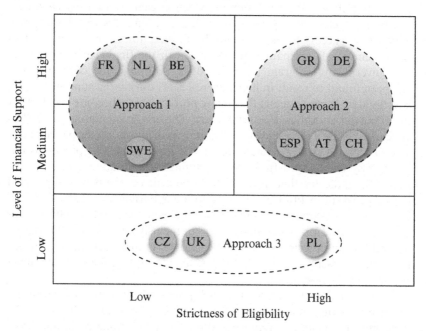

Figure 1.1   Assessment of programs based on financial support and strictness of eligibility

By mapping the respective programs on these two dimensions, the different approaches of the countries in our sample become apparent. In order to better understand these contrasting approaches, several interviews with representatives from selected countries following the different approaches were conducted. In the following, we discuss the advantages and disadvantages of the strategic positioning for both governments and participants based on the previous overview of support schemes, supplemented by information gained during the interviews, as well as corresponding publicly available information.

Differing Policy Approaches

Approach 1: Low strictness of eligibility/medium to high levels of financial support

Countries positioned in the top left corner of the categorization feature a rather generous policy scheme as almost anyone is granted the comparatively high financial support when engaging in an entrepreneurial activity. France represents an example for this type of policy orientation.

From a governmental perspective, granting large shares of the unemployed population financial support when engaging in entrepreneurship represents a relatively expensive approach, as even ideas with lower probabilities of success are supported. In France, for instance, more than 50 percent of all companies are started with the financial support from this government program (APCE, 2012). Although the current policy has been found to result in high survival rates during the support period, anecdotal evidence suggests that many problems only become visible after the financial subsidies are terminated. The governmental support thus appears to incite a false sense of economic security among the participants, as a disciplined strategy development and implementation process is not sufficiently encouraged from the beginning. Quantitative data from the year 2011 indicates that more than 80 percent of companies supported by the program in France are single-founder businesses, whereas around 80 percent of companies are service or commerce-related businesses (APCE, 2012). Correspondingly, such an inclusive program might have a limited impact in terms of national economic growth, demanding for differentiated measures of success that are able to capture the societal impact of this policy strategy.

From a participant perspective, such policy schemes are received rather positively, as the broader population of unemployed individuals has the possibility to explore entrepreneurship as a viable career path, and ideas with an extended exploratory phase—prior to knowing about the financial viability—can receive monetary support for an extended period. In this case, the participants are somewhat protected from too much pressure to identify a viable business model that would be present without the policy scheme. However, anecdotal evidence suggests that such unrestrained programs specifically targeted towards unemployed people can result in a substantial social divide, as the formal unemployment registration is required to be eligible for funding. Those starting a business while employed elsewhere thus tend to perceive such policies as somewhat unfair and unjust.

Approach 2: High strictness of eligibility/high level of financial support
The top right corner of the categorization indicates programs that can be characterized as generous, yet highly selective. One example of a country within this category is Germany.

From a government perspective, having strict eligibility criteria while simultaneously offering generous financial support leads to an increased selection effort during the early stage of the process. The focus of this approach is on those participants that have the highest probability of succeeding. According to the German employment ministry, this positioning is the result of a recent strategic shift towards an increased emphasis of re-employment of unemployed individuals rather than self-employment stemming from the currently (2013) optimistic economic situation in the country. As a consequence, the accessibility of these programs has been changed from being generally available for every unemployed person interested in becoming self-employed, to being a merely voluntary offering at the discretion of the respective employment agency. While supporting only the most capable citizens in becoming entrepreneurs might increase the life chances of such firms, this strategy denies large shares of the population the chance to explore whether self-employment represents a viable career for them.

From a participant perspective, this strategic shift has both positive and negative aspects. Those allowed into the program are likely to possess alternative employment options, whereas those denied might lack such options, thus potentially excluding some people from being able to participate in the labor market. Assuming a functioning selection process, the positive aspects of such a policy variant reside in the quick market feedback to the individuals, indicating whether their business ideas are economically feasible of having long-term survival prospects in the market.

Approach 3: Low level of financial support
The lower part of the categorization indicates programs featuring only a low level of financial support, thus reducing the importance of the eligibility requirements in this approach. Poland and the Czech Republic are examples of countries following this policy strategy in our study.

While government expenditures related to the provision of financial support are kept at a minimum in such a policy variant, only marginal positive externalities with respect to reducing unemployment and generating economic growth can be expected in return. New businesses have to find alternative ways to compensate their need for funding through other actors such as financial institutions and private investors, which might be an even more difficult endeavor for unemployed individuals compared to others who did not suffer from an unemployment spell.

From a participant perspective, this approach is similar to a total lack of support, as the restricted financial support is likely to be insufficient for the exploitation of most opportunities, increasing the chance of establishing under-resourced businesses with poor survival chances from the onset (ILO, 2002). Only business concepts requiring a minimal amount of financing, such as simple arbitrage or services businesses, can be exploited in case additional private funds are absent. The implementation of more complex, larger-scale business ideas is thus reserved to those having access to other capital sources in this policy approach. On a more positive note, the mere existence of a dedicated entrepreneurship support policy targeted at unemployed people is likely to entice at least some individuals to try out if self-employment presents a viable career option for them. Although we can only speculate about the impact of such a policy approach, participants lacking additional sources of financing might feel discouraged at a later point in time when having to realize that the available funding proves insufficient for the realization of many projects.

Key Insights

The categorization of countries provides a snapshot of the status quo of the pan-European policy landscape designed to help unemployed individuals transition into self-employment within a number of European countries. While this landscape can be expected to continue evolving in the years to come, several insights can be distilled from the current examination:

- Two central parameters, the level of financial support and the strictness of eligibility of the respective national policies, reveal several contrasting policy approaches with differing implications from both a governmental and a participant perspective.
- While some programs have a strategy of primarily promoting growth-oriented entrepreneurship, others follow a rather inclusive labor market approach, perceiving entrepreneurship as a potentially viable career option for larger shares of the population and as a

solution to increased rates of unemployment. Again others offer only very limited assistance for those seeking to create a business after a period of unemployment, revealing that entrepreneurship support policies are not a top policy priority. Correspondingly, the programs cannot be ranked in order of effectiveness or efficiency, as each policy scheme follows an approach that has been adapted to the specific national context, shaped by both economic and societal factors (Staber and Bögenhold, 1993).

- Even generous policies can have a negative impact on participants, as they might incite a false sense of economic security as indicated by the example of France. Survival rates during the support period would thus be artificially inflated but can be expected to drop sharply after the funding expires. Future studies are needed to improve our understanding if this effect is visible in larger-scale empirical research and identified in other countries as well.

CONCLUSION

This chapter provides an international comparative analysis of the policy initiatives designed to help those affected by unemployment transition into self-employment within a number of European countries. Following an overview of the history of the programs as well as a comparative analysis of currently existing programs across Europe, we identified and analyzed key program dimensions, including the overall program structure, the program eligibility requirements, and practices related to the provision of financial support and nonfinancial business support services. This analysis revealed several distinctive features about the current state of development of these policies:

- The program structure follows a centralized approach in the majority of countries with consistent national policy schemes that are being executed by regional employment agencies. Both dedicated, and generic self-employment support programs can be found.
- Most countries have introduced some sort of eligibility requirements that the applicants need to fulfill in order to receive the financial support including a well-refined business concept that needs to be approved by a qualified institution. As the criteria often leave room for interpretation by labor office employees, the assessments are likely to be influenced by subjective factors, resulting in potential regional differences of how the national policies are being implemented.

- While some form of financial support for the program participants, either direct or indirect, is available in all of the investigated countries, the type, amount and duration of monetary support differs widely. However, we could identify grant-based monthly contributions for half a year to a year being the most common approach. A basic fallback solution in case the entrepreneurial endeavor proves unsuccessful is available in all of the countries.
- The available business support services differ markedly across the countries, but also across different regions within the same country. One area for further policy development could focus on making information about the various types of support more transparent—an observation that is in line with prior research indicating that the publicity and visibility of support services is strongly limited for small and medium-sized companies (Thomas, 1994; Das Dores Guerreiro et al., 2000). Prior studies moreover suggest, that private organizations have advantages over government bodies in the provision of business support services (Kluve and Schmidt, 2002; Wössmann and Schütz, 2006) and that government-supported advisory services might be less proficient at supporting firm growth but instead better in rescuing ailing firms compared to services offered by the private sector (Bennett and Robson, 1999). Governmental interventions regarding business support services thus need to be carefully planned and potentially limited to market failures in the provision of support by the private sector.
- The program eligibility requirements and the level of financial support are central parameters revealing several contrasting policy approaches. Some policies primarily aim at promoting growth-oriented entrepreneurship, whereas others see entrepreneurship as a potentially viable option for larger shares of the population and as a solution to increased rates of unemployment. As prior studies have indicated that the costs of these programs are considerably lower than those of other ALMPs or the continued provision of unemployment benefits (OECD, 2000), the strategy of making entrepreneurship part of the solution towards reducing unemployment in many developed countries appears to be promising. Such policies can be an important instrument for generating positive economic and social externalities also in geographical areas where similar initiatives have thus far been scant or even absent. However, approaches offering only limited assistance for those seeking to create a business after a period of unemployment can also be appropriate in some contexts. A rank-ordering of program designs in terms of their general superiority is thus not feasible.

Outlook and Future Research

Despite an improved understanding of the structure and outcomes of the analyzed policy programs designed to help unemployed individuals transition into self-employment, further research is needed that can shed light on a number of issues:

- **Need for quantitative analyses:** We identified a need for additional international comparison studies that evaluate the programs in terms of their effectiveness and efficiency. Unanswered questions include: How can dedicated self-employment policies targeted at formerly unemployed individuals be compared quantitatively to generic programs open to anyone interested in starting a business? How might the eligibility requirements and the level of financial support be altered depending on the current economic circumstances and depending on the type of firm that is to be founded? What type of business support services can be provided in a cost-efficient manner by governments as well as private organizations? Inquiring into these topics can provide decision-makers with more quantifiable information in the future than what was available at the time of this study.
- **Need for additional performance measures:** To date, the central performance indicator of the programs has been the survival rate of firms supported by the programs. However, due to selection effects, the survival rates are not directly comparable as a result of the differing eligibility criteria. Policies featuring strict selection criteria thus are likely to lead to higher survival rates, as only the most capable individuals were previously admitted to the program. In case the policy schemes focus on increasing the country's economic output, the growth of the newly created businesses, measured for example in terms of tax revenue or by the creation of new jobs, should also be monitored and taken into account as a meaningful performance indicator. In case the policy schemes are part of the national social development strategies, the impact resulting from eligibility requirements needs to be more seriously considered in order to help a large proportion of those affected by unemployment discover whether self-employment represents a potentially viable career path for them. Measures such as levels of resulting work- and life-satisfaction might be valuable additions for these policy approaches. Programs aiming to pursue both goals simultaneously could benefit from more insights into the quantitative trade-offs of the different policy strategies outlined in the section "An Examination of Contrasting Policy Approaches."

- **Need for effective communication mechanisms:** While self-employment has the potential to be a rewarding professional career path, the reality that self-employment is also risky should not be neglected. A critical element for the successful implementation of functional programs thus represents an honest and authentic communication with prospective participants, rather than promoting self-employment as a viable path for everyone (Kellard and Middleton, 1998). Future research could help investigate the different mechanisms by which the government is able to communicate this reality to the prospective applicants.
- **Need for better understanding of support services:** There are several questions surrounding the provision of nonfinancial support services deserving further attention: Which type of business support is the most cost-effective from a government perspective? How can governmental agencies ensure that appropriate business support services are widely available? Which services are best provided privately, versus publicly administered and controlled? How can business support services be made more accessible to those interested in starting a business, including those located outside of metropolitan areas?

While more research is needed in order to shed light on these and other questions, the comparative analysis presented in this chapter was able to uncover several interesting facts about the current stage of development of policies designed to support the transition of formerly unemployed individuals to self-employment. Our work contributes to an improved understanding and a heightened awareness of the public policy schemes that were previously difficult to compare, facilitating the exchange of best-practice solutions in order to improve existing programs and in developing new programs. The programs have the potential to stimulate a number of positive secondary effects, such as a relief of the welfare system, increased societal well-being, and economic growth. It should not be forgotten, however, that such policy initiatives are only one tool within a larger set of active labor market policies, albeit an important one deserving further attention as acknowledged within the current "Europe 2020 Strategy" (European Commission, 2010). It is hoped that the increased transparency that this chapter created continues to stimulate the international dialogue on this topic.

ACKNOWLEDGEMENTS

This chapter would not have been possible without the generous support and help of a number of people. We would thus like to express our gratitude to those who have supported this study through their time and knowledge. First, we would like to thank Professor Marc Gruber and Professor John Dencker for their valuable insights and comments on the content, structure and contribution of this chapter. Second, we would like to thank those who have participated in the interviews that helped us improve our understanding of the specifics of the government programs. Specifically, we would like to thank Dietrich Englert from the German "Bundesamt für Arbeit und Soziales," Laurent Deloisen from the French Pôle-Emploi (Pays de la Loire), Martina Jakl from the Swiss-Czech Tech-Transfer Office and Lech Antkowiak from the Polish Department of Labor in Warsaw. Additionally, we want to thank David Halabisky and Paul Swaim from the OECD for providing valuable insights about existing analyses of policy schemes on a pan-European level, Víctor Martín-i-Sánchez and Argyro Nikiforou for having helped us gather information for Spain and Greece, respectively.

NOTE

1. The traditionally employed elements of ALMP comprised public employment services, subsidized employment within the private sector and labor market training programs, however all but the latter have been evaluated rather unenthusiastically in subsequent analyses (Heckman, Lalonde, and Smith, 1999; Martin and Grubb, 2001; Kluve and Schmidt, 2002; Boone and van Ours, 2004).

REFERENCES

APCE (2012, April). *La Création D'Entreprises en France en 2011*. L'Agence Pour la Création d'Entreprises. Paris.
Baumgartner, H.J., and Caliendo, M. (2008). Turning unemployment into self-employment: effectiveness of two start-up programmes. *Oxford Bulletin of Economics and Statistics*, 70(3), 347–373.
Bekker, S. (2010). *European Employment Observatory, EEO Review: Self-employment, Netherlands*. Birmingham.
Bennett, J.R., and Robson, P.J.A. (1999). The use of external business advice by SMEs in Britain. *Entrepreneurship and Regional Development*, (11), 155–180.
Benus, J.M. (fall 1994). Self-employment programs: a new reemployment strategy. *Entrepreneurship Theory and Practice*, 19(2), 73–86.
Blanchflower, D., and Oswald, A.J. (1990). *What makes an Entrepreneur? Evidence on Inheritance and Capital Constraints*. Cambridge, MA: National Bureau of Economic Research.
Block, J., and Sandner, P. (2006). The effect of motivation on self-employment duration in Germany: necessity versus opportunity entrepreneurs. *MPRA Paper series*, no. 215. Munich.

Block, J., and Wagner, M. (2010). Necessity and opportunity entrepreneurs in Germany: characteristics and earnings differentials. *Schmalenbach Business Review*, 62(4), 154–174.

Boone, J., and van Ours, J.C. (2004). Effective active labor market policies. *IZA Discussion Paper series*, no. 1335. Retrieved on February 16, 2016 from http://hdl.handle.net/10419/20604.

Bosma, N., Acs, Z.J., Autio, E., Coduras, A., and Levie, J. (2008). *Global Entrepreneurship Monitor, 2008 Executive Report*. Babson Park, MA: Babson College.

Brüderl, J., and Preisendörfer, P. (1998). Network support and the success of newly founded business. *Small Business Economics*, 10(3), 213–225.

Bundesagentur für Arbeit (2012). *Aufbau und Organisation*. Retrieved on February 15, 2013 from http://www.arbeitsagentur.de/nn_27200/Navigation/zentral/Servicebereich/Ueber-Uns/Aufbau-und-Organisation/Aufbau-und-Organisation-Nav.html.

Caliendo, M., and Kritikos, A. (2009). I want to, but I also need to: start-ups resulting from opportunity and necessity. *IZA Discussion Paper series*, no. 4661.

Caliendo, M., and Künn, S. (2011). Start-up subsidies for the unemployed: long-term evidence and effect heterogeneity. *Journal of Public Economics*, 95(3), 311–331.

Card, D., Kluve, J., and Weber, A. (2010). Active labour market policy evaluations: a meta-analysis. *The Economic Journal*, Wiley Online Library.

Carling, K., and Gustafson, L. (1999). Self-employment vs. subsidized employment: is there a difference in the re-unemployment risk? *Institute for Labour Market Policy Evaluation (IFAU)*, Working Paper.

Corral, A., Isusi, I., and Stack, J. (2006). *Support Measures for Business Creation Following Restructuring*. Dublin, Ireland: European Foundation for the Improvement of Living and Working Conditions.

Cueto, B., and Mato, J. (2006). An analysis of self-employment subsidies with duration models. *Applied Economics*, (38), 23–32.

Das Dores Guerreiro, M., Palma, S., Pegado, E., and Rodrigues, N. (2000, August). Relações Sócio-Laborais em Micro e Pequenas Empresas (Occupational and social relations in the micro and small enterprises). *OEFP*. Lisbon.

Dencker, J.C., Gruber, M., and Shah, S.K. (2009a). Pre-entry knowledge, learning, and the survival of new firms. *Organization Science*, 20(3), 516–537.

Dencker, J.C., Gruber, M., and Shah, S.K. (2009b). Individual and opportunity factors influencing job creation in new firms. *Academy of Management Journal*, 52(6), 1125–1147.

Désiage, L., Duhautois, R., and Redor, D. (2010). Do public subsidies have an impact on new firm survival? An empirical study with French data. TEPP Working Paper, no. 2010-4. ISSN 2110-5472.

Duggan, C. (1998). *Self-employment in the United Kingdom and Ireland. Current trends, policies and programmes*. Paper presented at the OECD Conference on self-employment, Burlington, September 24–26, 1998.

European Commission (1997). *The Way Forward: The European Employment Strategy*. DG V, Luxembourg: Office for Official Publications of the European Communities. Brussels.

European Commission (2010). *Europe 2020: A Strategy for Smart, Sustainable and Inclusive Growth*. Retrieved on January 15, 2013 from http://ec.europa.eu/europe2020/index_en.htm.

Fritsch, M. (2008). How does new business development affect regional development? Introduction to the Special Issue, *Small Business Economics*, (30), 1–14.

Guérin, I., and Vallat, D. (2000). *Les clefs du succès de la création d'entreprise par des chômeurs. A contribution to the International Labour Organization (ILO) Action Programme: Enterprise Creation by the Unemployed—Microfinance in Industrialized Countries*. Centre Walras, France.

Heckman, J., Lalonde, R., and Smith, J. (1999). The economics and econometrics of active labor market programs. In: O.C. Ashenfelter and D. Card (eds), *Handbook of Labor Economics*, Elsevier, 3, 1865–2097.

IAB Kurzbericht (2007). Ausgabe 10, April 10, 2007: Existenzgründungen: Unterm Strich ein Erfolg. *Bundesagentur für Arbeit*. Nürnberg.

International Labor Organization (ILO) (2002). *Micro-finance in Industrialized Countries: Helping the Unemployed to Start a Business*. Geneva: ILO.

Jakobsen, L., and Ellegaard, C.E. (2012). Danish Technological Institute. *Public measures to support self-employment and job creation in one-person and micro enterprises*. Report. European Foundation for the Improvement of Living and Working Conditions.

Kellard, K., and Middleton, S. (1998). *Helping unemployed people into self-employment*. Research Brief no. 46. Centre for Research in Social Policy. Department for Education and Employment. Leicestershire, UK.

Kluve, J., and Schmidt, C.M. (2002). Can training and employment subsidies combat European unemployment? *Economic Policy*, (35), 411–448.

Martin, J., and Grubb, D. (2001). What works and for whom: a review of OECD countries' experiences with active labour market policies. *Swedish Economic Policy Review*, 8(2), 9–56.

Meager, N. (1996). From unemployment to self-employment: labour market policies for business start-up. In G. Schmidt, J. O'Reilly, and K. Schömann (eds), *International Handbook of Labour Market Policy and Evaluation* (Chapter 16). Cheltenham, UK and Northampton, MA, USA: Edward Elgar Publishing.

Meager, N., Bates, P., and Cowling, M. (2003). An evaluation of business start-up support for young people. *National Institute Economic Review*, (186), 59–72.

Metcalf, H. (1998). *Self-Employment for the Unemployed: The Role of Public Policy*. Department of Education and Employment, Research Report RR47.

Nolan, A. (2003). *Entrepreneurship and Local Economic Development: Policy Innovations in Industrialized Countries*. Paris: Organisation for Economic Co-operation and Development.

O'Leary, C.J. (1999). Promoting self employment among the unemployed in Hungary and Poland. Working Paper. W.E. Upjohn Institute for Employment Research.

Organisation for Economic Co-operation and Development (OECD). (1992). Recent developments in self-employment. In *Recent Developments in Self-employment* (Chapter 4). Paris: OECD.

Organisation for Economic Co-operation and Development (OECD). (2000). The partial renaissance of self-employment. In *Employment Outlook* (Chapter 5). Paris: OECD.

Parker, S.C. (2004). *The Economics of Self-employment and Entrepreneurship*. Cambridge, UK: Cambridge University Press.

Pfeiffer, F., and Reize, F. (2000). Business start-ups by the unemployed—an econometric analysis based on firm data. *Labour Economics*, 7(5), 629–663.

Rodríguez-Planas, N. (2008). Understanding why public employment services

38 *Institutional case studies on necessity entrepreneurship*

and small-business assistance programs work at getting the unemployed back
to work: evidence from Romania. *Universitat Autònoma de Barcelona, IZA and
FEDEA.*
Rodríguez-Planas, N. (2010). Channels through which public employment services
and small business assistance programmes work. *Oxford Bulletin of Economics
and Statistics*, 72(4), 458–485.
Shane, S. (2003). *A General Theory of Entrepreneurship: The Individual–Opportunity
Nexus.* New Horizons in Entrepreneurship Series. Cheltenham, UK and
Northampton, MA, USA: Edward Elgar Publishing.
Sheikh, S., Pecher, I., Steiber, N., and Heckl, E. (2002). *Support Services for Micro,
Small and Sole Proprietor's Businesses: Final report.* Vienna: Austrian Institute
for Small Business Research (IFGH), and European Network for SME Research
(ENSR).
Staber, U., and Bögenhold, D. (1993). Self-employment: a study of seventeen
OECD countries. *Industrial Relations Journal*, 24(2), 126–137.
Statistics Sweden (1998). *New Started Enterprises in Sweden 1996 and 1997.*
Statistika meddelanden, SCB, Örebro.
Storey, D. (1994). *Understanding the Small Business Sector.* London: Routledge.
Thomas, K.-G. (1994). *Die mittelständische Unternehmung im Entwicklungsprozess*
(SMEs in their development process). Schriftenreihe Wirtschafts- und
Sozialwissenschaften, Bd.19. Ludwigsburg, Berlin.
Van Es, F. and Van Vuuren, D.J. (2011). A decomposition of the growth in self-
employment. *Applied Economics Letters*, 18(17), 1665–1669.
Veverková, S. (2012). *ERM comparative analytical report on public support instru-
ments to support self-employment and job creation in one-person and micro enter-
prises.* EMCC/Research Institute for Labour and Social Affairs.
Wössmann, L., and Schütz, G. (2006). *Efficiency and equity in European education
and training systems.* European Expert Network on Economics of Education
(EENEE). Analytical Report for the European Commission.

2. From unemployment to self-employment: government support programs in Greece

Argyro Nikiforou

INTRODUCTION

According to the most recent data released by the European Statistical Agency (Eurostat, 2013), the unemployment rate in Greece reached 27.9 percent in June 2013. Figure 2.1 shows that this is compared to 10.9 percent in the European Union as a whole (EU-27) and 12.1 percent in the Eurozone (EA-17), although Greece entered the crisis in 2008 with an unemployment rate similar to the European and Eurozone average. In Greece the unemployment rate has increased by more than 20 percent in just four years: 1.4 million individuals are unemployed, over 750,000 of

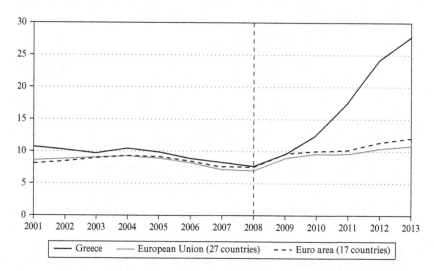

Figure 2.1   Unemployment rate (percent of civilian labor force), data from Eurostat (2013)

them are long-term unemployed, while approximately 400,000 families have no member earning an income. This situation threatens the social cohesion and stability and undermines the prospects for long-term sustainable economic growth.

To control and reduce unemployment a number of policy initiatives have been undertaken, including the support of unemployed individuals to become self-employed. Advancing our understanding of these programs is important, as they not only help the unemployed to go back to work, but they may also create new jobs for others (Caliendo and Künn, 2011; Caliendo and Kritikos, 2009; Dencker, Gruber, and Shah, 2009).

The purpose of this chapter is to provide a brief overview of the government programs that provide support to unemployed individuals to become self-employed in Greece. The target group, the duration and the financial assistance of the programs are presented, along with the eligibility criteria and other requirements of the programs. The key differences between the most recent (2010–2013) and the earlier programs are discussed in light of the economic and social restructuring that has taken place in Greece since the beginning of the global economic crisis.

OVERVIEW OF SUPPORT PROGRAMS IN GREECE

Two governmental bodies implement self-employment support programs in Greece: the Greek Manpower Employment Organization and the Ministry of Development, Competitiveness, Infrastructure, Transport and Networks. The Greek Manpower Employment Organization (Greek: Οργανισμός Απασχόλησης Εργαικού Δυναμικου/Ο.Α.Ε.Δ.) is the Greek unemployment agency and has a long history in implementing programs that support the transition from unemployment to self-employment. The Ministry of Development, Competitiveness, Infrastructure, Transport and Networks (Greek: Υπουργείο Ανάπτυξης, Ανταγωνιστικότητας, Υποδομών, Μεταφοπών και Δικτύων) has experience in conducting new venture creation support programs (for example, youth entrepreneurship, spin-off and spin-out ventures), but has only recently (2012) started to support specifically unemployed individuals to become self-employed.

The Greek Manpower Employment Organization Programs

The Greek Manpower Employment Organization (OAED) has implemented a large number of programs that provide support to unemployed individuals to create their own firms. These programs can be distinguished to the generic "New Freelancers" program, which is not addressed to a specific target group, and the specific programs, which can be categorized along several criteria, such as the gender, the age and the educational background of the unemployed individuals.

Generic program

The generic program of OAED "New Freelancers" is conducted every two to three years and is addressed to all unemployed individuals irrespectively of gender, geographical region and industrial sector of their prospective business activity. The program targets unemployed individuals registered in the unemployment registry of OAED. Its duration is one year, except for the last "New Freelancers 22–64 years old" program that was initiated in 2009 and lasted three years. Finally, the monetary support is provided in the form of grants. The financial support is up to 24,000 € (for the three year program) and depends on the duration of the program and the year of implementation.

Specific programs

The specific support programs are designed to target groups of population that are particularly vulnerable to unemployment, or to advance specific goals of broader social interest. They can be categorized along the following criteria:

- **Gender**: The most recent program of OAED, "Entrepreneurship of Unemployed Women 22–64 years old" (2010) was the first self-employment program of the unemployment agency that targeted women only.
- **Age**: In 2008, two programs targeted individuals of specific age groups. The "Young People and Entrepreneurship" program targeted unemployed individuals 22–32 years old, which was complemented by a program that targeted unemployed individuals 33–64 years old.
- **Educational background**: The "Young scientists" program (2009) was addressed only to scientists up to the age of 34 years old.
- **Family characteristics**: The "Entrepreneurship of Multimember Families" program (2006) was addressed to unemployed individuals, members of families with at least three children. At least one of the three children should be underage.
- **Geographical region**: There are programs that have been addressed to unemployed individuals who live in specific geographical areas of Greece. For example, the "Business Decentralization" program (2006) targeted unemployed individuals registered in the unemployment registries of the prefectures of Attica and Thessaloniki, in order to create firms outside these prefectures and in a distance of at least 100 km from the cities of Athens and Thessaloniki.[1]

Table 2.1   Examples of specific support programs

Gender	Entrepreneurship of Unemployed Women 22–64 years old (2010)
Age	Young People and Entrepreneurship, 22–32 years old (2009)
	New Freelancers 33–64 years old (2009)
Educational Background	Young Scientists (2009)
Family Characteristics	Entrepreneurship of Multimember Families (2006)
Geographical Scope	Integrated Intervention for Unemployed Individuals in Attica Periphery—Action of Self-Employment (2008)
	Business Decentralization (2006)
Sector	New Freelancers in the Culture Sector and Environment (2006)
	New Freelancers in the Culture Sector (2002)

- **Sector**: A small number of programs targeted individuals to become self-employed in specific sectors, including the culture sector and the environment.

Table 2.1 presents examples of specific support programs of OAED.
Despite the heterogeneity of the programs of OAED, there are some features common to the majority of them:

- **Target group**: The programs aim at unemployed individuals registered in the unemployment registry of OAED. Men should have fulfilled their military service obligations.
- **Duration**: The duration of the programs is limited to one year for the programs funded by national funds and three years for the programs that are co-funded by European and national funds.
- **Financial assistance**: The financial aid is provided in the form of grants through three to five periodic payments after the audit of the financial documents and the inspection of the business premises of the newly founded firms. The amount of the monetary support differs significantly among the programs and is up to 24,000 €. Some of the programs require the participants to show proof that they have supplementary funds to invest in their business activity.
- **Eligibility criteria**: Individuals are eligible for the programs, if they attended the entrepreneurship seminars, organized by OAED, and their business plan was approved. With few exceptions, the participants to the programs should not have prior entrepreneurial experience.

- **Other requirements**: The business premises of the participants should be clearly distinct from their home premises and the business premises of other entrepreneurs. A number of programs put restrictions on the maximum income of the unemployed individuals in the fiscal year before the application to the program.

The Ministry of Development, Competitiveness, Infrastructure, Transport and Networks Programs

Since 2012, the Ministry of Development has initiated two programs that have funded unemployed individuals to become self-employed. The target group, the duration, and the financial assistance of the programs are presented, along with the eligibility criteria and other program requirements.

Support of Entrepreneurship of Unemployed Individuals and of Start-ups Program (2012)

- **Target group**: The program targets unemployed individuals 18–64 years old and newly founded firms.
- **Duration**: The duration of the program is up to 24 months.
- **Financial assistance**: The monetary support is provided in the form of grants and ranges from 10,000 to 20,000 €. Extra financial support of 15,000 € is provided to the participants who create new jobs for others. The program can cover 100 percent of the expenses and provides the option to receive a 50 percent deposit by issuing a letter of guarantee.
- **Eligibility criteria**: The participation of the applicants to the program depends on the approval of their business plan.
- **Other requirements**: In contrast to earlier programs, the house premises of the participants could be used for their business activities. For unemployed men, the fulfillment of military service obligations stops being a criterion for their admission to the program.

Women Entrepreneurship Program (2013)

- **Target group**: The program targets women 18–64 years old who are:

  - registered unemployed individuals
  - employees who face a significant risk of becoming unemployed (that is, employees who have exercised their right to withhold labor)

- self-employed individuals who have terminated their business activity in the last three years or
- self-employed individuals with an income lower than the poverty threshold.

- **Duration**: The duration of the program is limited to 18 months.
- **Financial assistance**: The monetary support is provided in the form of grants and ranges from 10,000 to 20,000 €. Extra financial support of 12,000 € is provided to the participants if they create new jobs for others. The program can cover 100 percent of the expenses and provides the option for the participants to receive a 100 percent deposit by issuing a letter of guarantee.
- **Eligibility criteria**: The participation of the applicants to the program depends on the approval of their business plan.
- **Other requirements**: As in the 2012 support program, the house premises of the participants can be used for their business activities.

PROGRAM DIFFERENCES IN THE COURSE OF THE FINANCIAL CRISIS

Four key differences can be observed between the most recent (2010–2013) and the older government support programs in terms of (1) the target group of unemployed individuals, (2) the emphasis given on job creation, (3) the financial assistance, and (4) the business premises of the newly founded firms.

- **Target group of unemployed individuals**:

  - **Gender**: Two out of the three most recent programs are addressed to women only. This shows a significant change in the support programs, as no previous initiative targeted women only.
  - **Age**: The 2012 and 2013 support programs decrease the minimum age limit for individuals from 22 years old to 18 years old.
  - **Unemployment status**: As discussed in the previous section, the most recent support program (2013) is not restricted to unemployed individuals who are registered in the unemployment registry. Instead, it adopts a less strict definition of unemployment and also targets employees who face a high risk of becoming unemployed, self-employed individuals who have

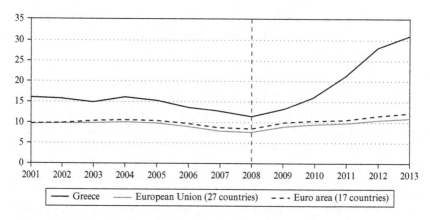

Figure 2.2   Female unemployment rate, data from Eurostat (2013)

terminated their business activity in the last three years, and self-employed individuals with an income below the poverty threshold.

- **Stronger emphasis on job creation**: The programs initiated in 2012 and 2013 put strong emphasis on job creation by offering extra financial support (15,000 and 12,000 € respectively) for new job creation.
- **Financial assistance**: In contrast to a number of previously conducted programs, the 2012 and 2013 programs do not require from the participants supplementary own funds. They further provide the formerly unemployed entrepreneurs with the option to receive a 50 to 100 percent deposit of the funds by issuing a letter of guarantee.

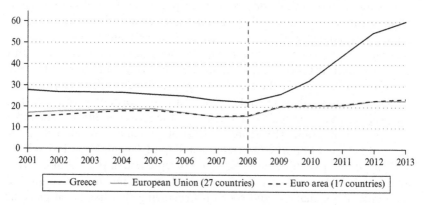

Figure 2.3   Youth unemployment rate, data from Eurostat (2013)

- **Business premises**: In contrast to earlier programs, the 2012 and 2013 support programs permit self-employed individuals to operate their business from home.

The aforementioned differences reflect the substantial labor market and economic restructuring that has taken place in Greece since the beginning of the global financial crisis. The crisis has disproportionately affected women and the youth. According to Eurostat in June 2013, the unemployment rate for females reached 31.9 percent, considerably higher than the rate for males (24.9 percent), while youth unemployment rate reached 61.5 percent. At the same time, female and youth unemployment in the EU-27 was 11 percent and 23.2 percent respectively (Figures 2.2 and 2.3). These differentials are calling for policy initiatives that reduce unemployment among these groups.

The emphasis on new job creation by the newly founded firms highlights the fact that government support programs aimed at unemployed individuals can help achieve this goal not only by helping individuals transition from unemployment to self-employment, but also by creating jobs for others (Dencker, Gruber, and Shah, 2009). Finally, the option for the participants to receive a 50 to 100 percent deposit of the funds and the possibility of operating their business from home compensates the decrease in the Greek household income and their inability to secure sufficient funds to invest in a new business.

CONCLUSION AND FUTURE RESEARCH

This chapter provides a brief overview of the Greek government programs that support the transition from unemployment to self-employment. Despite the heterogeneity of the programs in terms of the target group, duration, financial support provided and other features, two common patterns can be observed. First, the financial support offered by both OAED and Ministry of Development programs is quite generous. Lasting from one to three years, the financial support offered for self-employment initiatives is up to 35,000 € and is provided in the form of grants. Second, the programs have been altered to adapt to the crisis conditions. The three most recent programs (Entrepreneurship of Unemployed Women 22–64 years old, 2010; Support of Entrepreneurship of Unemployed Individuals and of Start-ups, 2012; and Women Entrepreneurship Program, 2013) reveal that policy initiatives have evolved by taking into account the economic, labor market, and social restructuring that has taken place in Greece in the last four years.

However, to better understand the support programs in Greece, more work is needed to shed light on several issues such as the ones indicated below.

Support Mechanisms

The examination of the support mechanisms can help the governmental bodies that implement the self-employment support programs to provide better services before, during and after a firm's creation. Several questions revolving around the support mechanisms require further consideration: How efficiently do the governmental bodies communicate the support programs to unemployed individuals across the country? How satisfied are formerly unemployed individuals with the grant application process? Are there any nonfinancial support services currently in place (for example, access to network contacts, coaching and training) that can help entrepreneurs during and after business creation?

Program Outcomes

- **Firm survival and job creation**: Prior research has shown that firms created by unemployed individuals seem to have slightly higher survival chances than other populations of newly created firms (Dencker, Gruber, and Shah, 2009; Brüderl, Preisendörfer, and Ziegler, 1992) and may also create jobs for others (Caliendo and Künn, 2011; Caliendo and Kritikos, 2009; Dencker, Gruber, and Shah, 2009). In order to evaluate the effectiveness of the support programs in Greece, the survival rate and job creation of the firms that were founded by formerly unemployed individuals need to be measured and compared with those of new firms created by other categories of individuals.
- **Firm revenues**: Firm revenues constitute an important indicator for new firm performance (Eisenhardt and Schoonhoven, 1990). Monitoring firm revenues and revenue growth, that is, the increase of revenues over time could help policymakers to measure how fast the firms created by unemployed individuals are expanding in relation to other populations of newly created firms.
- **Work and life satisfaction**: In addition to more traditional performance measures, the evaluation of work and life satisfaction of the formerly unemployed entrepreneurs is critical, because Greece's financial crisis has significantly affected the mental health of its people. It has led to a substantial increase in suicide rates (Kentikelenis et al., 2011) and in all types of psychological disorders,

including anxiety, depression and antisocial behavior (Chaffin, 2012). High levels of work satisfaction and life satisfaction among the entrepreneurs that started their firms as a means to get out of unemployment can to some extent protect entrepreneurs and their families from psychological strain, thereby contributing to the psychological well-being at the society level.

Comparisons Across Programs and Geographical Areas

The heterogeneity of the programs allows comparisons across the different support schemes. For example, it would be interesting to examine whether there are any systematic differences in firm survival and job creation across programs that provided different levels of monetary support, or whether there are any substantial differences in the satisfaction outcomes across the targeted groups of the programs (for example young people versus 33–64-year-old people). The geographical diversity and the different population density levels in Greece also favor meaningful comparisons across the different geographical areas of the country. Questions such as the following can be asked: Does the impact of the support programs differ in the prefecture of Attica, where more than a third of Greece's population resides, from their impact in the different regions of the country? Are the self-employment support programs equally effective in the urban and the rural areas of Greece? Gaining insights into these topics could help policymakers offer more targeted support to the unemployed who choose to become self-employed.

NOTE

1. Athens, the capital of Greece, is located in the prefecture of Attica; Thessaloniki is the second largest city in Greece.

REFERENCES

Brüderl, J., Preisendörfer, P., and Ziegler, R. (1992). Survival chances of newly founded business organizations. *American Sociological Review*, 57(April), 227–242.
Caliendo, M., and Kritikos, A.S. (2009). I want to, but I also need to: start-ups resulting from opportunity and necessity. *IZA Discussion Papers*, paper 4661.
Caliendo, M., and Künn, S. (2011). Start-up subsidies for the unemployed: long-term evidence and effect heterogeneity. *Journal of Public Economics*, 95(3), 311–331.
Chaffin, J. (2012, December 27). Crisis takes toll on Greeks' mental health.

Financial Times. Retrieved on October 2, 2013 from www.ft.com/intl/cms/s/0/2c7f2302-49c0-11e2-a625-144feab49a.html#axzz2gYkhyvOk.

Dencker, J.C., Gruber, M., and Shah, S.K. (2009). Individual and opportunity factors influencing job creation in new firms. *Academy of Management Journal*, 52(6), 1125–1147.

Eisenhardt, K.M., and Schoonhoven, C.B. (1990). Organizational growth: linking founding team, strategy, environment, and growth among U.S. semiconductor ventures, 1978–1988. *Administrative Science Quarterly*, 35(3), 504–529.

Eurostat (2013). Unemployment statistics. Retrieved on October 2, 2013 from http://epp.eurostat.ec.europa.eu.

Kentikelenis, A., Karanikolos, M., Papanicolas, I., Basu, S., McKee, M., and Stuckler, D. (2011). Health effects of financial crisis: omens of a Greek tragedy. *The Lancet*, 378(9801), 1457–1458.

3. Pete Suazo Business Center

Gladys Gonzalez, Robert Heyn
and Jessica Pino

INTRODUCTION—PSBC FOUNDERS AND HISTORY

In 1991, Gladys Gonzalez, a native Colombian woman, arrived to Utah with her children looking for a safe place to escape from the war on drugs and the guerrillas that were destroying her country. At first, her transition was hard: she was cleaning floors, delivering newspapers, working three jobs at a time and attending university. In 1993, Gladys and her daughter Sandra founded the Hispanic newspaper *Mundo Hispano* in an effort to give a voice to the Hispanic community and promote the integration of Hispanics to the mainstream community. In 1995, *Mundo Hispano* was about to collapse because of cash flow problems. Gladys and Sandra needed $10,000 to solve their problems, but neither of them had collateral to offer in order to obtain a loan. After several attempts to secure a business loan proved unsuccessful, they felt that they had no other resources available to them. Gladys had worked for an American Bank in Colombia, so she knew the requirements to obtain a loan and she felt that she would be perceived as an ignorant woman seeking for a loan with no collateral. She also felt inadequate because of her strong Spanish accent.

In a last ditch effort to save *Mundo Hispano*, Gladys and Sandra shared their struggles with their good friend, and Hispanic Senator of Utah, Pete Suazo. Upon hearing from Gladys and Sandra, Senator Suazo explained that, if they had a letter of refusal from a bank for a loan and a solid business plan to present to interested parties, he would help them connect with the Utah Microenterprise Loan Fund (UMLF), a non-profit organization dedicated to helping small business owners to obtain loans when they were declined by a regular bank. Shortly after their meeting together, Gladys was in front of the UMLF loan committee presenting her request, with the business plan, and within a week she had the $10,000 check. This was the day the Pete Suazo Business Center model was born.

Gladys photocopied the check and outlined what she envisioned to be a business center located in Salt Lake City to help other minorities like her who were (1) struggling to keep their businesses alive or (2) trying to start a new small business. The more Gladys thought about the idea the more excited she became. She was able to empathize with other minorities in the area who desperately needed to learn hard business skills, such as: financial literacy, sales models, marketing models, inventory control systems, legal structures, and so on. Gladys also recognized the need to teach local minorities the soft skills necessary to develop or grow a small business in the United States, to become productive citizens, and to foster economic development for the state of Utah. The outline slept in the drawer of her night table for about six years; she would read it from time to time, seeking guidance to fulfill her dream.

In 2001 Gladys was appointed by U.S. Senator Robert Bennett to represent Utah's Hispanic community in the Congress Hispanic Task Force in Washington DC and during the interview the Senator manifested his desire to help Utah minority communities. At this time, Gladys believed it was the moment of opportunity to start the business center for minorities. She talked to the Senator about the outline she had written and he requested to see it. Three weeks later, Tim Sheehan, the State Director for the Senator, called Gladys to let her know the Senator liked what he read and was willing to help her to develop the project.

In August of the same year (2001) Utah's Senator Pete Suazo passed away in an accident, leaving behind his family and a devastated Hispanic community. After receiving permission from Senator Suazo's family, Gladys registered her business center under the name "Pete Suazo Business Center" (PSBC).

PSBC has a two-pronged mission in its effort to serve Utah's Latino/Hispanic and other under-served populations: (1) Provide education on what is needed to start and run a successful business in the United States and (2) Serve as an access point for organizations, institutions and other existing entities that wish to offer their services to the under-served community in this area.

MINORITY FOCUS

The center educates a large portion of the adult minority communities who are disenfranchised from education due to various circumstances such as age, cultural and language barriers, lack of financial resources and need of evening schedules. Furthermore, coming from different cultures makes it harder for students to learn a financial subject while trying to fit among mainstream peers; studying business concepts exclusively in English in an unfamiliar environment is not an easy task.

INSTITUTIONAL FINANCING/FUNDING

The PSBC had a very humble beginning in a tiny office rented at the Salt Lake Neighborhood Housing that hosted the center for two years until Senator Bennett and Robert Heyn helped the institution to obtain a $500,000 grant from HUD to build its own facilities. A few of PSBC's corporate sponsors are:

- Zions Bank
- Goldman Sachs
- Morgan Stanley
- Governor's Office for Economic Development of Utah
- Mexican Government—IME
- Department of Workforce Services
- United Way of Salt Lake.

PSBC Courses Include:

- Business Plan Development
- Accounting
- Electronic Bookkeeping
- Taxes for LLCs
- Business Finances
- Sales
- Financial Literacy.

PERSONAL FINANCE TRAINING

PSBC provides current and prospective entrepreneurs, and their families and friends, with a strong foundation on personal finances through our Personal Wealth workshops:

- **Personal Wealth I: Budgeting and Saving (Family Finance Credit)** is a three-hour session of theory and hands-on instruction of basic financial management skills. Participants are exposed to family budgeting skills, consumer credit and challenges frequently associated with credit and family financial planning and wise investments.
- **Personal Wealth II: Managing Credit Wisely (Family Finance Wealth)** is a three-hour session of theory and hands-on instruction of basic wealth building skills taught in a workshop setting. Participants are

given an in-depth understanding of making sound purchases, wise savings and sound investments. Exposure is given to retirement planning, stocks and bonds, and real estate investments.

MENTORING

As a complement to their business classes, PSBC students have access to one-on-one mentoring. In mentoring sessions, students learn how to apply the concepts they learn in class directly to their businesses. Weekly mentoring sessions are set up with professionals who have experience and education in diverse areas of business, such as:

- Finance
- Marketing
- Sales
- Accounting
- Operations
- Management
- Construction
- Food industry.

TECHNOLOGY ASSISTANCE

PSBC provides its students with the opportunity to participate in hands-on workshops covering essential computer skills with the following courses and programs:

- Windows® Operating System
- Internet Browsers
- Email Applications
- Word®
- Excel®
- QuickBooks®.

MICRO-LOANS

PSBC students who demonstrate a high commitment to their business education at the center and present a viable business plan may become eligible for a loan. Micro-lending: the maximum money lent is $5,000. These small loans have helped small businesses to buy equipment, have working capital or get a business started more quickly.

Screening Loan Applicants

In order to receive a PSBC loan applicants have to:

- Have taken classes and seminars at the center
- Be under the direction of a mentor at the center
- Complete a business plan
- Fill a loan application
- Make a presentation to the PSBC loan committee.

Post-loan Process

Loan recipients continue with frequent meetings with a mentor at the center. In addition, loan recipients meet with the Executive Director every other quarter to review their business progress.

CURRENT STATUS

During 2012 PSBC served 311 companies, helped to incorporate 132 new companies, provided 1,625 counseling hours, taught 252 classes and seminars, had 2,166 attendees to classes/seminars and served 802 households. One of the most important goals for the future is to make the PSBC more self-sufficient by becoming less reliant upon donations. Today, the Pete Suazo Business Center stands on the west side of Salt Lake City as a witness of what it means to live the American Dream achieved through hard work, integration to Utah's society, generosity of donors and trust in God.

PART II

Private/non-governmental programs

4. Bharatiya Yuva Shakti Trust

Raj K. Shankar

INTRODUCTION[1]

Bharatiya Yuva Shakti Trust (BYST) is a not-for-profit organization that assists disadvantaged Indian youth in converting business ideas into viable enterprises under the guidance of a mentor. The program supports young entrepreneurs in the age group of 18–35, who are either unemployed or underemployed, by providing financing, business support services such as training, networking, monitoring and mentoring. The young entrepreneurs are nurtured until they become self-sufficient.

Over the past two decades, BYST has expanded and set up eight regional clusters (Delhi, Rural Haryana, Chennai, Rural Tamilnadu, Pune, Hyderabad, Rural Maharashtra and Assam) in India and financed close to 3,000 entrepreneurs creating employment for over 30,000 people. Ten percent of BYST supported entrepreneurs have become millionaires. BYST through its training and signposting initiatives has reached out to close to 100,000 young people nationwide (Narasimhan, 2014; Marich, 2012).

BYST works, with the captains of Indian industry, to support young underprivileged entrepreneurs and helps to create employment across the country. BYST's co-founder Lakshmi Venkatesan says,

> BYST's major focus is on the youth, both men and women entrepreneurs and those with physical disabilities. Amongst the youth, young entrepreneurs are particularly at a disadvantage, as banks do not finance them for want of collaterals. In fact there are several levels of disadvantages youth face such as economic, social, gender based etc. Money alone also cannot solve these problems; guidance and hand-holding is [sic] equally required. (Rai, n.d.)

According to estimates, 69 percent of India's population is below 35 years of age and a large majority is underemployed (Rajendram, 2013). It is also said that 4 percent of the total adult population in India are driven to entrepreneurship due to necessity or lack of better job opportunities (Saraf and Banerjee, 2015). A solution needs to be found or else it could turn into a demographic disaster. To turn this disaster into dividend, BYST has taken it upon itself to create an ecosystem which is more nurturing of the young people. It intends to create an ecosystem in which young entrepreneurs can set up their own business, thrive and become self-sufficient.

The trust is supported and managed by the Confederation of Indian Industry (CII), India's premier business association, as part of its corporate citizenship initiative.

THE INSPIRATION

Being the daughter of the President of India could have enabled her to choose a comfortable life, but Lakshmi V. Venkatesan, daughter of former President Mr. Venkataraman, had different plans. During one of the state visits in which she accompanied her father to London, she was deeply influenced by the foundation run by Prince Charles, which was mentoring school drop-outs and equipping them with skills and work experience.

Unable to contain her entrepreneurial self, inspired by the above, she left her comfortable job at a multinational organization to launch a trust, which would enable the youth of India to aspire and live the entrepreneurial life. She decided to support grassroots youth, both unemployed and underemployed, and enable them to dream and achieve a respectable life. The tool used was entrepreneurship with self-sustenance and job creation as the program's aim. The project launched in association with Youth Business International, UK has served as a blueprint for rollouts across many other countries.

BRIEF HISTORY

BYST was inspired by, and officially launched by, HRH Prince Charles, in 1992 in New Delhi. The late Bharat Ratna, JRD Tata, a doyen of Indian industry was an encouraging and inspiring supporter of the initiative. After successfully launching and running programs in urban areas of Delhi and Chennai by the end of 1993, a need was felt to explore enterprise development amongst rural youth. With this objective, BYST started its operations in the villages of Rural Haryana in 1994. Escorts Limited, a leading Indian corporate house, supported BYST in fulfilling its agenda of developing dynamic microentrepreneurs in the villages. The rural success has resulted in BYST being operational in over 90 villages across Haryana. As BYST increased its activities on the field of youth entrepreneurship development throughout the country, early results got attention. The corporate sector started recognizing the work of BYST and acknowledged the need for generating employment through entrepreneurship.

In the middle of 1994, BYST was approached by Diageo (multinational) to launch a youth entrepreneurship development program in Pune (Maharashtra, Western India). CII, which was already supporting BYST in Delhi and Chennai, came forward to provide the infrastructure and managerial support. Inspired by the overwhelming success of the urban Pune program BYST extended the work into rural Maharashtra.

After the success of various regional programs, BYST was recognized as a developing country model for youth entrepreneurship development. It was another milestone for BYST when American Insurance Group (AIG), a leading multinational, came forward to lend support to BYST's program in Hyderabad. The Hyderabad program was similar to other urban locations such as Delhi, Chennai and Pune, and was launched in 1998. BYST also has been a pioneer in catalyzing non-collateral funding through banks, mentor development and most recently micro-equity growth funding. The program, apart from expanding to eight regions of India, has also come a long way in supporting and establishing similar initiatives across the world.

UNIQUENESS OF BYST: THE 'GURU-SISHYA TRADITION'

BYST accepts applicants from doll making to hi-tech electronics without asking for 'financial down payments or collaterals'. Seed capital is provided as a low-interest, non-collateral loan, which entrepreneurs use alone or in conjunction with financing from banks and other financial institutions. But apart from this financial assistance, BYST differentiates itself by being there for the entrepreneur in a way that matters most to them.

The ancient Indian principle of 'guru–sishya parampara', envisaged a close relationship between the guru (teacher) and sishya (disciple). Not only did the guru impart skills to the sishya, but also developed a sense of self-confidence and values. Along the same lines BYST pairs each entrepreneur with a mentor—a guide who acts as a 'guru'. The mentor is a friend, philosopher and guide to the entrepreneur. Mentors spend two to three hours of quality time in a fortnight to instill confidence, provide psychological support, help understand simple business management techniques and facilitate independent decision-making.

This 'people helping people' is what BYST is all about. The model, apart from contributing to the program's success, has also given BYST its uniqueness.

OBJECTIVES OF BYST

The immediate objective of BYST is to empower young dynamic disadvantaged microentrepreneurs and integrate them into the mainstream of society. BYST also intends to be a role model, nationally and internationally, for mentoring and nurturing necessity-driven start-up businesses through the active involvement of the corporate sector.

In the long term, BYST aspires to be in the forefront of entrepreneurship development for underprivileged youth, create employment opportunities and contribute to national development. BYST will develop and nurture entrepreneurial qualities among youth of India, support self-employment in manufacturing and services, and make available mentors/volunteers who can provide timely advice for growth of entrepreneurial ventures.

ORGANIZATION STRUCTURE

BYST's Board of Trustees is comprised of some of the most eminent members of the Indian business community. Currently, Mr. Rahul Bajaj (Chairman, Bajaj Group) is the Chairman of BYST. Other members of the Board of Trustees include: Ms. Lakshmi V. Venkatesan (Co-founder), Mr. Sunil Bharti Mittal (Chairman, Bharti Enterprises), Mr. Jamshyd N. Godrej (Chairman, Godrej and Boyce), Ms. Anu Aga (former Chairperson, Thermax Ltd), Mr. Suresh Neotia (Group Patriarch, Ambuja Realty Group), Mr. Yogesh C. Deveshwar (Chairman, ITC Ltd), Mr. Gautam Thapar (Chairman, Avantha Group), Mr. Nachiket Mor (Board member, RBI and CARE) and Mr. Tarun Das (former Chief mentor, CII).

Policy decisions are taken by the trustees during the quarterly board meeting. The co-founder and Executive Vice President Ms. Lakshmi Venkatesan, leads and manages the day-to-day operations. She is assisted by heads of policy and operations respectively. Branch managers are responsible for the running of respective regional offices.

HOW DOES BYST OPERATE?

Business proposals from potential entrepreneurs typically in the age bracket of 18–35 are received directly or through vocational schools, entrepreneurial training institutions and other non-governmental organizations (NGOs). Most of these necessity-driven youth are unemployed or underemployed, but have sound ideas and tremendous will for success. In many cases, assistance is also provided to help formulate these proposals.

The proposals are screened by an Entrepreneur Selection Panel (ESP). ESP is comprised of experts from the industry in marketing, finance, management, and so on. On approval of the proposal by the panel, a number of business support services are offered. A mentor is assigned who provides guidance until the venture becomes sustainable. BYST's plan of support is comprehensive and complete ranging from loans, business mentors, training, networking and marketing.

The services provided can be broadly classified into three groups:

1. Entrepreneur Support Services

BYST offers support to young people at various stages of the business start-up process. It provides support from identifying potential opportunities, building business plans and also setting up the enterprises.

- Training on key aspects of managing small businesses is delivered across all regional offices.
- The online BYST portal acts as a one-stop-shop of information for the entire stakeholder community, primarily designed to facilitate connections, discussion and knowledge-sharing.
- A quarterly newsletter in numerous regional languages provides a shared platform for entrepreneurs to exchange views, ideas and other business tips.
- Referral of performing entrepreneurs with a good track record in loan repayments to banks and other financial institutions for further financial assistance.
- Creating opportunities to increase exposure for entrepreneurs by making new contacts and helping realize market potential.
- Business Excellence Awards: The JRD Tata Young Entrepreneur Award in memory of BYST's Founding Chairman, Mr. JRD Tata. It rewards entrepreneurs in three performance-related categories and serves as an encouragement to aspire higher.
- Entrepreneur recognition: BYST actively nominates and supports their entrepreneurs to win accolades. Many of BYST's entrepreneurs have won 'Citi Micro Entrepreneur Awards' as well as the prestigious YBI Young Entrepreneur awards a number of times.

2. Mentoring

Mentoring is the crux of BYST's program. Mentors are volunteers from many walks of life such as business, accounting, marketing and academics. They are professionals who dedicate a part of their time to share experience and skills with entrepreneurs. As BYST expanded the scope of its activities, it developed a more formalized and comprehensive mentoring program.

Mentor model
BYST mentors are a key link between the entrepreneur and BYST. BYST has developed a flexible mentoring model to meet the challenges that arise as a result of both the size of the country and the mix of rural and urban entrepreneurs:

a. **One-on-One Mentoring**—Young entrepreneurs are matched with a personal mentor, who typically meets the entrepreneur regularly. This is mostly practiced in urban areas and relationship continues over a period of time.
b. **Mobile Mentor Clinics**—Since mentor availability in rural areas is limited, mentors drawn from diverse backgrounds travel together to visit and guide entrepreneurs. This ensures access to a range of skills typically unavailable in rural settings.
c. **Emergency Mentor Clinics**—At times entrepreneurs have specific challenges and need immediate support. Mentor groups based on expertise are formed in order to help respond to such unique situations. This is predominantly practiced in rural areas.

BYST has ambitious plans to significantly expand its mentor pool. Currently it has close to 1000 mentors, recruited through a number of routes, including arrangements with organizations such as Rotary Clubs, corporate partners and business schools. BYST holds a database of industry and resource personnel, NGOs and professional associations, and frequently targets them through direct mailings to mobilize additional mentors.

Mentors and entrepreneurs are required to meet at least once per month. In practice, many exceed this, meeting fortnightly, weekly and at times every day. BYST mentors are also required to monitor and report regularly on the progress of their entrepreneurs. This supervision proves crucial, particularly during the first two years of the enterprises' life, while reducing default rates on loan repayments.

Recognizing and accrediting mentors
Mentors are the backbone of BYST's success. They help young entrepreneurs across urban and rural areas at the early stages to enable them to scale new heights. Accredited mentors are those senior business professionals who have completed ten hours of volunteer mentoring in BYST to budding entrepreneurs and have completed and passed all the modules of

the six-hour online mentor course offered through City & Guilds (C&G) London, the UK's largest and best known vocational training and certification body. Since mentoring is a highly valued skill in today's world there is a huge demand for accredited mentors. It is strongly believed that this accreditation will give universal recognition to the mentors and instill a sense of pride in them.

3. Funding Assistance

Though it is the wise counsel of a seasoned mentor that truly shapes entrepreneurs and their enterprises, the importance of finance cannot be undermined. While BYST initially focused on providing seed funding, it is now constantly working to increase the number of funding options, especially growth capital for its entrepreneurs.

Collateral free loan assistance

BYST has arrangements with banks to enable eligible enterprising entrepreneurs to gain collateral-free loans. BYST screens aspiring entrepreneurs, maps them to a mentor who works along with them and makes them investment worthy. Once they are ready for availing financial support, BYST recommends the entrepreneur and their start-up to the identified financial institution. After scrutiny by the financial institution, the collateral-free loan is made available to the entrepreneur.

In recent times due to the success of many of BYST's entrepreneurs, there has been a need to increase the quantum and type of funding. Hence BYST has signed a memorandum of understanding with Indian Overseas Bank (IOB), a public sector bank for making available funds to its entrepreneurs. According to this arrangement, IOB will provide loans up to 50 lakh for manufacturing units and 25 lakh for services plus units supported by BYST (Narasimhan, 2014). Apart from identifying the eligible entrepreneurs, BYST will also provide business mentoring, business planning and marketing support to these young entrepreneurs. BYST also has similar arrangements with other financial institutions.

A micro-equity growth fund

BYST's experience in the field has brought to its notice a group of entrepreneurs who can neither access equity nor loans. BYST calls it 'the missing middle'. But many of these enterprises have potential for scale and larger social impact. To catalyze the growth of these small, disadvantaged, yet smart entrepreneurs, BYST in association with Ventureast (Venture Capital Firm) and International Finance Corporation (IFC), has set up a unique growth fund. This fund will invest in those small businesses, which can neither raise equity (since there is no exit option), nor raise debt (because of the lack of collateral). Typically, the BYST fund invests anywhere between 10 lakh and 50 lakh in such ventures for a time period of say five to eight years. The investee company provides returns in the form of share of profits or revenues. Being a futuristic model it seems to have its own growth pains, some of which include: establishing scale, finding the right microentrepreneurs and making microentrepreneurs understand this model and structuring of the financial return model (Premkumar, 2011; Seth, 2009).

Where does BYST get its funds from?

Funding is always a challenge for every social venture. Funding is required not just to set up and sustain the operations, but also for the growth of the enterprise. With regard to the sources of funding, Lakshmi Venkatesan reflects on her earliest days,

> When we started off we had no funds. We approached Banks and even went to public sectors but got no support. For 12 years we gave our own funds through credit guarantee scheme for upcoming entrepreneurs. We supported them via growth funds such as the micro equity funds. Subsequently through IFT, SIDBI and some high net individuals we would take and give Rs.50,000 and turn several entrepreneurs into crorepatis. (Rai, n.d.)

Once the success of the program became clear to people, a lot more individuals and institutions came forward to provide resources, both monetary and otherwise. BYST has two broad sources of income (YBI, 2012):

Partnership income

Corporations, governments and international agencies provide close to 80 percent of the program's necessary funding. BYST receives a significant amount of general corporate donations towards its corpus. Alternatively, partnerships are also used to run specific programs or establishment of regional initiatives (for example, Escorts for Rural Haryana and AIG for Hyderabad).

BYST has also developed strong relationships with other partners for non-monetary services. The Confederation of Indian Industry (CII), India's leading industry association, provides office space and administrative support free of charge for BYST headquarters and regional operations.

Internal income

The remaining 20 percent of funds is generated through interest earned from investment of up to three quarters of the core funds as fixed deposits. Small service charges (varies according to size and length of loan), paid by successful BYST supported entrepreneurs, contribute to the funding. This was first piloted in the financial year 2007–2008, and it has provided close to Rs 4.68 million (US$101,000) for BYST as early as the end of October 2009.

The bank partnerships allow BYST to reduce its operating costs, making the program more sustainable, thereby positioning it for scale and growth.

BYST's Board of Trustees is comprised of prominent industrialists who are themselves great donors for social causes. Their networks also help in reaching the right individuals and institutions for raising resources and support.

INSTITUTIONAL PARTNERSHIPS

Youth Business International (YBI)

Youth Business International, UK (an association of youth business initiatives around the globe) comprised of 35 nations, has set up several youth business initiatives to help disadvantaged young people in starting up businesses and becoming entrepreneurs. YBI was founded as a joint venture of The Prince of Wales International Business Leaders Forum (IBLF) and The Prince's Trust.

BYST is a founding partner of YBI and in this capacity has helped other countries like Sri Lanka, Mauritius, South Africa, and so on, set up similar development models. BYST also works with YBI created forums to exchange best practices with other developing countries. Many developing countries like Namibia, Uganda, Ghana, Kenya, South Africa, Mauritius and Bhutan have approached and been helped by BYST for support in setting up youth business initiatives in their respective countries.

United Nations Development Program (UNDP)

The United Nations Development Program (UNDP) is the UN's principal provider of development advice, advocacy and grant support. It has long enjoyed the trust and confidence of governments and NGOs in many parts of the developing world, as well as the developed world.

As part of its global initiatives to tackle the youth unemployment problem, the UN Secretary-General has formed a Youth Employment Policy Network (YEPN) combining UNDP, ILO and the World Bank. BYST plays a key role as part of YEPN's task force to reduce unemployment.

International Labour Organization (ILO)

The International Labour Organization is the UN specialized agency which seeks the promotion of social justice and internationally recognized human and labor rights. It promotes the development of independent employers' and workers' organizations and provides training and advisory services to those organizations.

BYST was chosen as an effective practice program by the ILO Sustainable Employment and Economic Development (SEED) program. It has been highlighted, in particular, for its mentoring model and has been designated as a Center of Excellence for its mentoring model. It has also been asked to develop a mentoring tool kit, to compliment the other tools being developed and disseminated. BYST has also written an article on its mentoring model for a publication that is being produced with support from the ILO and International Development Research Centre in Canada.

BYST works closely with number of educational institutions. It shares the experience gained from entrepreneur development programs, mentoring processes and showcasing success stories of entrepreneurs. BYST also engages in activities that inspire students to take up entrepreneurship as a career option. BYST was the host of the 2011 Global Entrepreneurship Week in India taking the message of entrepreneurship to the masses (Marich, 2012).

INDIAN CORPORATE CONNECT

The Indian business community actively supports the Trust. Their voluntary support extends from donations, professional assistance and sponsorship of events to assigning mentors. Some of the key Indian businesses supporting the Trust today include:

- TATA Group: The TATAs have donated liberally towards the BYST corpus fund. They also donate money for the JRD Tata Young Entrepreneur Award, which was instituted in the name of the late Mr. JRD Tata.
- Escorts Ltd: The late Mr. H.P. Nanda, one of the founding trustees of BYST and also the Chairman of the Escorts group, cherished a dream of nurturing rural entrepreneurs. This resulted in the formation of BYST in Rural Haryana in 1994. Presently BYST is operational from the Escort's Rural Development Department. Apart from providing space and other support in kind, Escorts also provides funds for the BYST corpus.

- Bajaj group: Mr. Rahul Bajaj, Chairman and Managing Director of Bajaj Auto Ltd, is the current chairman of BYST. He ensures that the Trust gets adequate funds and mentors for running the entrepreneurship development program.

MULTINATIONALS

Apart from getting help from the Indian Business Community, BYST has also forged partnerships with various multinationals.

- Diageo (UK): With the help of Diageo, BYST set up the Pune (Maharashtra) program in 1996. Apart from providing the funds to run the program, Diageo provided mentors to young entrepreneurs assisted by BYST.
- American International Group (AIG): The collaboration between AIG and BYST was another success story of rich dividends reaped. Joining hands to launch the Hyderabad program in 1998 has yielded many entrepreneur success stories.
- The Keep Walking Fund (KWF): After the success of the Rural Haryana Program, the Johnnie Walker KWF joined hands with BYST to launch the rural Maharashtra program in 2001. Like other corporate and business partners, KWF provides the much-needed mentors and funds for the running of the program.
- The Confederation of Indian Industry (CII): The apex industrial institution has been a keen supporter of BYST since inception. It provides support in the form of administrative and infrastructure support at head office as well as regional offices.

Help is also received in the form of smaller donations in cash or as volunteer time of owners and employees. Promotions of BYST initiatives, sourcing of entrepreneurs (deserving ones) as well as high quality mentors are various ways in which help is offered by individuals and organizations. All donations made to BYST are eligible for deduction under section 80-G of the Indian Income Tax Act. The Trust is also registered under the Foreign Contribution Regulation Act (FCRA) for receiving overseas contributions.

IMPACT OF BYST

'Ten percent of BYST supported entrepreneurs have become millionaires,' says Lakshmi Venkatesan (Santhanam, 2010). Success is natural when one provides the right ecosystem to entrepreneurial minds. The Bharatiya Yuva Shakti Trust has supported and financed over 2000 entrepreneurs which in turn have created 30,000 jobs. A representative set of success stories below showcase the impact of BYST's work in the field.

Story 1: Sharad Tandale, Innovation Engineers and Contractors

Sharad comes from an economically marginalized community of farmers, in which less than 1 percent of people start a business. His family and community were opposed to his entrepreneurial ideas. Sharad managed to get a degree in engineering from a rural institute, with the help of a government scholarship.

After his studies, he landed his first job in the city of Pune, but was unable to sustain himself. He went on to take up a number of engineering work orders, but lacked the capital to execute them. No bank or financial institution was willing to support him without collateral or guarantee. It was during this period that he came across BYST. BYST and the bank's joint selection panel were impressed by the way in which Sharad had broken through the barriers of his tribal background to build up work contracts. They approved Sharad a loan amount of US$20,000 for raw materials and equipment.

Apart from being a finalist in YBI Entrepreneur of the Year 2013, Sharad's success is in positioning himself today as a community icon at the national level. Sharad's half a million dollar business in infrastructure services, 'Innovation Engineers and Contractors,' provides infrastructure engineering services such as laying underground cable, building roads, water pipe fitting, mobile towers and electrical services and employs more than 200 people. These are rural youth who have limited potential for skilled work, and are provided on-the-job training. He provides support for his night shift employees, educational support for employees' children and annual rejuvenation trips for supervisors. Sharad insists on all standard safety precautions and gives his employees accident insurance coverage. Sharad also provides advisory help to his friends to start up their own businesses (YBI, 2014a).

Story 2: Sonam Patil, Shree Group Designers and Manufacturers

In the male dominated world of Indian garment manufacturing, Sonam has made great strides in creating an impressive business in designing and manufacturing clothing, particularly uniforms for schools and companies. Sonam was compelled to consider entrepreneurship after her husband took ill, because without any work experience no employer would hire her.

Sonam approached BYST with her business proposal and secured a collateral-free loan of US$16,000 which she used to start her business at her warehouse. Due to an unfortunate fire at her warehouse, she had to call on support from many parts of the community—including customers, who agreed to pay higher advances and suppliers who gave her additional credit. She acknowledges that her survival through this turbulent period has been made possible by the support of BYST, especially her BYST mentor who helped her sail through the difficult times.

Established in the year 2009, 'Shree Group,' today is a new name in the field of manufacturing and supply of uniforms and garments. Within four years, Sonam achieved a turnover of US$350,000, provided direct employment to 120 people (80 women) and provided indirect employment to 480 people. Their product range encompasses uniforms for schools, offices, security personnel and the police force. Through her business, Sonam has been able to demonstrate her social commitment in a number of ways, including providing a doctor free of charge to employees, sponsoring school education of one child for every employee, providing school uniforms to employees' children, and encouraging five women to start up their own businesses (YBI, 2014b).

Story 3: Arun Awatade, Iris Polymers

Poorly managed agriculture, along with unpredictable weather patterns, has caused huge problems for farmers in Maharashtra. Arun's company, Iris Polymers, manufactures mulching film—a plastic product which covers the soil, conserving water and strengthening the nutrients in the soil. As a result of his business, not only is he helping farmers and supporting the environment, but he has also created employment for 25 staff.

When Arun completed his education, he was looking for a way to start a business. Having grown up with an understanding of the challenges faced by landless laborers and farmers in rural communities, he developed an interest in the mulching technique. With a small amount of savings, he teamed up with a childhood friend and started his business using scrap machinery. But he was unable to sustain the business.

Fortunately, he was introduced to BYST. Recognizing his potential, BYST provided Arun with a mentor and financing, through a partner bank—enabling Arun to start a sustainable business in June 2012.

Arun was named the Social Entrepreneur of the Year by Youth Business International (YBI) and Barclays at the YBI Young Entrepreneur Awards in London. Arun Awatade's range of plastic mulch is helping farmers to reduce their reliance on water and pesticides, helping to reduce costs, increase yields and maintain the environment. Arun cites one of his customers, a tomato grower, was able to reduce usage of pesticides up to 80 percent in his two-acre land after using mulching film (YBI, 2014c).

Story 4: Godavari Satpute, Godavari Akashkandil

Godavari Satpute from Nari Village in India's Maharashtra region, founded and runs Godavari Akashkandil, a thriving start-up business which turns waste material into decorative paper lamps. Providing financial security for her family and financial independence for herself were the main reasons behind starting-up.

Commercial banks rejected Godavari's business proposal and she wasn't offered any business support. She started up with a very small US$700 loan from a relative which allowed her to make a prototype and explore routes to selling her products. It was at this time that BYST stepped in, providing a US$3,600 loan and mentoring. This transformed Godavari Akashkandil from a one-woman business to an enterprise employing 79 people with an annual turnover of US$50,000 (YBI, 2013). The task of creating awareness for an eco-friendly product was challenging enough, but then Godavari was able to decipher the marketing code with the help of her BYST mentor. She says she could not have got to where she is now without the support and guidance of her mentor.

While getting the business off the ground and making money was a huge milestone for Godavari, she being named YBI Woman Entrepreneur of the Year in September 2013 by Youth Business International (YBI), and Barclays at the YBI Young Entrepreneur Awards in London, was a greater rewarding moment. She provides crèche and education facilities for her employees' children and has also appointed a doctor for any medical emergencies that might happen on site. After expanding to a number of places within India, Godavari is also exploring the export market. Besides all these, she is also looking at options of starting a second business with her husband (YBI, 2013).

Impact—Riches of a Different Kind

The stories above clearly highlight the impact that the creation of entrepreneurs at the grassroots level can have in an economy. These enterprises may not have become the Apples and Googles of the world (clearly a possibility in the future), but they share wealth, create employment and inspire self-employment in their local communities. When carefully crafted, these entrepreneurs can turn the potential demographic dividend into social capital.

BYST—GOING FORWARD

Expanding Domestic Reach

Like all purpose-driven organizations, BYST is clearly laying the foundation for its next step of growth. BYST's mentor-supported entrepreneur creation model is widely acknowledged as an effective one, especially at the grassroots level. Entrepreneur creation remains the top priority for the institution. Hence increasing the availability of BYST centers and serving more parts of the country is a definite aim. There is also growing interest from the private sector to join hands in this endeavor.

Increasing Mentor Pool

A vital component of the BYST model of grassroots entrepreneur development is the 'mentor' assigned to every entrepreneur. The case studies of necessity-driven entrepreneurs described above confirm this. BYST is expanding its pool of available mentors through its outreach programs. BYST has also begun the process of educating and accrediting mentors. Their use of an online program to deliver this makes it futuristic and scalable. This program will ensure that there is a certain level of quality among mentors. Increasing the certified mentor pool will also increase the possibility of serving a larger group of entrepreneurs.

Going Global

BYST has signed MOUs with a number of countries, both with government as well as non-governmental institutions to share knowledge and learning from the India program. The focus of most of these MOUs include exchange of knowledge, building of linkages amongst entrepreneurs and mentors between countries, and building of new content and methodologies using technology for mutual benefit.

BYST has collaborated with a number of institutions such as Instituto Negocios da Juventude do Brasil (INJ) of Brazil, South Africa's Youth Business Trust, Nepali Young Entrepreneurs Forum (NYEF) and Federation of Nepalese Chambers of Commerce and Industry (FNCCI), Nepal's Youth Business Trust. BYST also helped launch Youth Business China to enable young and aspiring youth to take up entrepreneurship as a career option.

'Missing Middle'—The New Focus

BYST research has identified that it could increase its impact if it focused its support on India's 'missing middle' with an emphasis on job creation as well as business start-ups—the enterprise multiplier effect. The 'missing middle' denotes those potential entrepreneurs who risk being left out between traditional microfinance/start-up support and SME/venture capital support. They are mostly informal enterprises which are sustainable, but aspiring to grow.

The focus on 'growth-oriented microenterprises' is with the objective of maximizing socio-economic impact. This could also enable BYST to differentiate itself within the market, making it easier to raise its profile and attract resources. About 10 percent of BYST's entrepreneurs themselves have reached this level where they require growth capital. A futuristic beginning in this direction is the creation of the 'micro-equity fund' that BYST has created with Ventureast.

CONCLUSION

While the intention is noble, expanding a socially valuable enterprise such as BYST has its own challenges. Since the model of BYST hinges on the 'mentor–entrepreneur' relationship, it becomes extremely critical for the institution to constantly keep a watch on the quality of both mentors, as well as entrepreneurs. Finding enough of the right mentors and ensuring they are equipped to help their entrepreneurs is a challenging task. Though the business community has been supportive of BYST's cause, increased support from a wider base of organizations in terms of funding, training and mentoring, needs to be mobilized to achieve greater scale.

BYST's long held belief that India's ancient 'guru—sishya parampara' (loosely equated to mentoring) is the ideal way to create the next generation of necessity entrepreneurs has been tested and now waits to be scaled. BYST's founding Chairman, Bharat Ratna the late Mr. JRD Tata captured the spirit when he said, 'no success or achievement is worthwhile unless it serves the needs and interests of the country and its people'.

NOTE

1. This case study has been prepared based on secondary information available about BYST in the public domain. The intent is to showcase how the program has successfully created necessity entrepreneurs in the Indian context.

BIBLIOGRAPHY

All web links were accessed during January–February 2015.

Advance (n.d.). Lakshmi VenkataramanVenkatesan, *Advance*. Retrieved from www.yasni.info/ext.php?url=http%3A%2F%2Fadvance.org%2FLakshmi-Venkataraman-Venkatesan%2F&name=Lakshmi+Venkatesan&showads=1& lc=en-us&lg=en&rg=us&rip=in.

BharatiyaYuva Shakti Trust (BYST), www.bystonline.org.

EntrepreneurIndia(2010). Education: No Bar, Success: Baar Baar, *EntrepreneurIndia. com*. Retrieved from www.entrepreneurindia.com/article/features/ecosystem/ Education-No-Bar-Success-Baar-Baar-234/.

India Inc. (2013). Special Report: Royal stamp for Indian entrepreneurship. *IndiaIncorporated.com*. Retrieved from www.indiaincorporated.com/features/ item/2752-special-report-royal-stamp-for-indian-entrepreneurship.html.

IPF (n.d.). BharatiyaYuva Shakti Trust – A Noble Initiative, *IPFonline.com*. Retrieved from www.ipfonline.com/IPFCONTENT/articles/bharatiya-yuva-shakti-trust---a-noble-initiative.php.

Marich, M. (2012). GEW 2011 in India. *Global Entrepreneurship Week (GEW.co)*. Retrieved from www.gew.co/blog/gew-2011-india.

Mitra, M. (2009). BharatiyaYuva Shakti Trust: turning minorities into entrepreneurs, *TheEconomicTimes.com*. Retrieved from http://articles.economictimes. indiatimes.com/2009-11-20/news/28464494_1_byst-entrepreneurs-bharatiya-yuva-shakti-trust.

Narasimhan, T.E. (2014). IOB ties up with industry bodies to boost lending, *Business-Standard.com*. Retrieved from www.business-standard.com/article/sme/ iob-ties-up-with-industry-bodies-to-boost-lending-114012701115_1.html.

Premkumar, S. (2011). The early bird in the Indian venture capital industry, *TheSmartCEO.com*. Retrieved from www.thesmartceo.in/the-early-bird-in-the-indian-venture-capital-story.html.

Rai, N. (n.d.). BYST: the launch pad for budding entrepreneurs, *SmallInterpriseIndia. com*. Retrieved from http://smallenterpriseindia.com/index.php?option=com_ content&view=article&id=378:byst-the-launch-pad-for-budding-entrepreneurs &catid=68:women-in-business&Itemid=99.

Rajendram, D. (2013). The promise and peril of India's youth bulge. Retrieved from http://thediplomat.com/2013/03/the-promise-and-peril-of-indias-youth-bulge/.

Ravindranath, S. (2010). Mushrooming entrepreneurship, *TheFinancialExpress. com*. Retrieved from http://archive.financialexpress.com/news/mushrooming-entrepreneurship/633259/1.

Santhanam, K. (2010). Scripting success stories, *TheHindu.com*. Retrieved from www.thehindu.com/life-and-style/scripting-success-stories/article263037.ece.

Saraf, N. and Banerjee, B. (2015). *Global Entrepreneurship Monitor 2013 India Report*. New Delhi: Emerald Group Publishing.

Seth, M. (2009). IFC, VenturEast, and BYST set up fund to support grassroots entrepreneurship in India, *International Finance Corporation, IFC.org*. Retrieved from http://ifcext.ifc.org/IFCExt/pressroom/IFCPressRoom.nsf/0/839768F2074 727B58525754700793AD7?OpenDocument.

Sify (2004). India, Brazil welcome youth entrepreneur, *Sify.com*. Retrieved from www.sify.com/carnaticmusic/fullstory.php?id=13370738.

YBI. (2012). How three YBI network members are supporting young entrepreneurs around the world, with lessons for best practice? The second report in YBI's Making Entrepreneurship Work series. Retrieved from http://www.youthbusi ness.org/wp-content/uploads/2012/08/TheYBINetworkapproach.pdf.

YBI. (2013). Godavari Satpute. Retrieved from www.youthbusiness.org/wp-content/ uploads/2013/08/Godavari-Satpute1.pdf.

YBI. (2014a). Sharad Tandale. Retrieved from www.youthbusiness.org/sharad-tandale-of-india-wins-ybi-young-entrepreneur-of-the-year-award/.

YBI. (2014b). Sonal Patil. Retrieved from www.youthbusiness.org/case-studies/ sonal-patil/.

YBI. (2014c). Arun Awatade. Retrieved from www.youthbusiness.org/case-studies/ arun-awatade/.

5. Hanhua Guarantee

Lingzhi Zhang and Spencer Brown

INTRODUCTION

Capital is one of the most important factors in starting a business. But for many small- and mid-sized companies, borrowing money from banks is difficult because small loans have high marketing costs (Zsrongzhi160, 2014). Guarantee companies provide financing strategies that give smaller companies access to capital. These guarantee companies allow clients to borrow money from banks by guaranteeing the full payback of client debts. Hanhua Guarantee, a subsidiary of Hanhua Financial Holding, is one of the largest guarantee companies in China. Hanhua's guarantee and microcredit programs help borrowers establish small businesses. This chapter will provide background information on Hanhua, explain how it assists clients in obtaining funding and business training, and forecast possible challenges facing Hanhua in the future.

ORGANIZATION BACKGROUND

Description of Program

Hanhua Guarantee Ltd (formerly Chongqing Hanhua Credit Guarantee) was established by Guoxiang Zhang in 2004. Hanhua is supported by the All-China Federation of Industry and Commerce (ACFIC) and approved by the Finance Office of Chongqing People's Government. The company receives capital from 25 private enterprises and individual shareholders. Hanhua is currently one of the top ten most influential guarantee agencies in China, with 20 branches in 17 different provinces.

Mission/Vision

Hanhua's mission is to help clients increase welfare, build mutually beneficial relationships and create a sustainable cycle between capital providers and clients. Its services include fundraising, petty loan, equity investment and asset management.

Program Goals

Hanhua Guarantee's short-term goals are to increase its number of clients to 30,000 and to increase its bank guarantee balance (the reserves the company uses to guarantee loans) to US$8.3 billion (163, n.d.-a). Its long-term goal is to become the largest guarantee company in China.

Major Changes/Challenges

Hanhua Guarantee faces big changes as it prepares to become a listed company. In July 2004, when Hanhua was established, its original registered capital was only US$16.5 million. In December 2004, Hanhua joined the Chongqing Guarantee Associate. The company then began implementing a series of strategies, including deterritorialization, establishing branches, increasing capital and expanding total shares. From 2005 to 2006, Hanhua opened four branches in Chengdu, Beijing, Shenyang and Guiyang provinces. In May 2009, the company moved to Yubei District in Chongqing.

In February 2013, Hanhua was chosen as the Deputy-Chairman Enterprise of the Financing Guarantee Association by the Ministry of Civil Affairs of the People's Republic of China, an association responsible for preserving order and improving management in China's credit market. In March 2013, its registered capital reached US$495.7 million (Baidu, n.d., Han Chinese guarantee). In addition, Hanhua Guarantee earned an AAA rating in the credit market and an AA rating in the capital market. Meanwhile, it is the only guarantee organization to win the China Renowned Brand award.

Impact

Hanhua's success is due in large part to its cooperation with banks (163, n.d.-b). Relationships with banks give Hanhua a large capital base that has allowed it to increase its lending power. In March 2013, Hanhua opened several more branches and increased its registered capital in order to become a listed company.

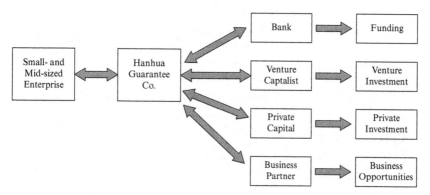

Figure 5.1   Hanhua organizational service chart, data from Hanhua (n.d.-a, About Us)

ORGANIZATION STRUCTURE

Organization Chart

Hanhua Financial Holding is comprised of 36 subsidiaries in six main departments: Hanhua Guarantee, Hanhua Micro-credit, Hanhua Assets Management, Hanhua Credit Management, Hanhua Factoring and Hanhua Technologies. This chapter focuses on Hanhua Guarantee, which is the largest of these departments. Please see the organization chart (Figure 5A.1) at the end of this chapter (Hanhua, n.d., About Han).

Organizational service chart
In order to provide more first-rate services to help clients solve financing problems, Hanhua Guarantee has built a mature system to meet clients' needs. Figure 5.1 shows the basic process for services.

Figure 5.2 is the organizational chart and different departments: and functions of Hanhua Guarantee.

The main process of service is depicted in Figure 5.3.

Leadership

Guoxiang Zhang is the Founder and President of Hanhua Guarantee. Zhang graduated from Liaoning Bank School in Urban Finance (Miagoo, n.d.), and afterward earned a Chinese law license. He enjoyed a 20-year career in the banking industry before establishing Hanhua. His visionary leadership has contributed to the success of Hanhua

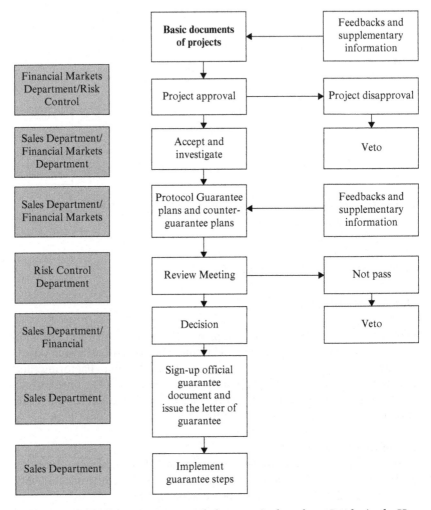

Figure 5.2   Hanhua organizational chart no. 2, data from Baidu (n.d., Han Chinese SMEs)

Guarantee. In 2008, only 1 percent of all employees held a doctorate degree, 21 percent held a master's degree (Mianyang City, n.d.), and 52 percent held a bachelor's degree. Five years later, in August 2013, Hanhua Guarantee employed approximately 1,600 people, 80 percent of them with bachelor's degrees. The average age among Hanhua employees is 32, and the average working experience in finance is eight years (Baidu, n.d., Zhang Gouxiang).

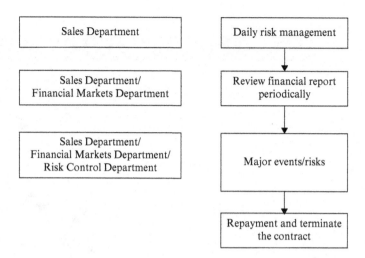

Figure 5.3 Main process of service, data from Baidu (n.d., Han Chinese SMEs)

Branches

Hanhua Guarantee has two headquarters and 20 branches in 17 provinces. The headquarters offices are located in Chongqing and Beijing. Other branches are in Liaoning, Sichuan, Jiangsu, Shaanxi, Dalian, Tianjin, Shandong, Guizhou, Suzhou, Hubei, Guangxi, Gansu, Hebei, Heilongjiang and Shenzhen (Figure 5.4).

ORGANIZATION SERVICES

Debt (Loans)

In 2008, Hanhua expanded its market share by focusing on small and mid-sized organizations and individually owned businesses, which had difficulty borrowing money from banks or other channels. In 2008, Hanhua released 805 loans totaling about USD$362.6 million, including 708 business guarantees (US$304.6 million) and 97 loan transactions (US$58 million) (CQ News, n.d.-a). By the end of 2009, Chongqing and Chengdu branches had released 1,241 loans. The total amount loaned reached US$93.7 million (US$75,371 per loan) (Xiaoying, 2010). The smallest loan was US$1,653.00 (Table 5.1).

Table 5.2 shows the total number of guarantee contracts (USD).

Figure 5.4   Branches in China (original map from www.cia.gov)

Basic information for the clients of loan applications

Hanhua Financial Holding provides two kinds of services: guarantee and microcredit. Guarantee services include financing assurance, financial product guarantees and performance guarantees. Financial assurance relies on bank support. Hanhua provides liquidity loan guarantees, banker acceptance bill guarantees, letter of credit guarantees, fixed asset guarantees, comprehensive credit guarantees and many others. Financial product guarantees include bond guarantees, trust plan guarantees, principal-guaranteed funds,

Table 5.1   Loan balance and transaction amount per contract

	Loan balance (USD)	Transaction amount per contract (USD)
2010	152,435,094	79145.94704
2011	267,207,615	88042.04778
2012	324,172,465	90931.96774

Table 5.2   Total number of guarantee contracts

	Dec 31, 2010		Dec 31, 2011		Dec 31, 2012		Dec 31, 2013	
Transaction Amount	# of contracts	% of total	# of contracts	% of total	# of contracts	% of total	# of contracts	% of total
<$495,777	1061	55.1%	1515	49.9%	1840	51.6%	2034	50.0%
$495777–$826,296	379	19.7%	694	22.9%	807	22.6%	968	23.8%
$826296–$1,652,592	333	17.3%	550	18.1%	566	15.9%	693	17.0%
$1652592–$4,957,776	130	6.7%	246	8.1%	323	9.1%	350	8.6%
>$4,957,776	23	1.2%	30	1.0%	29	0.8%	26	0.6%
Total	1926	100.0%	3035	100.0%	3565	100.0%	4071	100.0%

asset securitization and bill guarantees. Performance guarantees comprise several fields, such as engineering, contract, bill, equipment leasing, credit sale and preservative measures (Hanhua, n.d., Services, Business process). Microcredit services allow individuals, small and mid-sized companies, and privately and individually owned businesses to borrow money (Hanhua, n.d., Services, SME loans).

For private businesses, loan applicants must be between 23 and 55 years old to qualify. Their businesses must be at least one year old. Applicants must provide account records for the previous six months (including receipts for three consecutive months) (Rong 360, n.d.).

Materials

1. A copy of business license
2. A copy of legal person code certificate
3. Copies of Tax Registration Certificate (from both national and local tax bureaus). The above-mentioned copies shall all bear the seal of the supplier

4. A copy of the capital verification report
5. Copies of Corporation's Charter, legal person qualification certificates and his/her identity card, and certificate of authorization and identity card of the specific operator
6. The resumés of officers (Chairman, manager and finance director)
7. A written decision about loans from outside and application for guarantee from the board and shareholders
8. Current financial statements, recent two-year certified financial statements from accounting firm and explanation about financial statements
9. A description about corporation's general condition and main service
10. Corporation's honor certificates.

Interest

Hanhua Guarantee provides two types of charges for lending money to clients. For six-month loans, Hanhua charges a 3 percent one-time handling rate, along with a 1 percent monthly handling charge. For 12-month loans, the company charges a 7.2 percent one-time handling charge, along with a 1 percent monthly handling charge.

Equity (Venture Capital)

Hanhua Guarantee is a joint-stock company. Its main equity is capital stock from shareholders. Figure 5.5 shows the proportion of all shares.

Business Training

Hanhua Guarantee provides training services in seven categories: industrial chain, business chain, real estate, justice, individual, appreciation in organizational management and general field (Hanhua, n.d., Product). In the field of industrial chain, Hanhua Guarantee provides four major plans for its clients. For example, for rapidly expanding science and technology enterprises, Hanhua requires that clients have strong management and technology teams and room for increasing profit and expanding new markets. Within this plan, Hanhua provides three training options for these enterprises: a guarantee share option plan, a guarantee dividend plan, and a guarantee investment plan. For industrial park enterprises, Hanhua Guarantee's services include: (1) a mortgage guarantee for standard workshop, which can help developers rapidly collect sale capital and avoid large circulating funds to be received; (2) a series of matched methods of debit guarantee to solve capital problems; (3) a financing guarantee for park

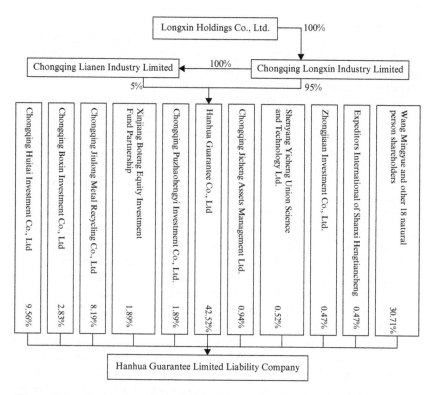

Figure 5.5   Proportion of Hanhua's shares, data from Baidu (n.d., Han Chinese SMEs)

land. In addition, Hanhua provides financial and production assistance to mainframe businesses. Hanhua also offers industrial chain service, including guarantees for product quality, service quality, shipments and payments (Hanhua, n.d., Product).

Hanhua Guarantee's primary business chain service includes contract bidding and guarantees for payments, contractual delivery, product quality, and financial lease. Hanhua also conducts financial planning for merchants of clients. Services include guarantees of loan liquidity, banker's acceptance bills, and credit extensions (Hanhua, n.d., Product).

In the real estate industry, Hanhua Guarantee's primary service is to ensure the bidding of industrial projects, contract follow-through, project quality, contractor payments, project funds, worker salaries, subcontracts and bank guarantees. Its exclusive guarantee service includes loans and circulating funding for development, circulating funding and equipment leasing of construction companies, and implementing high-quality programs. Hanhua also provides easily accessible credit for developers and construction companies, allowing these organizations to solve unforeseen financial problems. Hanhua also assists small and mid-sized companies in carrying out municipal projects and receiving engineering materials for building highways (Hanhua, n.d., Product).

In the field of justice, Hanhua Guarantee's provides property preservation guarantee. Hanhua also assists individual clients in applying for self-employment loans. Other organizational management services include finance consulting, investment consulting, management consulting, asset evaluation and financial consulting (Hanhua, n.d., Product).

Hanhua Guarantee offers start-up capital and growth capital loans to clients but does not charge other fees except interest payments. Besides, each Hanhua branch provides free financial advisory training according to client needs. Seventy percent of Hanhua's clients are male. The average loan applicant is 40 years old and has worked on his/her business for three years before coming to Hanhua. The company seeks to provide loans to applicants with stable jobs and developing businesses, rather than those with little to no income or business experience. Loans can be approved in as little as eight hours. Loan application materials are included in the previous subsection "Materials."

Once a loan application is approved, the client will receive money in three to five business days. Hanhua's financial consultants continue to visit clients to evaluate needs and provide further business assistance. Hanhua reports near-perfect success rates in its clients' businesses (L. Zhang, Telephone Interview, March 26, 2014).

FINANCES

Budget for the Last Five Years

Chinese companies keep company financial information confidential. Hanhua staff member Yiran Liu stated that Hanhua's budget is focused on employee salaries and technological upgrades, including business systems, intranet system (such as email accounts) and the internal IM system (L. Zhang, Telephone Interview, December 13, 2013).

Funding

Like other guarantee companies, Hanhua Guarantee receives capital through two channels: private savings and banks. Private savings is the most popular channel, but Hanhua also uses its brand value to leverage its capital through banks. Generally speaking, guarantee companies have the advantage of leverage, which allows money to multiply in value. A US$10 million deposit may increase in value as much as ten times, in accordance with Chinese government regulations. Hanhua lends to other organizations from this capital base (163, n.d.-b).

Expenses

According to the most recent data, the average Hanhua employee earns US$755.50 per month. In addition, Hanhua provides endowment insurance, unemployment insurance, medical insurance, work-related injury insurance, maternity insurance, housing funding, free annual health examinations, subsidies for festivals and paid vacation after working for one year (Yjbys, n.d.).

Hanhua Guarantee spends more than US$1.22 million annually on employees' basic salaries. The company also pays more than US$6.61 million on systems software (Mianyang City, n.d.).

The most recent balance sheet of Hanhua Guarantee is shown in Table 5.3.

Client Relations

Since its creation Hanhua Guarantee has served over 13,000 petty loan clients, totaling 30,000 loans and more than US$1.65 billion in transactions (ChinaHR, n.d.). Mr. and Mrs. Jiang of Chongqing, China own one of the many small-sized companies that have been positively impacted by Hanhua. This disabled couple run a bicycle store in their small town. They did not possess the resources to open a new store and expand their business. However, after seeing a Hanhua advertisement, Mrs. Jiang contacted the Chongqing branch of Hanhua Guarantee. Three days later, the couple's application was approved and they received funding. Now, their second bicycle store is running profitably (CQ News, n.d.-b).

ORGANIZATION RELATIONSHIPS

Government

Each Hanhua Guarantee branch is approved by the Chinese government, which gives Hanhua credibility among clients. Local government support also strengthens relationships between Hanhua Guarantee and other banks. However, Hanhua does not gain funding from local governments. As a result, banks are more willing to loan capital to Hanhua.

Table 5.3   Hanhua balance sheet, data from Mianyang City (n.d.)

MFI ID	143089	Intangible assets other than goodwill	1264.04
MFI name	HanHua	Net fixed assets	201207.7
Fiscal Year	2012	Liabilities and equity	119950009.6
Period	ANN	Liabilities	61181786.68
Annual Diamonds (Mixmarket. org rating)	3	Deposits	0
Currency	USD	Borrowings	24077046.55
As of date	12/31/2012 0:00	Retained earnings	10614129.86
Assets	119950009.6	Other short term financial liabilities	24446909.63
Cash and cash equivalents	496472.07	Trade and other payables	12657830.5
Trade and other receivables	3522037.08	Deferred tax assets	73000.32
Net loan portfolio	115515052.7	Equity	58768222.95
Gross Loan Portfolio	117564262	Paid in capital	48154093.1
Impairment loss allowance	2049209.31		

Corporate

Hanhua Guarantee cooperates with twelve large banks and several other smaller local banks. Hanhua benefits from these organizational relationships in a number of ways. First, Hanhua can utilize the customer resources and clients of other companies, expanding its market share. Cooperating with these companies also lowers the risk of credit funds. Additionally, collaborating with banks allows Hanhua to build a platform of social credit in order to develop new financial services for the companies they service. Moreover, Hanhua depends on distribution channels of other companies to integrate industrial chains and expand its financial services market base. Finally, Hanhua makes use of its relationships with other companies to fix unhealthy financial assets and maximize valid assets (Hanhua, n.d.-b, About Us).

The twelve large banks are China Development Bank, China Construction Bank, Industrial and Commercial Bank of China, Bank of

China, Agriculture Bank of China, Bank of Chongqing, China Merchants Bank, China Everbright Bank, Industrial Bank Co., Ltd, Shenzhen Development Bank Co., Ltd, Chongqing Rural Commercial Bank and Bank of East Asia.

ORGANIZATION FUTURE

Plan

Hanhua Guarantee is currently carrying out strategies to enter H stocks (the Hong Kong foreign share listing for companies registered in mainland China). Hanhua expects to enter the capital market within three years, hoping to capitalize on the high-growth potential in that market. The future of the guarantee industry will be in systematism, chain-orientation, and diversification, and Hanhua appears to be focusing on these strategies. Its chain-orientation method is particularly consistent with the developing market trend, enabling Hanhua to expand into other market channels, cooperate with companies in other fields, lessen risk and avoid sales fluctuations (Hexun, 2013).

Challenges

High-debt mode

As with all guarantee companies, Hanhua Guarantee's capital is limited. The company must borrow money from other resources in order to carry out operations. As a result, Hanhua uses a high-debt approach that may present potential challenges to its shareholders in the future.

High-interest for financing

Guarantee companies typically provide high-interest returns to individual investors. When a large project fails, these companies cannot afford to pay off their debts. This presents a potential challenge for Hanhua, as a major failure could significantly reduce future funding.

Macroeconomic impact

Recently, China has implemented an economic control policy, which includes monetary policy, fiscal and economic policy, law, and administration (Xinhua, 2007). This policy affects many fields including real estate, stock futures, the mineral industry and precious metals. As a result, companies in these fields may have difficulty receiving capital from individual investors. In the event of a credit scandal, investors will quickly withdraw their savings. Meanwhile, receiving capital from clients will become increasingly difficult. Furthermore, the recent guarantee company scandal in Wenzhou, China caused many private investors to withdraw their capital from guarantee companies. Thus, the risk of a broken capital chain presents another challenge to Hanhua's future (Hanhua, n.d., Anticipation).

Recommendations

Hanhua Guarantee must innovate, adapt to new market environments, improve its services, make use of different capital markets and strengthen its ability to manage risks in order to establish itself as a leading microfinance organization in China (Bjdbxh, 2013).[1]

NOTE

1. The Yuan–US dollar exchange rate in the article is based the rate on January 28, 2014. US$1.00=6.05110 CNY.

REFERENCES

All online references were accessed between February and September 2014.
163 (n.d.-a). *163.com.* Retrieved from http://money.163.com/13/0519/14/8V8D9 GIG00253DC8.html.
163 (n.d.-b). *163.com.* Retrieved from http://news.163.com/11/0805/00/7ALCSG2 C00014AED.html.
Baidu (n.d.). Han Chinese guarantee, *Baidu.com.* Retrieved from http://baike. baidu.com/view/6200242.html.
Baidu (n.d.). Han Chinese SMEs private debt secured by letter of instructions, *Baidu. com.* Retrieved from http://wenku.baidu.com/view/5f5ef08283d049649b665853. html.
Baidu (n.d.). Zhang Gouxiang (Han Chinese Guarantee Co., Ltd., shares), *Baidu. com.* Retrieved from http://baike.baidu.com/subview/1161682/8802278.htm?fro mId=1161682&from=rdtself.
Bjdbxh (2013). Guarantee: Risks and Future (Part One), *Bjdbxh.com.* Retrieved from http://www.bjdbxh.org.cn/news/QTXH/2013/121/13121144179B86A113H DGECG91FIII.html.
ChinaHR (n.d.). Company introduction (Han Chinese Guarantee Corp), *ChinaHR. com.* Retrieved from http://page.chinahr.com/default/20120612006758_1265108_ 10465/index.aspx?ADPara=193,178375,12,3&prj=promo.
CQ News (n.d.-a). *CQNews.net.* Retrieved from http://cq.cqnews.net/cqztlm/cj/ cqssjsjzyycpx/sjzyrchxrwd/200912/t20091224_3916341.html.
CQ News (n.d.-b). *CQNews.net.* Retrieved from http://cq.focus.cn/news/2012-02-10/1763888.html.
Hanhua (n.d.). About Han Chinese, *Hanhua.com.* Retrieved from www.hanhua. com/CN/AboutUs/CommonView?nodeId=355&menuId=1&aIndex=2.

Hanhua (n.d.-a). About Us, *Hanhua.com*. Retrieved from www.hanhua.com.cn/about.php?rcc_id=7&id=10.

Hanhua (n.d.-b). About Us, *Hanhua.com*. Retrieved from www.hanhua.com.cn/about.php?rcc_id=7&id=9&nid=18.

Hanhua (n.d.). Anticipation Mayor Han Chinese visit Investigation, *Hanhua.com*. Retrieved from www.hanhua.com.cn/news_c.php?rcc_id=2&brawarid=25&warpid=700.

Hanhua (n.d.). Product Catalog (by clients), Hanhua Guarantee, *Hanhua.com*. Retrieved from www.hanhua.com.cn/product.php?rcc_id=3.

Hanhua (n.d.). Services (Business process), *Hanhua.com*. Retrieved from www.hanhua.com/CN/Service/InfoDetails?guid=3eca46bd-a5fb-4b3e-83a2-4d8e58d149a1&menuId=3&aIndex=0.

Hanhua (n.d.). Services (SME loans), *Hanhua.com*. Retrieved from www.hanhua.com/CN/Service/InfoDetails?guid=ca9ad299-e39e-4087-8316-e79068ad4995&menuId=3&aIndex=1.

Hexun (2013). Han Hua Holdings proposed landing H shares in the industry say a huge future space, *Hexun.com*. Retrieved from http://stock.hexun.com/2013-05-09/153918103.html.

Miagoo (n.d.). Zhang Guoxiang—Han Chinese Guarantee Co., Ltd., introduced, *Miagoo.com*. Retrieved from http://mingren.maigoo.com/9551.html.

Mianyang City (n.d.). *Mydbxdxh.com*. Retrieved from www.mydbxdxh.com/index.php?m=content&c=index&a=show&catid=26&id=322.

Rong 360 (n.d.). Han Chinese small loans, *Rong360.com*. Retrieved from http://shenyang.rong360.com/p_07816lrbo.

Xiaoying, C. (2010). Zhang Guoxiang professional excellence: From Bank to guarantee giants, *CQWB.com*. Retrieved from www.cqwb.com.cn/news-files/201002/02/20101902041900323303.shtml.

Xinhua (2007). What is macro-control?, *Xinhuanet.com*. Retrieved from http://news.xinhuanet.com/fortune/2007-12/24/content_7303696.htm.

Yjbys (n.d.). *Yjbys.com*. Retrieved from www.yjbys.com/wage/company-1193056.html.

Zhang, L. (December 13, 2013). Telephone Interview.

Zhang, L. (March 26, 2014). Telephone Interview.

Zsrongzhi160 (January 14, 2014). Seok Investment Guarantee Corporation chosen to talk about why the election secured loans (Blog post). Retrieved from http://blog.ifeng.com/article/31654888.html.

APPENDIX

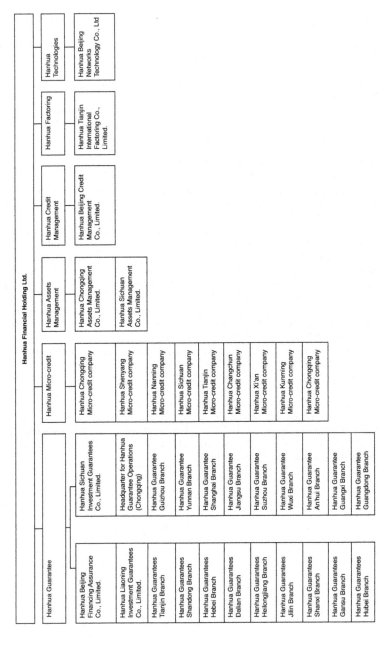

Figure 5A.1   Hanhua Financial Holding Ltd

6. Prospera: a case for microenterprise among necessity entrepreneurs

Macarena Hernández, Gabriela Enrigue and Justin Oldroyd

INTRODUCTION

Prospera is a social enterprise working in urban areas throughout Mexico. Prospera seeks to empower female-led micro businesses and connect them with citizens/consumers looking to create a more equal and engaged society. To achieve its mission, Prospera combines economic development strategies and training programs, to allow urban micro businesses to develop innovative and competitive products, with civic engagement activities, to incorporate consumers/citizens in the creation of these local products.

To drive innovation and civic engagement, Prospera deploys the collective power of hundreds of urban citizens and consumers to help microenterprisers with their product development and access to market challenges. Prospera designs and launches its own social and consumer movements using entrepreneurship for civic engagement while working with organizations and progressive companies; this helps them mobilize large-scale purposeful action to bring about a more dynamic, productive and equitable society.

Prospera's mission and innovation potential is twofold. First, Prospera strengthens local economies by leveling the playing field for urban microenterprisers to take advantage of growing urban markets. Second, Prospera inspires and empowers Mexican consumers to support their own economy by engaging in the design, development and purchase experience of local products to transform Mexico into a more equitable society where microenterprisers and citizens can participate and thrive.

WHAT IS PROSPERA?

In Mexico, microenterprises have an average of ten employees and have annual sales of approximately $100,000 MXN (about US$10,000).

Furthermore, approximately seven out of ten jobs in Mexico are provided by microenterprises. However, while the vast majority of employment is provided by microenterprises, an overwhelming amount (nearly 70 percent) of microenterprises in Mexico last, on average, twelve months before closing down. Additionally, an estimated 85 percent of microenterprises in Mexico are not profitable and nearly all operate in urban areas of the country and in the informal sector. Their products fail to reach consumers because of inadequate sales and communication channels. As a result, 48 percent of Mexico's GDP is generated by 0.2 percent of businesses—making Mexico one of the most unequal countries in Latin America (Secretaría de Economía, 2010).

Prospera is a social enterprise working in urban areas, where 75 percent of the Mexican population lives, to empower female-led micro businesses and connect them to citizens/consumers looking to create a more equal and engaged society. To achieve its mission, Prospera combines economic development strategies with training programs in an effort to allow urban micro businesses to develop innovative and competitive products, with civic engagement activities, to incorporate consumers/citizens in the creation of these local products. Prospera's vision is to create a more equitable Mexico full of opportunity for local entrepreneurs.

FOUNDERS

Prospera was founded by Gabriela Enrigue González. Gabriela was born and raised in Guadalajara, Jalisco, Mexico and started focusing on poverty alleviation and economic development while in college. When she turned 23, she worked at the Mexican Supreme Court, focusing on judicial issues, evaluating its performance and implementing initiatives to increase access to justice, especially for the poor. After three years of government work, González realized that neither the public sector nor academia were ideal places for her to give back or make a lasting impact in Mexico.

Graduate studies at UC Berkeley gave González the opportunity to improve her technical and managerial skills. Moreover, her studies gave her the chance to spend three months in the Philippines, where she saw the capacity of social entrepreneurs to change the world. This inspired her to believe in, and work toward, one single goal: to provide every hardworking man and woman in Mexico with the ability to improve the lives of their families by becoming entrepreneurs from their own homes, without having to risk their livelihoods by migrating or looking for a job at a large corporation where they are likely to be laid off in the future. Committed to making her vision a reality, González founded Prospera.

Since 2008, González has been a consultant for the International Finance Corporation (IFC), a subsidiary of the World Bank Group, where she has had the opportunity to work with Secretaries of State and specialists in designing public policies for countries like Mexico, Colombia, Brazil, Indonesia, Kenya and South Africa. Additionally, González has been a consultant to officials of these countries in the field of process optimization, simplification of procedures and trade regulations (for example, starting a business, paying taxes, licensing) to improve the business environment and incorporate small entrepreneurs around the world within formal markets.

The experience González has gained over the last ten years has allowed her to witness the impact of the use of information technology around the world to incorporate marginalized segments of the population into the formal economy. For this reason, in 2009 she decided to officially form Prospera, in order to contribute more directly to the growth of Mexico, increase the productivity of marginalized sectors and reduce the economic inequality in her country.

MISSION AND VISION

Initially Prospera offered two tools for necessity entrepreneurs involved in microenterprises:

- **Learn and Prosper**. A free training program which aims to provide necessity entrepreneurs with the necessary tools to productively operate microenterprises. This program consists in two blocks: The first is a group workshop where the tools are given in general and applicable to all types of microenterprise. The second is an advisory "one on one" mentoring program where the business idea of each specific microenterprise is studied, and results in a unique business plan and a list—this is a defined action plan that helps the entrepreneur to start immediately.
- **Save and Prosper**. Prospera offered necessity entrepreneurs with microenterprises discounts on raw materials to increase the competitiveness of their products.

The training program "Learn and Prosper" is a program financed by the local government where Prospera trained about 30 microenterprises per week. As for the second program, "Save and Prosper," Prospera experienced several challenges: the number of microenterprises trained did not represent the amount of packaging required for wholesale discounts. This meant that Prosper had to buy large amounts of stock without immediate customers for them, which in turn caused:

1. Large investments in inventory
2. High inventory costs
3. Wastage, damage and losses of inventory.

In addition, profit margins that Prospera obtained from the sales of these materials were minimal, because it had to maintain an attractive price that would allow microenterprises to be competitive in the market.

EARLY STAGE "PIVOTS"

Shortly after launching the "Learn and Prosper" training program, Prospera saw the need to pivot their model. In addition to working with innovative governments, Prospera began working with socially responsible companies and foundations.

To improve the "Save and Prosper" program, Prospera decided to create alliances with major suppliers of raw materials. Through these alliances, microenterprises given referrals from Prospera were able to obtain preferential discounts, and by reducing inventory, Prospera was able to free up capital previously tied up in raw materials.

In addition to improving the "Learn and Prosper" program, Prospera created two additional programs:

1. **Be responsible and Prosper**. A movement that involves increasing the awareness of citizens about the importance of consuming products of local microenterprises. The goal of this program is to sell the products of microenterprises trained by Prospera in "unconventional channels." These are channels in which the microenterprises don't yet sell and which are very difficult for *Prosperandos* (entrepreneurs trained by Prospera) to enter on their own. In order to do this, Prospera becomes a client of the Prosperandos, directly buying their products and distributing them in these "unconventional channels."
2. **Share and Prosper**. A communication platform that connects microenterprises with organizations that can help them grow. In the *Prospera* network, international agencies, universities, distributors, raw material producers, buyers and governments work in a coordinated manner toward one goal: the development of competitive microenterprises with efficient operations and functional products that are distributed in global markets. Through this technology platform, Prospera and its

allies can analyze real-time behavior of microenterprises, new market trends, and challenges they face in order to respond and allocate resources more efficiently, timely and more fully focused on the specific needs of the microenterprises.

PROSPERA'S SOCIAL CHANGE MODEL

The programs "Learn and Prosper," "Be responsible and Prosper" and "Share and Prosper" currently comprise the Prospera social change model. This social change model seeks to solve three basic problems that microenterprises face:

1. They do not have useful information or the practical tools required to develop a business.
2. They are isolated—no one knows them.
3. Their structure does not allow them to compete with large companies.

Prospera's approach to solving these three models through the three programs can be summarized by the following formula: Tools + Market Linkages + Civic Engagement Activities.

Through this social change model, Prospera has:

- Provided tools and training to more than 3,000 microenterprises.
- Introduced more than 80 products through 20 sales channels, including an online platform for local purchase: http://Prosperando.org/tienda-se-responsable.
- Created a network of 150 professionals who provide mentoring to microenterprises and promote the consumption of their products.

COLLABORATION THAT TRANSFORMS LIVES

Through the movement "Be responsible and Prosper," Prospera sought to generate demand for the products of the Prosperandos. To further educate citizens of their responsibility to consume products of local microentrepreneurs, Prospera launched the program: "Talentos responsables" (Responsible talents).

On June 6, 2012, Prospera had the opportunity to meet María del Refugio López, Head of household, entrepreneur and participant in the first generation of "Programa de talentos responsables Cemex-Prospera." Days before, Macarena Hernández and María Fernanda Lopez Obeso

Córdova, then coordinator and sub-coordinator of the unit "Be responsible and Prosper," got together to plan the third meeting of Best Practices of Social Responsibility in Jalisco, in which Prospera will participate as a speaker. It was during this meeting that they had the pleasure to meet Edith Couvillier Salazar, Director of Social Responsibility and Community Relations at Cemex Guadalajara.

Cemex is one of the largest and most important companies in Mexico. Cemex produces the majority of cement used in the country. It also has one of the largest social responsibility departments in Mexico and has Community Development Centers in almost all the cities which have production plants.

María del Refugio had already spent six months attending many workshops offered by the Community Development Center in Cemex Guadalajara, in the colony of "Las Juntas," in which she lived. This center was led by Edith, and offered various courses like sewing, baking, computer skills, and so on. Edith realized that these temporary workshops gave some skills to the entrepreneurs, but they did not create a tangible source of income that could transform the quality of life for families in the community.

When Edith learned of the program that Prospera offered she found that in fact there was a way to generate microenterprises through the workshops offered in the Community Development Center, and that this may transform the lives of María del Refugio and all the other entrepreneurial women that were participating in her programs.

María del Refugio was one of the 20 participants in the first generation of entrepreneurs of "Programa de talentos responsables Cemex-Prospera."

Before the program began, María del Refugio obtained income to support her family by selling jewelry in her community. Jewelry sales however, were also performed by three other ladies in the same community, which made business very difficult. Through the "Programa de talentos reponsables Cemex-Prospera," María del Refugio transformed her business idea, found a market niche, found additional sales channels and found a business partner (Angélica León).

María del Refugio and Angélica formed a microenterprise called Bysan, making handcrafted bath and beauty products: oatmeal soap, cocoa soap, body lotion and hand sanitizer. In conjunction with Prospera they created the line "Selva vanilla," which is characterized by the aroma of vanilla.

How Does the Relationship Between Bysan and Prospera Work?

1. Prospera provides Bysan with containers for the body lotion and the hand sanitizer. Bysan does not produce enough volume by itself

to qualify for wholesale prices, and without Prospera, the cost of raw materials, especially containers and packaging, would represent 60 percent of the total costs of its products. This is because they can't get wholesale prices due to the volume that they produce. Prospera, through the conjunction of many microenterprises, has bought large volumes of packaging suppliers and has created a close relationship with these suppliers, who have become strategic partners of Prospera. This allows Prospera to get wholesale prices. Prospera buys the packages with preferential prices and offers these wholesale prices to Bysan. This tool has allowed Bysan to reduce their variable costs and thereby deliver a product with a more attractive and competitive price.

2. Prospera provides Bysan with the labels for the "Selva vanilla" line. Year after year, Prospera is supported by design students from the "Instituto Tecnológico y de Estudios Superiores de Occidente" (ITESO), a Jesuit university in Guadalajara. These students work with Prospera to gain professional experience and give back to the community. Through this alliance with ITESO and the participation of the design students, Prospera generated a design for the bath and beauty line "Selva vanilla." With this support, Bysan was able to standardize the image of their products and have an attractive product line, which will lead to increased sales and brand recognition.

3. Prospera purchases the products of the bath and beauty line "Selva vanilla." In September 2012 Prospera began designing the 2012 Christmas catalog. This catalog consolidates the products of the most outstanding Prosperandos as responsible Christmas gift ideas. One of the Christmas gifts that were offered was "Las esferas," which was a gift formed from the bath and beauty line "Selva vanilla" created by María del Refugio and Angélica León. Thanks to the Christmas initiative, Bysan had the opportunity to have an income of 700 dollars in just one month, tripling its sales. Its products also reached 85 new customers who may soon become direct consumers of their products.

Prospera created an online platform for purchase of products: www. Prosperando.org/tienda-se-responsable. Through this site, anyone can purchase the products of the best microenterprises trained by Prospera. Each product is linked to the entrepreneurial family who produces it, so customers not only know the product information, but are also able to learn about the people who produce the products. María del Refugio and Angélica are part of this platform which allows anyone to know their story and buy their products (López, 2013).

During Prospera's workshops, María del Refugio and Angélica learned strategies to develop their own distribution channels and to reach their target customers. In addition to this, Prospera is dedicated to finding alternative marketing channels to generate sales volume for the entrepreneurs. Looking to generate this sales volume, Prospera make a Corporate Gift Catalog, in which Prospera offers to companies, organizations, foundations and institutions the opportunity to personalize their gifts and customize according to their needs for any event or important date. By purchasing these gifts, these groups are able to promote the creation of jobs in microenterprises in their country. In a single purchase they can have a variety of products made by different entrepreneurial families. You can find the bath and beauty line "Selva vanilla" in Prospera's Corporate Gift Catalog.

One of Prospera's goals is to act as a link between microenterprises and responsible consumers, who are identified by Prospera's team as people who care about what they consume and the repercussions and impacts connected to their purchase. These are Prospera's target consumers. To learn more about these responsible consumers and better inform them how they can become agents of social change by purchasing local products, Prospera often has speakers at events of Corporate Social Responsibility. During these events, in addition to talking about Prospera's social change model, Prospera talks about the lives of the entrepreneurial families who have been trained in its program and show the best products created by them in previous months. It is at these events where many of the citizens involved in movements of social responsibility become responsible consumers and begin to change their consumption habits.

In order to further promote civic engagement, Prospera organizes local fairs within large corporate and multinational companies—home to a large body of professional leaders and activists. María del Refugio and Angélica, along with other outstanding entrepreneurs, participate in these fairs. This gives them the opportunity to show and promote their products while speaking face to face with potential customers.

In addition to generating sales for the microenterprises, these fairs give them the opportunity to personally interact with their target market, promote their products through word of mouth, and receive direct feedback from their customers and improve both their products and their value proposition.

At the same time, the customers (professionals that work in these corporations) have the opportunity to meet the families who produce the products, allowing them to realize how consuming these products can transform the lives of people that live in their community.

In addition to the Prospera Christmas initiative, María del Refugio and Angélica have participated in special date campaigns. In these campaigns Prospera provides businesses, governments and activists with special gifts for special occasions, such as: Valentine's Day, Mother's Day, Teacher's

Day and Mexico's Independence Day. To the customers of Prospera, these gifts have become an opportunity to show appreciation on these special dates, strengthen relationships and position themselves as agents of change by supporting the social development of their country.

María del Refugio and Angélica bring their products to Prospera's office, where they are distributed through various distribution channels, developed by the program "Be responsible and Prosper." In addition to these channels, inside the office is a space called "Tiendita Prospera" (Prospera mini store), where anyone can find the products created by microenterprises of the region.

This "store" has become a special point of sale; it is a place where anyone can find handmade, natural and organic products, all made by local microenterprises. Prospera's team is in charge of attending to customers who come to the shop, so it's the perfect time to establish a relationship and discover what other needs they have and transform their needs into products in conjunction with microenterprises.

One of the objectives of the program "Share and Prosper" is to share with the world, through the platform of Prospera, the work that Mexican microenterprises do every day. It was through this platform that individuals on the other side of the globe, Sylvain Delavergne, Marc Giraud and Rémi Sierakowski, founders of Wifuproject, first learned about Prospera. Based in France, Wifuproject (www.wifuproject.com) seeks to find the best social cause organizations from around the world, and they chose Prospera as one of them.

On November 29, 2012, María del Refugio and Angélica had the opportunity to share with Sylvain and Marc their experience with Prospera. Today they are part of a project that is going around the world and their products were chosen as gift for French families of the founders of Wifuproject.

After their workshop with Prospera, María del Refugio and Angélica, like all Prosperandos, wrote their own story to share through the Prospera platform. These stories inspire and empower other entrepreneurs. Here is what they wrote:

> Our business is about making and selling handcrafted bath and beauty products. We are two entrepreneur mothers: Angélica and Mary López.
> When we first met and talked, we expressed our ideas and we have gradually developed them. What motivates us is the good feeling we have as humans because we know that we are improving ourselves.
> Being women entrepreneurs makes us feel proud because we are an example for our children that they can do anything as long as they are convinced and want to do it, and this makes us very happy.
> Today we are "Prosperandos". This represents a new opportunity for us. Prospera believed in us, and we are happy for it. Thank you! (María del Refugio López, 2013)

HOW TO FURTHER IMPROVE MEXICAN MICROENTERPRISE

"Learn and Prosper"

The program "Learn and Prosper" empowers microenterprises and provides them with a basis to make their business a successful and profitable one. The current goal of this program is to increase the number of microenterprises trained; the goal for 2014–2015 is to have 10,000 microenterprises trained by Prospera.

To achieve this, it is necessary to replicate the Prospera social change model in other regions of Mexico. That's why Prospera has decided to create a network of strategic partners that can take the model to other communities. An example is the alliance with the BRED (Bank of clothing and household goods) Foundation.

The BRED Foundation provides basic goods to people in poverty with dignity and self-sustaining recovery, channeling these articles through Banks of clothing, footwear and household goods, and ensures that the conditions in which they operate are financially self-sufficient, professional and transparent. Currently they are operating seven BREDs: Hermosillo, Culiacán, Guadalajara, Oaxaca, Querétaro, México DF and Tlaxcala.

The alliance Prospera–BRED Foundation aims to bring training programs to the communities where these banks are. There they will train the family leaders to develop or improve their microenterprises and thereby transform their quality of life.

"Be Responsible and Prosper"

This is a key program within Prospera because it is the unit able to verify that the model of social change is transforming the lives of Mexican microenterprises. This is why much of Prospera's resources are focused on growing this unit and thus growing the sales and customers of microenterprises.

Customer Development

The customer is the best ally of Prospera. They are who will ask what? how? where? and why? regarding the products created by microenterprises. This is why Prospera has decided to establish a closer relationship, a personal relationship, with the customers in which they become allies, mentors and new product developers.

Customer development is divided into three stages:

- Get—Strategies to attract new customers and grow sales. Goal for 2013: triple the number of clients for the microenterprises through Prospera's distribution channels, compared to 2012.
- Keep—Strategies to keep the customers you already have. The purpose of this stage is to establish a relationship after the sale to find out the customers' reasons and motivations for purchasing the products. Once Prosperandos understand customer motivations, they can give them reasons to come back and consume the products again. Goal for 2013: keep at least 80 percent of customers from 2012.
- Grow—Strategies to grow the average purchase per customer. For this stage it is necessary to create a collaborative relationship with the customers. The customers have to become mentors to micro-enterprises. Microenterprises become their students, and these customers are no longer just consumers but become the evangelizers to attract more customers. Goal for 2013: top 20 customers of 2012 become mentors of the microenterprises.

Product Development

By the end of 2014 Prospera hoped to have 50 new innovative products developed by Prosperandos.

Prospera does not train microenterprises to develop products to compete in a massive market. Through customer development strategies, Prospera intends to find opportunities to generate innovative and competitive products, specializing in niche markets. These innovative products must be able to be easily produced at home or in the microenterprise's workshops.

Distribution Channels

Prospera has been given the task of analyzing where the target consumers are. This analysis allowed Prospera to identify a list of distribution channels which can be utilized for products in 2013:

- Companies recognized as "Great place to work" that offer healthy and nutritious products for their employees
- Events of Social Innovation
- Cultural events
- Tourism events
- Recognized hotel brands

- Boutique hotels
- Social clubs
- Universities.

Partnerships for Sales

The challenge with "Be responsible and Prosper" is achieving high volume sales that represent significant income for microenterprises. That is why Prospera intends to create alliances with retail chains and coffee chains in order to increase sales volume.

Prospera needs to create a specialized display shelf that differs from the other shelves in the store so that customers understand the impact being generated if they buy local. This would also be a tool of awareness and consumer education.

"Share and Prosper"

"Share and Prosper" aims to promote the participation of different actors through the Prospera platform. The goal is to reach 10,000 users and ensure that they interact on the platform, so that they share their knowledge and get other change agents to become part of the network.

Most of the people who are in Prospera's platform have had access to the best education in the country and to sophisticated tools. "Share and Prosper" should be a springboard for knowledge where tools can be shared effectively with microenterprises who are looking to get ahead.

WHAT MOVES PROSPERA AND ENABLES THE GROWTH OF MICROENTERPRISES IN MEXICO?

Seeing the life transformation of Mexican families through the microenterprises is what drives Prospera to continue working.

Prospera has managed to empower microenterprises to move from fear to innovation. Microenterprises now see themselves as innovative and as capable of transforming the reality of their country.

Prospera's team is aware that problems faced by microenterprises are very complex problems and can't be solved overnight. That's why the Prospera model seeks to cut these problems in small pieces and solve them one by one. Tackling these problems step by step has been the secret of Prospera's success and growth.

But you can't walk alone. The problems faced by microenterprises can't be solved by a single person. We need the collective wisdom. It takes an interdisciplinary team, with different visions and different opinions, through collaboration. Prospera has made an interdisciplinary team through these years of work and they are convinced that, as an African proverb says: "If you want to go fast, go alone. If you want to go far, go together."

Prospera's team is a group of constructive visionaries that can't wait for the answers to the problems of prosperity, employment and economic development of the region to come from outside. We are working today to transform the lives of Mexican microenterprises and build a country with more equality, justice, participation and opportunities for everyone.

WHAT'S NEXT?

The Prospera social change model is not finished. Every day, Prospera's team works hard, together with the microenterprises, to prove that being an entrepreneur is profitable and is a viable solution for the economic development of Mexico.

It's not only that the microenterprises feel better and more capable with the training tools given by Prospera; the challenge is to transform the reality of these microenterprises to improve, generate more income to have a better quality of life and provide more and better opportunities for future generations.

"The best we can do with our neighbor is to give him tools to become the master of his own destiny," Gabriela Enrigue, Founder of Prospera.

REFERENCES

Both websites were accessed in August 2014.

López, M.R. (2013, January 24). [Blog Entry]. Retrieved from www.Prosperando. org/blog/2013/01/24/bysan.

Secretaría de Economía (2010). Boletín PYME: PYMES. *Nuestras Empresas 1*(1). Retrieved from www.concanaco.com.mx/documentos/BoletinPyME1.pdf.

7. The Academy for Creating Enterprise

Jeremi Brewer and Stephen W. Gibson

THE CO-FOUNDERS

In 1998, using their personal financial resources, Stephen W. Gibson and his wife Bette M. Gibson, founded the Called2Serve Foundation, which uses the trade name of the Academy for Creating Enterprise (the Academy). The Academy is a not-for-profit, non-governmental organization dedicated to educating and training necessity entrepreneurs living in developing nations how to start and grow microenterprises. The Academy only trains individuals who are members of the Church of Jesus Christ of Latter-day Saints.

HISTORY

After harvesting their family business in Colorado, Stephen and Bette Gibson relocated to Provo, Utah, where Bette was hired to teach Early Childhood Development in the College of Education at Brigham Young University (BYU). Shortly thereafter, Stephen was invited to join the faculty of the Marriott School of Business to teach entrepreneurship. The Gibsons believed that, "because of their success in business," they had a "moral obligation to give back to the community" (S. Gibson, personal communication, February 15, 2011).[1]

While teaching at BYU, Stephen was invited to participate with an NGO known as Enterprise Mentors International—an organization helping Filipinos have access to capital to start/grow microenterprises.

THE PHILIPPINES

In his own words, Stephen Gibson expressed why he and Bette decided to move to Cebu, the Philippines:

When I first started working with necessity entrepreneurs in the Philippines, I participated in micro-credit loans. In the beginning, I believed that a lack of capital was one of the major obstacles faced by necessity entrepreneurs. However, I quickly recognized that their failure to grow their businesses was due to a lack of business education and access to the resources and tools to achieve business success. And, by resources and tools I am not referring to money, I am referring to knowledge and culture.

Continuing his explanation of the specific challenges that he has observed among necessity entrepreneurs, Stephen states:

I have observed necessity entrepreneurs in developing nations and I have noticed that the majority, not all, but the vast majority of necessity entrepreneurs in developing nations tend to transfer their macro-culture habits and traditions into their business transactions. For example, they are afraid to have written agreements or charge their customers for their products and services. When I saw these habits and attitudes, I realized that culture had more to do with their failure than anything else. The problem is a business culture of poverty. The solution is education. (S. Gibson, personal communication, February 15, 2011)

Gibson notes that the vast majority of necessity entrepreneurs in developing nations fail because they subscribe to a business culture of poverty—a culture that stems from a lack of formal business training—and not because they have little access to capital.

Funding

Using their own resources, the Gibsons secured a private home on the island of Cebu, the Philippines that could house 40 students. Believing that the majority of necessity entrepreneurs living in the Philippines subscribed to a culture of poverty, and believing that education is the solution to the problems faced by necessity entrepreneurs living in the Philippines, the Gibsons felt strongly that, in order for these necessity entrepreneurs to change their habits and traditions, they would most benefit from an isolated, intensive, educational experience. As Bette Gibson explained:

The Academy in the Philippines requires every student to pay tuition. It costs them US$50. Students have to cover their own expenses to and from the Academy campus. This means that they have to move from their respective islands to an area that, in many cases, they have never been. They have to leave their families for eight weeks and live far apart from them without much communication. Many of our poorest students worry about whether or not their children and spouses are eating every day. Students enter the Academy discouraged and broken, but they leave much more confident and better prepared to run their small businesses. (S. Gibson, personal communication, February 15, 2011)

The Gibsons are not afraid to say that some cultures are better than others at creating economic prosperity; they would prefer to have hurt feelings for a short time than to have starving children, generationally.

The Academy is primarily led under the direction of co-founders Stephen and Bette Gibson. Nevertheless, the Gibsons have meticulously constructed the governing body of the Academy, which is comprised of a Chairman, CEO, Executive Director and an Advisory Board. The advisory board is comprised of individuals who are chosen according to their experience in education, their understanding of culture and their conviction that poverty can be eradicated through microenterprise training.

Teaching Model

From inception, the Academy was established as a full-time boarding school where students from throughout the nation could come and reside for a period of eight weeks. In 2010, the Academy's teaching model in the Philippines pivoted from a residential school to a regional training model known as On-Site Training (OTP) where the Applied Entrepreneurship Program (AEP) was implemented. A review of these models will be covered later in this chapter.

Location

The Academy-Philippines campus was originally located at 11 Aquamarine Street, Saint Michael Village, Banilad, Cebu City, Island of Cebu, in the Philippines. The school was situated on a 1.3-acre lot in the eastern-most part of the island. Students enrolling in the Academy's residential model came from each of the different islands as well as from different socio-economic backgrounds.

Physical Facilities

The Academy's residential school was a large renovated home with capacity to house up to 40 individuals. There were 11 bedrooms—referred to as "dormitories"—seven of the bedrooms were used to house the male students and the remaining four bedrooms were used to house the female students. The dormitories at the Academy were not coed. The home also had two kitchens and a large area in the main floor (35 feet wide by 70 feet long) used as the classroom. The Academy also provided students with a library where students could check out books on business administration and related topics.

Enrollment

Individuals interested in attending the Academy were required to comply with the following three requirements to be considered as residential candidates: (1) Be a member of the Church of Jesus Christ of Latter-day Saints (LDS),[2] (2) Be a returned missionary of the LDS church, and (3) Hold a current temple recommend.[3] Both men and women were encouraged to apply and attend the Academy; there was no specified age limit. Each cohort, or "batch," of students was comprised of approximately 30 students, with a 66 to 33 percent men-to-women ratio. While on campus, students were assigned separate wings of the dormitory living quarters. Both married and single individuals were accepted as students. Preference, however, was given to men who are married with children. The average age of students who attend the Academy was 30 years old for men and 28 years old for women. Students attended classes, studied, followed an exercise program, and lived full-time on campus.

Student Tuition Fee

In order to attend the Academy, each student was required to cover his or her own traveling costs, both to and from the school. In addition to paying their travel costs, students were required to pay a US$50 tuition fee.[4] This US$50 cost provided each student with a bed, three meals a day, books and education for eight weeks. The cost of tuition was subsidized (nearly 95 percent) by The Called2Serve Foundation.

When asked why the students are required to cover their own traveling costs, as well as the US$50 tuition, Bette Gibson responds, "We have found that when our students pay a portion of their educational experience, they are more dedicated to the program" (S. Gibson, personal communication, February 15, 2011). Answering the same question, Stephen Gibson adds:

> I must note here that no student has ever been denied acceptance into the Academy because they do not have the funds to attend. While we will not cover their cost of travel, we do offer work-study programs for those students that truly are unable to cover the cost of tuition. We know that not every prospective student has the financial capacity to cover travel and tuition, and this is why we don't mind helping them pay what they can't afford. We are, however, very explicit with our students that the Academy is not a "give-me-free" institution. When they make the sacrifice to come by covering their expenses, the students are much more motivated.

The Gibsons required their students to make a financial sacrifice to attend the Academy because they believe it helped the students arrive more dedicated and more emotionally prepared to learn, apply and achieve their goals.

Directorship and Teachers

James Fantone is the Country Director of the Academy in the Philippines. He is the President and Chief Trainer of NXT Level Training and Consulting. He holds a degree in Business Management from Rizal Technological University—Manila. He is an equity partner in several small businesses throughout the Philippines. As the Country Director of the Academy, Mr. Fantone employed a staff of approximately 15 Filipinos with the residential model, and currently employs a staff of seven Filipinos with the OTP/AEP model.

There are two stipulated requirements for any individual interested in working for the Academy: (1) Every staff and faculty member must be a graduate and (2) Every staff and faculty member must be Filipino. "The staff must be graduates because it allows them to relate better with the current students," says Bette, "and it improves the overall educational experience for the current students to relate with their teachers." Regarding the second requirement, Stephen Gibson notes, "The current Director of the Academy is a Filipino and this is very important to us because he speaks their language, he knows their culture, and he can show the students that change is possible" (B. Gibson, personal communication, February 15, 2011).[5]

Instruction and Methodology

The Academy students encounter their first culture shock once they attend their training seminars. Contrary to the cultural norm of education in Asia, where students sit in silence and copiously note every word their professor speaks, the Academy employs the "discovery learning," or "guided learning," methodology—the same methodology that Professor Clayton Christensen uses with his students at Harvard's Business School. In his book *Disrupting Class*, Christensen explains, "With this methodology the responsibility of teaching is shifted from the teacher to the students [as] the teacher becomes a facilitator of knowledge and the students 'discover' the principles and lessons through guided questions" (Christensen, Horn, and Johnson, 2008, p. 13). This is the same role that the teachers at the Academy play when teaching in the classroom; they are not lecturers, they are facilitators. Bette Gibson explains why the Academy uses the "discovery learning" principle:

The premise of the "discovery learning" methodology is to transfer knowledge from teacher-to-student by using the ideas and words of the students. The teacher asks lots of questions. The teacher facilitates discussion. The students are the ones involved in the discussions, sharing their ideas, creating theories, and challenging one another. We love to use debates in the classroom because it is such a foreign concept to our students. They are not used to discussing or debating ideas with their peers. They are trained in school from the time they are very young to sit down, take notes, and not ask questions. In the Academy, they are expected to do just the opposite. We want them to share their opinions. We want them to share their ideas. They are supposed to speak up and share their insights. This makes for a much better learning environment. The learning is personalized and the learning is individual. In our opinion, when the teaching only comes from one source, too much is lost. (S. Gibson, personal communication, February 15, 2011)

For Bette, the "discovery learning" methodology is a *cultural* technique implemented to enhance the learning experience that the students have at the Academy. Adding to Bette's words, Stephen mentions the following about the use of the "discovery methodology":

One of the principal ways that we put into practice the discovery methodology is through case studies. By case studies, I mean simple, but entirely true, stories of what micro-enterprisers are doing *inside* their businesses. Our case studies take up a bulk of the curriculum that the students receive while enrolled at the Academy. These case studies allow for great discussion among students, especially because the answers are not cut-and-dry. The case studies require reflection, introspection, analysis, and collaboration. The students solve the case studies in small groups and then as a cohort. Because there are many ways that each case study can be solved, and because they are not fill-in-the-blank tests, the Academy students are forced to focus on what is happening in the business and find solutions to the problems. By doing this they acquire the skill-set to go back home and not make the same mistakes. Lastly, if the most prestigious business schools in the world use case studies coupled with the discovery methodology, why wouldn't the Academy?

The case studies used by the Academy demonstrate to the students the *cultural* aspects that the owner and operator of the small business had to implement in order to succeed. The embedded assumption in the Academy's *Where There Are No Jobs* curriculum[6] is that most Filipino necessity entrepreneurs remain impoverished because they subscribe to the "culture of poverty"—a culture that the students who attend the Academy readily accept as a fitting description of their own belief system (S. Gibson, personal communication, February 15, 2011). Most importantly, it is a culture that they are willing to overcome by adopting the "progress-prone" cultural values taught at the Academy that will positively impact their enterprises (Harrison, 2006).

Launch & Learn

As the name indicates, students enrolled at the Academy start ("Launch") an income generating activity (IGA), which allows them to apply ("Learn") the various business principles that they acquire during their classes. According to Stephen, "Launch & Learn is the most critical component of the educational experience that each student has" and "that is why every Academy student is required to participate in this portion of the program." "Launch & Learn is our way of ensuring that the Academy does not just teach theory to the students," says Bette Gibson, "it ensures that students immediately apply what they learn in the classroom." Expounding on the purpose and mission of Launch & Learn, Stephen Gibson mentions further:

> Launch & Learn works. There is only one sure way to learn how to do business and that is by doing business. It pushes the students to overcome fear and allows them to make mistakes in a safe environment. Even if they fail miserably on one day, they are able to come back to the campus knowing that they will have food to eat. They can literally sit down to dinner, talk with their teammates, discuss their experiences with their classmates, overcome their failures, and go out ready to do business the next day. It is the basis of what makes the Academy so powerful. In the morning they have the theory and in the afternoon and evening they go out and apply it. Launch & Learn works. (S. Gibson and B. Gibson, personal communication, February 15, 2011)[7]

The balance between theory and application provides each student with the necessary time to learn what should be done in business and then the opportunity to immediately go out and apply that knowledge.

Teaching Models

- **Eight-Week Residential Model.** The Academy's residential course has a duration of eight weeks. Students spend 30 percent of their time in the classroom learning the theory of business administration and 70 percent of their time in the field practicing the theory.
- **One-Week Executive Batch.** The primary purpose of the Executive Batches is to reach out to the men and women who currently operate microenterprises but need a quick training of basic business principles on how to improve their purchasing power, bookkeeping practices, negotiation skills, and human resource knowledge. The major differentiator between the eight-week, residential program and the one-week Executive Batch program is the fact that the one-week students own and operate a business prior to entering the Academy.

- **On-Site Training Program (OTP).** As its name suggests, the advantage of OTP is that the necessity entrepreneurs who do not have the financial capacity or the time to attend a one-week training program can attend classes in their respective cities. Students enrolled in the OTP classes are expected, but not required, to have experience in small businesses. Students enrolled in the OTP classes pay a minimal enrollment fee, which is used to cover the materials used. OTP classes are held two days a month for three months.

2010—Institutional Innovations and Growth

In 2010, two significant institutional innovations were implemented. First, in the Philippines, the Academy's *modus operandi* transitioned from the ten-year-old residential center into a regional-training center approach fortified by more than 50 learning centers, also called "Chapters." These chapters follow the support group model for behavior change that has proven so successful with Weight Watchers, Alcoholics Anonymous and Microcredit borrowing groups.

The second significant innovation occurred in Mexico City, where the Academy secured a 3.7-acre campus, enabling the residential center method to begin there until sufficient Alumni Learning Centers are established. Following is an overview of the Academy-Mexico.

MEXICO

History

The Academy began pilot-trainings in Mexico City in 2008. Dr. Jeremi Brewer and Dr. Rebecca Brewer were the primary teachers. Pilot-trainings were also conducted in Mexico City in 2009 and in Puebla, Mexico in 2010. In October, 2010 the Academy secured the physical facilities used currently for operations.

Campus

The Mexico City campus sits on a 3.7-acre campus in the north of Mexico City. The campus can house up to 64 students, with dormitories for both men and women. The Director of the Academy-Mexico was Dr. Brewer (2010–2012). In 2012, the leadership of the Academy was handed over to Mexican national, Gandhi Blas Pérez.

Directorship and Teachers

The Academy-Mexico was launched by Dr. Jeremi Brewer, Dr. Rebecca Brewer, and Mr. Gandhi Blas Pérez. Within the first 20 months of operation, the Academy-Mexico had a staff of 22 employees, five of which carried much of the teaching load. In August 2012, Mr. Blas was promoted as the Director of the Academy-Mexico.

The Academy-Mexico Teaching Models

- **Residential:** Students from across the Republic of Mexico travel to Mexico City and live on the Academy's campus for a period of six weeks. Students are required to pay their own travel to-and-from their homes. Students enrolled in the residential model also pay US$310 (60 percent subsidized) for the six-week program. Individuals who are unable to pay the tuition are provided with need-based scholarships.
- **Night Courses:** The Academy-Mexico began teaching night courses to individuals living in the Mexico City area who were involved in microenterprise. Individuals who wished to enroll in the night courses would pay US$200 and attend classes three nights a week for six weeks.
- **Regional Training:** Regional Training is conducted in the same fashion as the Philippines. Regional Training is given over a ten-day period, five hours a day.

Current Status

From January 2011 to the present day, more than 4,100 individuals have been trained by the Academy-Mexico. An estimated 500 new income generating activities have been created and nearly 700 new jobs have been created. In 2012, Dr. Jeremi Brewer was promoted to the Executive Directorship and had charge to govern the Academy's training programs in the Philippines, as well as help with the expansion of the Academy into Zimbabwe, Peru, Brazil, and Cambodia. On December 31, 2013, Dr. Jeremi Brewer resigned as the Executive Director and was replaced by Mr. Robert Heyn.

Curriculum

The Academy produced five volumes of curriculum called "handbooks," all of which share the same title: *Where There Are No Jobs*. These handbooks are comprised of self-explanatory lessons that can be taught in any developing nation. The Academy hopes that these handbooks will reach individuals around the world who are motivated to take part in poverty eradication through microenterprise education. Following is a brief overview of each handbook:

- **Volume 1:** *Where There Are No Jobs: The 25 Rules of Thumb.* This volume explains some of the most essential business principles that, when implemented, will help business owners establish a solid foundation for their businesses and help business teachers establish a solid foundation for their classes. The 25 Rules of Thumb are discussed in detail so that microentrepreneurs can gain an appreciation for the importance of implementing correct practices in their businesses.
- **Volume 2:** *Where There Are No Jobs: 26 Complete Micro-Enterprise Lessons.* This volume contains lesson plans designed to explore in more depth some of the Rules of Thumb. The lesson plan topics range from record keeping to increasing sales, and from basic marketing to opportunity identification. From these lessons, business owners can learn how to start and grow their small businesses by applying each rule of thumb.
- **Volume 3:** *Where There Are No Jobs: 18 Complete Micro-Enterprise Case Studies.* This volume is a collection of 18 microenterprise case studies. It is designed for the facilitator, mentor, coach, teacher and discussion leader to use in teaching analytical skills to microenterprise students and owners.
- **Volume 4:** *Where There Are No Jobs: The Micro-Franchise Handbook.* This volume is a collection of case studies that describe the microfranchising efforts of 39 businesses that operate in different parts of the world. Each case study describes what the microfranchise does, how it operates, and what makes it successful.
- **Volume 5:** *Where There Are No Jobs: Creating Family Prosperity.* This volume is a collection of 12 simplified lessons that focus on cultural norms, which impede the progress of business. They are based on popular questions that necessity entrepreneurs often ask when administering their microenterprises. This volume is currently used in 23 countries around the world and has been translated into four languages (Spanish, English, Portuguese and French).

THE 25 RULES OF THUMB

The curriculum created by the Gibsons derives from thousands of hours of classroom discussions with students. When the Gibsons began teaching in the Philippines, Bette's major contribution was transcribing Stephen's lessons and then converting them into the books and short stories (case studies). Since then, more manuals have been developed and published under the direction of Dr. Jeremi Brewer. Referring to the creation of the Academy's curriculum, Bette explains:

> When we first moved to the Philippines, we didn't have an established curriculum, per se. Steve knew *what* to teach the students because he had started and sold many businesses over the years and he had several years' experience working in the Philippines with EMI. He also knew *how* to conduct a classroom because he had taught for many years. Additionally, he knew *why* to teach the students what he taught, but he didn't have practice putting it on paper so that other people could replicate his lessons. The students would come back from applying the different principles that they had learned in their IGAs and Stephen would help them "discover" what it was that was working and what was not working. That is where my background in education came into play the most: I sat through thousands of hours of lessons and created the lessons that Stephen taught in the classroom. I knew that if we could be successful in creating a curriculum that worked in the Philippines that we could eventually teach these same lessons in every nation where the culture of poverty exists and replicate the Academy there. (B. Gibson, personal communication, June 7, 2011)[8]

Commenting on his perspective of the curriculum development, Stephen shares the following:

> I knew that the culture of poverty existed in the Philippines because I saw it every day I was there. I knew that our students would have to overcome the traps (habits and customs) associated with the culture of poverty in order to have profitable businesses. Each day, I would teach a lesson and then the students and I would come up with a "Rule of Thumb" that we could write in one or two sentences. I wanted to come up with simple, straightforward business principles that the students could remember while working in their businesses. More importantly, I wanted these "Rules of Thumb" to help students remember how to overcome the culture of poverty habits and replace them with the habits found in the culture of business success. Thus, the 25 Rules of Thumb were created by the students through the "discover and define process." That is why they are so powerful. (S. Gibson, personal communication, June 7, 2011)[9]

Stephen's decades of experience in entrepreneurship, coupled with Bette's background in education, made for the ideal curriculum development team. Stephen taught the lessons by guiding the students through personal analysis of their Launch & Learn activity while Bette transcribed the lessons.

The 25 Rules of Thumb are one of the founding pillars upon which the Academy's curriculum is based. Table 7.1 gives an overview of the 25 Rules

Table 7.1   The 25 Rules of Thumb

Rule	Explanation
Sell What the Market Will Buy	Solving a critical, recurring problem is the best way to create a business.
Practice Separate Entities	Keep personal and business money separate.
Start Small, Think Big	Learn basics when small and less costly. Then grow.
Be Nice Later	Don't give your product or business capital away to friends and relatives.
Keep Good Records	Success comes from beating yesterday's sales and profit records.
Pay Yourself A Salary	This eliminates taking cash out of the business for living expenses.
Buy Low, Sell High	The bigger the difference, the greater the potential profit.
Don't Eat Your Inventory	Consuming inventory or seed capital will kill your business fast.
Use Multiple Suppliers	Negotiating with several suppliers for the best price is critical to success.
Buy on Credit, Sell for Cash	Selling product before payment is due increases cash flow.
Purchase in Bulk	Suppliers usually sell products cheaper if purchased in volume.
Use Suggestive Selling	Suggest to each customer other items they might like or need.
Increase Sales, Decrease Costs	As the gap grows bigger, net profits also grow bigger.
Turn Your Inventory Often	Profit is made every time inventory is priced right and sold.
Value Your Customers	Keeping them coming back and buying more is a key to success.
Differentiate Your Business	Give customers a reason to return; better, cheaper, faster.
Hire Slow, Fire Fast	Screen potential employees carefully. Terminate bad hires quickly.
Inspect More, Expect Less	Consistent performance comes from inspecting not expecting.
Have Written Agreements with Partners, Suppliers, Landlords and Employees	The dullest pencil is better than the sharpest mind.
Work on Your Business 10 Hours a Day, Five and a Half Days a Week	Anything less is a hobby.
Practice Kaizen	Kaizen means continual improvement. This is vital to income growth.
Make a Profit Every Day	If a workday goes by without profit, it's a loss.
Work on Your Business, Not Just in Your Business	Stand back and watch, then fix.
Write Daily/Weekly Business Goals	Stretching for more will move business forward faster.
Focus, Focus, Focus	A concentrated effort in one venture pays huge returns.

of Thumb that the Academy uses to teach students in the classroom as they experiment with small businesses during the "Launch & Learn" program over the eight-week course. Following Table 7.1, the history of the creation of the 25 Rules of Thumb will be shared.

The Creation of the 25 Rules of Thumb

The 25 Rules of Thumb are not taught in a hierarchical order of importance. Nor are they taught chronologically to the students. Instead, the 25 Rules of Thumb are taught to the students as they "discover" them through the "Launch & Learn" program of the curriculum. "As the students 'discover' these different business rules," says Stephen, "they are much more likely to remember them because the rules are attached to a personalized learning experience" (S. Gibson, personal communication, June 7, 2011). In addition to the discovery of the Rules of Thumb, Stephen Gibson mentions that the "power of the 25 Rules of Thumb is that many of them challenge the common cultural practices that I found present in the microenterprises created by Filipino necessity entrepreneurs." When asked to discuss how the 25 Rules of Thumb were created, Stephen responds:

> During my first year in the Philippines conducting business lessons with our students, I would ask them a lot of questions and require them to defend their actions. I did this because, having had successful businesses myself, I noticed that our students were transferring widespread cultural practices from their homes into their businesses and all too often those cultural practices were not helping the IGAs of our students to grow; in most cases they caused their businesses to fail. Seeing this, I was motivated to inquire about why they priced their products the way they did; I wanted to know why they ate their products without paying for them; I questioned their sales techniques; I challenged their lack of record keeping habits. Then, I would ask them to come up with a rule that would help them to remember what they should do in sales, pricing, record keeping, and goal setting. This is why the 25 Rules of Thumb are so powerful. First, the rules were created by the students, not me. Second, almost every single Rule of Thumb confronts a cultural habit found in the Philippines and it comes from the students. (B. Gibson, personal communication, June 7, 2011)

By observing the habits, traditions, and cultural norms employed by his Filipino students, Stephen Gibson knew that they were not conducting IGAs or microenterprises in a fashion that would lead to success. However, instead of directly telling the students that they were making mistakes, he allowed them to make the mistakes and then he would question them about why they did what they did. Eventually, the students began to learn from their mistakes and implement new strategies.

Alumni Learning Centers "Chapters" (Post-Graduate Continued Education)

The Academy offers their alumni a peer-mentoring program that allows for graduates living in areas close to one another to convene and continue learning. These small groups of alumni are called "Chapters." Each month, the Academy alumni meet together in their Chapters and continue learning and mentoring one another with help from videos they receive from the Academy-Headquarters (Provo, Utah) each month. The videos highlight interviews from entrepreneurs, CEOs, professors and leaders who wish to educate the nearly 6,000 Academy alumni. As of June 2013, the Academy had nearly 100 Chapters in the Philippines, Mexico, and Zimbabwe, and soon Brazil and Peru.

Conclusion

As the Academy becomes more and more streamlined, and the budget for the program decreases each year, the Gibsons desire to reach as many necessity entrepreneurs as possible throughout the world. Nevertheless, the founders of the Academy recognize that because they have limited resources and because their mission is placed solely on training Latter-day Saints, they are only reaching a portion of the nearly two billion necessity entrepreneurs around the world. Plans for 2014–2015 included replicating a residential center in Brazil, as well as creating virtual chapters in Peru through the Regional Training Models.

NOTES

1. Stephen Gibson (Founder, The Academy for Creating Enterprise, Brigham Young University; Provo), Interview by Jeremi Brewer, February 15, 2011.
2. The abbreviation LDS will be used in lieu of the full name of the Church of Jesus Christ of Latter-day Saints.
3. A temple recommend is renewed every two years by the presiding bishop of the individual's local Church and requires that the individual adhere to the principles of the LDS Church.
4. According to the International Monetary Fund, the average per capita monthly income of the Philippines is approximately US$150–200 per month.
5. Bette Gibson (Founder, The Academy for Creating Enterprise, Brigham Young University; Provo), Interview by Jeremi Brewer, February 15, 2011.
6. *Where There Are No Jobs* is comprised of five volumes that cover basic business principles.
7. Stephen Gibson and Bette Gibson (co-founders, The Academy for Creating Enterprise, Brigham Young University; Provo), Interview by Jeremi Brewer, February 15, 2011.
8. Bette Gibson (Founder, The Academy for Creating Enterprise, Brigham Young University; Provo), Interview by Jeremi Brewer, June 7, 2011.

9. Stephen Gibson (Founder, The Academy for Creating Enterprise, Brigham Young University; Provo), Interview by Jeremi Brewer, June 7, 2011.

REFERENCES

Christensen, C., Horn, M., and Johnson, C. (2008). *Disrupting Class: How Disruptive Innovation Will Change the Way the World Learns.* New York: McGraw Hill, 13.
Harrison, L. (2006). *The Central Liberal Truth: How Politics Can Change a Culture and Save It From Itself.* New York: Oxford University Press.

PART III

Promising high-impact programs

8. Entrepreneurship Finance Lab

Asim Khwaja, Bailey Klinger and Colin Casey

EFL'S MISSION

The Entrepreneurship Finance Lab's (EFL's) mission is to expand access to finance in emerging markets by equipping banks with better tools to measure credit risk. Built with the aim of tackling a $2.5 trillion dollar financing gap for micro, small and medium enterprises (MSMEs) around the world, EFL's digital psychometric credit assessment evaluates small business owners on key elements of entrepreneurship in a scalable and automated manner. This breakthrough technology helps banks provide financing to market segments previously out of reach, and helps bring the developing world's most capable, yet previously un-bankable, entrepreneurs into the formal financial fold. Emerging from a research initiative at the Harvard's Center for International Development, EFL now works with leading financial institutions across Africa, Asia and Latin America, and has facilitated over $275 million in lending to MSMEs. We've been recognized by leading development organizations such as the IFC, Inter-American Development Bank, and the G-20.

ORGANIZATION BACKGROUND

EFL began in 2006 as a collaboration between Dr. Asim Khwaja, a professor at the Harvard Kennedy School, and one of his PhD students, Bailey Klinger. A great deal of research had pointed to the "missing middle": a dearth of small and medium enterprises (SMEs) across the developing world. Indeed, while in developed countries SMEs accounted for, on average, 57 percent of employment, in developing countries that number was less than 20 percent. Instead the vast majority of employment was concentrated in informal "micro" businesses and in large corporations. McKinsey had estimated that the global financing gap for SMEs was more than US$2 trillion (Figure 8.1).

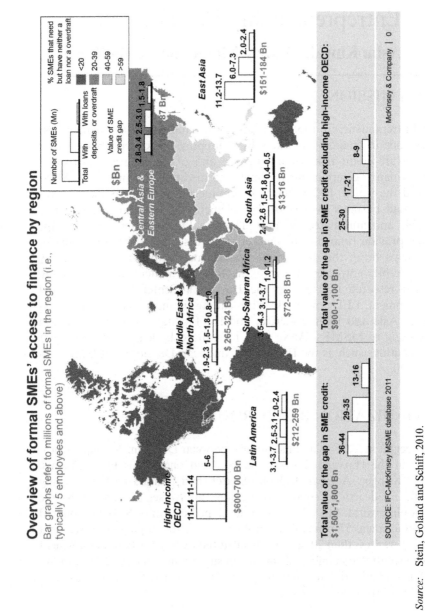

Source: Stein, Goland and Schiff, 2010.

Figure 8.1 SMEs by region

122

The SME financing gap had a variety of systemic causes, from ease of doing business to physical availability of bank branches. But one critical, universally consistent cause was information scarcity. Klinger and Khwaja found that banks and lending institutions everywhere relied on a similar set of criteria to evaluate risk: things like borrowing histories, credit scores, formal financial statements and collateral. In developed markets, this system works relatively well. Most people have access to the information they need, so banks have no problem determining who should get a loan and who should not. In emerging markets, however, the situation looks altogether different. Credit bureaus are less prevalent, regulations are less established, information sharing across institutions is hampered by data quality and other technological hurdles, and assets are fewer and farther between. In turn, very few people have recorded credit data, many businesses are informal, and entrepreneurs have less with which to securitize a loan. All of this means that lenders have little with which to determine which businesses are creditworthy, regardless of their potential.

Microfinance institutions get around this problem by lending to groups, not individuals, effectively outsourcing the credit review process to the borrowers themselves. On the other side of the spectrum, commercial banks investing in bigger, established businesses are able to engage in exhaustive due diligence processes, because bigger loan sizes mean bigger returns, and bigger returns mean more money to spend on credit review. But for SMEs, couched in between micro-loans and corporate loans, there was no clear solution: they were too big for group loans, but too small to justify the exhaustive review of bigger commercial loans. So, banks chose simply to invest their money elsewhere.

EFL grew out of an attempt to address this issue of information scarcity by developing an alternative approach to measure risk that would not require retrospective credit information that many in emerging markets lacked. Klinger and Khwaja's solution was to use psychometric assessments as a viable low-cost, automated screening tool to identify high-potential entrepreneurs and evaluate risk. Academic research had demonstrated strong statistical associations between entrepreneurial success and personal attributes measured with psychometric instruments. Such research had shown that successful entrepreneurs consistently display differences that can be detected with such tools, meaning even in markets where traditional credit data is unavailable, psychometric principles can allow lenders to see the true potential of SMEs. Using these questions, Klinger and Khwaja constructed EFL's first psychometric credit scoring model which, similar to classic creditscoring models, used a set of algorithms to calculate the ranking or score for

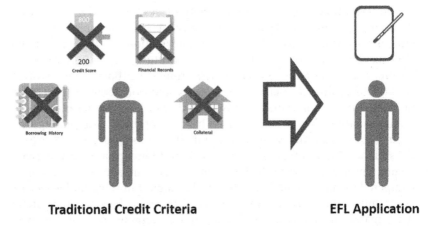

Traditional Credit Criteria   **EFL Application**

Figure 8.2   EFL application

that person. The EFL application takes between 30 and 60 minutes to complete, can be administered by a loan officer online or offline, and is returned to banks' credit teams within 30 minutes of synchronization (Figure 8.2).

In 2007, the first tests of this new assessment were performed in South Africa. In 2008, EFL received funding from Google.org to expand the scope of the pilot, and over the next year, ten financial institutions across eight African and South American countries began using EFL's psychometric assessment to assess loan applicants. The results from the pilot were encouraging: EFL's models had performed on par with traditional credit scoring methodologies in developed, information-rich markets, and were enabling partner lenders to grow lending threefold and reduce default rates by 25 percent or more.

In 2009, DJ DiDonna joined Klinger and Khwaja from the Harvard Business School to scale EFL as a private, for-profit company. Since launching in 2010, EFL has partnered with leading commercial banks across Africa, Asia and Latin America to disburse nearly $300 million dollars to micro, small and medium enterprises (Figures 8.3 and 8.4). EFL has been recognized by the G-20 as one of the most innovative solutions to SME finance globally, and has partnerships with the Inter-American Development Bank, Equifax and MasterCard Worldwide.

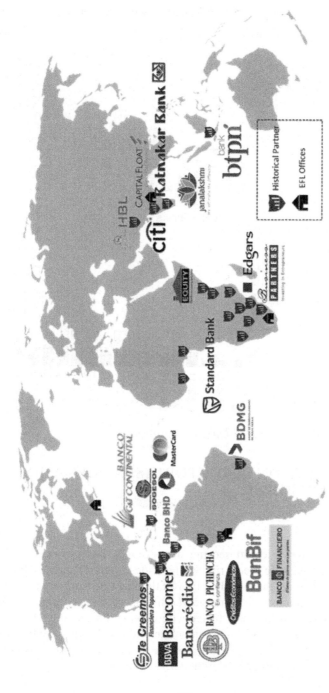

Figure 8.3   EFL offices and historical partners

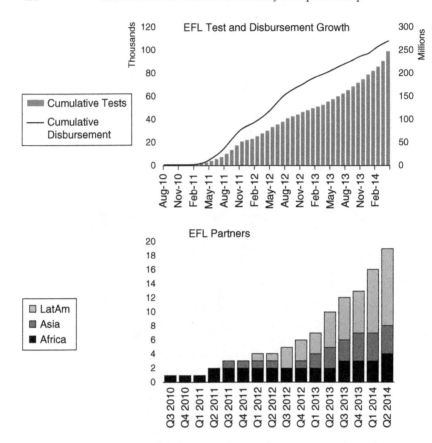

Figure 8.4   EFL test and disbursement growth

ORGANIZATION STRUCTURE (SERVICES AND RELATIONSHIPS)

Impact

EFL's psychometric credit scoring methodology has proved the ability to accurately measure credit risk with a wide variety of partner financial institutions around the world. Importantly, these institutions have leveraged EFL's technology for a range of lending ambitions, from expanding lending with controlled risk, to reducing risk within an active loan portfolio, to utilizing the EFL score in conjunction with other credit scoring services. Two case studies of EFL's work with partner institutions provide a glimpse into the range and depth of EFL's impact:

- Banco Financiero: a top ten Peruvian commercial bank.
- JFS: a fast growing Indian MFI used EFL to graduate group borrowers to larger, individual loans.

BANCO FINANCIERO

Executive Overview

- Banco Financiero, a top ten Peruvian commercial bank, engaged EFL in July of 2013 to help drive growth in the microfinance segment through better credit analytics.
- Banco Financiero created a new loan product using the EFL tool to measure risk, targeting applicants declined by other lenders due to insufficient credit history and documentation.
- Over the course of the first 12 months of the engagement, Banco Financiero administered nearly 5,000 EFL applications and disbursed nearly 2,900 new loans using the EFL tool.
- Encouraged by EFL's ability to measure risk and aid growth, Banco Financiero has invested in the expansion of the EFL tool in its Peruvian branch network.

Figure 8.5 below demonstrates EFL's risk separation power: the bottom 20 percent of Banco Financiero's portfolio according to EFL was 2.5 times more likely to default than the top 20 percent.

Additionally, EFL enabled Banco Financiero to screen out the riskiest

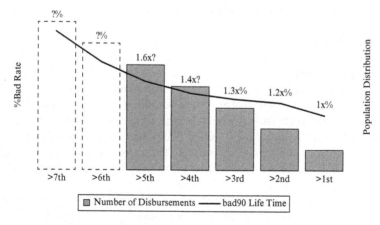

Figure 8.5   Cumulative bad rate by score bucket

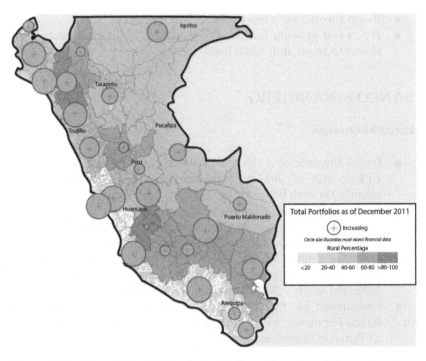

Figure 8.6   Map of financial inclusion in Peru, data from Mixmarket.org
*   (Peru, n.d.)*

segment of the applicant population (Figure 8.6). By identifying and declining these clients, EFL was able to reduce risk and improve the performance of Banco Financiero's lending efforts.

Partner Overview

A changing Peruvian market
As is the case throughout much of Latin America, Peruvian banks have for most of their history focused either on the upper income segment or microfinance segment of the Peruvian market. In both of these extremes, banks have excelled: Peru has an advanced corporate banking sector, and has been ranked the most microfinance-friendly country on earth for six consecutive years (Economist Intelligence Unit, 2013).

Recently, increased competition and a growing demand for financing in the middle and lower ends of the nation's economic pyramid have pushed many financial institutions to focus more on the micro segment.

Historically corporate-focused banks like BanBif (BanBif, n.d.) and Banco de Crédito (BCP) through its Edifycar subsidiary are reaching down-market to make smaller loans to smaller companies and servicing many levels of the economic pyramid.

Targeting these micro, small and medium enterprises (MSMEs), however, requires overcoming an imposing challenge: many Peruvian MSMEs lack basic credit criteria like borrowing history, credit scores and income statements. Less than 40 percent of Peruvians are covered by credit bureaus, and the vast majority of those covered are concentrated in Peru's high-income segment (World Bank, n.d., Private Credit Bureau Coverage). In Peru's poorest 40 percent, for example, fewer than in one in ten are able to access loans each year (World Bank, n.d., Global Findex). For companies that are too big for group facilities, but too small for traditional commercial loans, this information scarcity presents a formidable barrier to financial access. And for the banks jostling for position in an increasingly competitive microfinance market, it means a significant barrier to growth.

Banco Financiero's ambitions in the MSME space

Banco Financiero launched in 1996 under the primary ownership of Banco Pichincha, the leading bank in Ecuador. Since the early 2000s, Banco Financiero has targeted the bottom of Peru's economic pyramid as its key source of growth. The bank offers a variety of small business and consumer loan products to individuals and micro, small and medium enterprises (MSMEs) and today has the sixth largest loan portfolio in all of Peru. Banco Financiero continues to expand lending with a particular focus on the microfinance segment across its 3,800 branch network, achieving over 30 percent growth in micro-lending in 2013.

As Banco Financiero has grown over the last decade, however, it has been challenged to find new ways of measuring applicant risk without relying on the retrospective credit data that many of its target clients lack. Without a way of accurately quantifying the repayment potential of borrowers without traditional credit criteria, Banco Financiero and others have been able to capture only a small portion of the potential Peruvian micro market.

Project Overview

New product launch

Banco Financiero engaged EFL in July of 2013 to help expand lending to microentrepreneurs. More specifically, Banco Financiero identified a

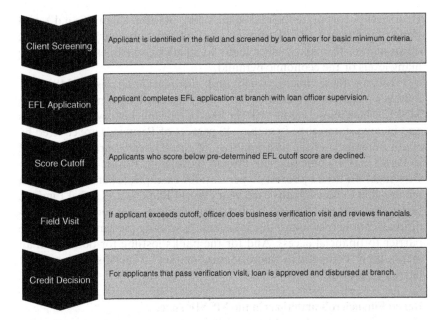

Figure 8.7   Five-step credit screening

significant market opportunity in entrepreneurs whose lack of business documentation, formal financial records, and insufficient or inadequate borrowing history had precluded them from borrowing from other banks. Many of these small business owners had the ability and willingness to repay loans, Banco Financiero believed, but without traditional credit criteria to illustrate their potential they appeared too risky for most lenders.

To serve this market, Banco Financiero developed a new, short-term working capital loan product and introduced EFL's psychometric credit application as an automated and scalable way to measure risk. By assessing clients' willingness and ability to repay through the EFL application, Banco Financiero was able to mitigate risk and lend with confidence as it moved into a relatively unknown market segment.

New EFL-enabled product offering

- Average loan size: US$800
- Average term: nine months
- Basic minimum criteria

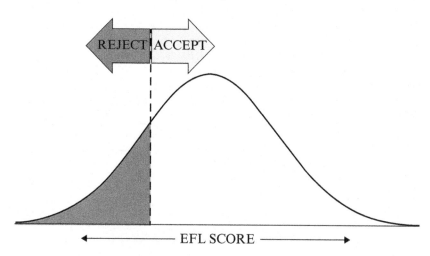

Note: The bell curve above is stylized, distributions are not typically standard normal.

Figure 8.8   Initial screen

- Minimum age
- Minimum business age
- National ID
- Collateral and/or guarantor required.

Using the EFL score

Banco Financiero integrated the EFL application into a five-step credit screening process (Figure 8.7).

The EFL score is used to measure and segment credit risk among prospective borrowers. All micro applicants that meet Banco Financiero's basic minimum requirements are required to complete an EFL application. EFL applications take an average of 45 minutes to complete and scores are returned to the bank within 30 minutes of synchronization.

Targeting a pre-determined applicant acceptance rate, Banco Financiero and EFL set an EFL cutoff score, below which applicants would be declined and above which applicants would be moved on to the later stages of credit review (Figure 8.8).

Rolling out EFL

Banco Financiero launched its new micro product in six branches in Peru's capital city of Lima, known for its high density of informal microentrepreneurs. In doing so, Banco Financiero was able to achieve high application

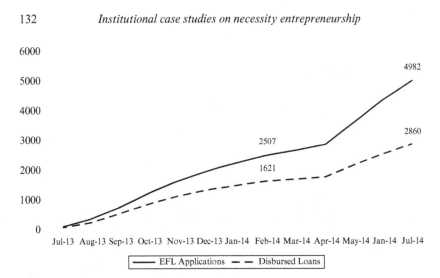

Figure 8.9   Evolution of EFL applications and loans

volumes in a well-controlled environment, thereby gaining a strong understanding not only of the viability of its new loan product, but also the
success of the EFL tool.

Results

The quality of any credit scoring tool lies in its ability to differentiate risk.
Those who receive higher scores should perform better, that is, default less
often, than those who score lower. The stronger the credit score, the better
it can differentiate between good and bad clients, and the more it can help
lenders control risk in their loan portfolios.

After 12 months, Banco Financiero had administered nearly 5,000 EFL
applications and disbursed nearly 2,900 loans to microentrepreneurs using
the EFL score (Figure 8.9). By looking retroactively at the relationship
between applicants' EFL scores and their respective loan performance, we
can evaluate the predictive power of EFL's scoring methodology among
Banco Financiero clients.

Figure 8.10 divides Banco Financiero's borrowing population into five
equally sized groups, or quintiles, based on applicants' EFL scores. Those
who scored in the top fifth are grouped into the column on the far right,
and vice versa. The "bad" rate, or ratio of borrowers that did not pay for
90 days or more (bad90) to the total borrowing population in that quintile
is illustrated by the downward sloping line.

Figure 8.10 demonstrates that EFL's psychometric credit model was

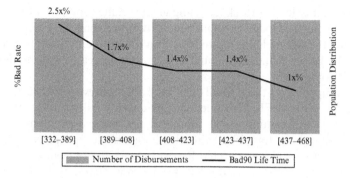

Figure 8.10   Default rate by score bucket

able to accurately differentiate credit risk in Banco Financiero's Peruvian borrowing population. Specifically, the bottom quintile was 2.5 times more likely to default than the top quintile. The bottom two quintiles were more than 70 percent more likely to default than the top two.

Figure 8.10 also illustrates the potential to control risk within a borrowing population. By screening out higher percentages of the applicant population, a lender can reduce default rates in the resulting loan portfolio. Had Banco Financiero chosen only to accept the top four quintiles and reject the bottom one, for example, it would have removed a segment that defaulted 80 percent more often than the rest of the borrowing population.

Figure 8.11 further conveys the opportunity for portfolio segmentation by showing cumulative portfolio defaults by score bucket. Had Banco Financiero chosen to lend only to the top 60 percent of approved applicants, it would have reduced total default rates by 20 percent. As the bank chooses to lend to a bigger population it deliberately chooses to

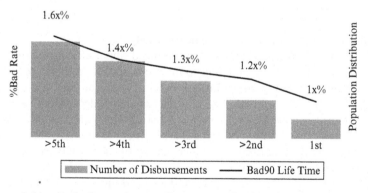

Figure 8.11   Default rate by cumulative score bucket

take on higher levels of risk, enabling greater value captured through risk-based pricing and loan size adjustments. By increasing the interest rate or reducing the size of loans offered between the third and fifth quintiles, for example, Banco Financiero could mitigate the increased risk of the borrowing population.

As compelling as these results are, they only represent part of the value added by EFL. EFL allows lenders to control risk in their portfolios not just by differentiating risk among those that receive loans, but also by rejecting those too risky to receive loans in the first place. While we don't know exactly how rejected Banco Financiero applicants would have performed had they received loans, we do know that they constituted the riskiest segment of the applicant population according to EFL's scoring methodology. By identifying and screening these clients, EFL was able to reduce risk and improve the performance of Banco Financiero's portfolio.

Moving Forward

EFL's psychometric credit scoring methodology has proven the ability to accurately measure risk in Banco Financiero's Peruvian borrowing population, enabling Banco Financiero to effectively expand in the micro sector. Encouraged by the first year's results, Banco Financiero is continuing to hone its product offering and develop effective methods of graduating borrowers to larger loans. Over the next year, Banco Financiero plans to expand the use of the EFL score to additional branches in Peru, relying on EFL as a key pillar of its growth strategy in the micro segment.

JFS

Partner Overview

Understanding the Indian microfinance market

India's microfinance segment has experienced unparalleled growth in the last decade. The total amount lent to microenterprises has increased nearly 90 percent in recent years (Durgadevi Saraf, n.d.) as new players have entered the market and existing players have expanded. Today there are more than 200 registered microfinance institutions with 35 million active borrowers and more than 5 billion dollars in micro-loans across the country, making India the largest microfinance market on earth (Mix Market, n.d., India) (Figure 8.12).

The enthusiasm for lending to India's working poor is balanced by lessons learned from a microfinance crisis that shook the nation in 2010.

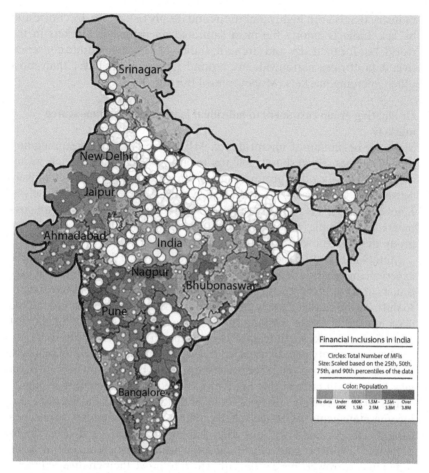

Figure 8.12 MFI penetration in India, data from Mixmarket.org (India, n.d.)

Ensnared in debt by some MFIs' predatory pricing and coercive collections policies, as well as widespread client over-borrowing and poorly crafted regulatory efforts, borrowers began defaulting in huge numbers. The crisis forced well-established MFIs to close their doors, sent a shockwave through the Indian microfinance community, and called into question the practices of MFIs around the world. The Indian government responded to the crisis with a series of regulatory changes to protect borrowers, and to control the exposure and restrain the risk of microfinance lenders.

The events of the last decade have given shape to an Indian microfinance industry that is both highly ambitious and deeply risk averse, by choice and by law. India is among the most saturated microfinance markets in the world, but for their size and strength, Indian MFIs remain quite conservative: default rates nationwide are around 1 percent, far lower than most other emerging markets (Moneycontrol Bureau, 2013).

Graduating group customers to individual loans in information-scarce markets

Since the beginning of microfinance, MFIs have practiced group-lending methodologies. By disbursing loans to groups and making each group member liable for other group members' repayment, MFIs have effectively outsourced the process of credit review onto the borrowers themselves. Knowing that she is responsible for every other group member's loan payments, for example, a borrower will only bring other borrowers into her group that she knows are likely to repay.

Many MFIs around the world have been able to scale these simple models, experiencing great success in delivering small loans to a large number of customers in need. More recently, however, microfinance ambitions have begun to shift. As the market for new group facilities begins to dwindle and a middle class in need of larger working capital loans emerges, many of the largest microfinance banks see individual loans as the future of lending in India.

The opportunity in individual lending is immense and widely recognized, but it is not without risk. The vast majority of business owners in India lack basic credit criteria that are typically used to assess creditworthiness: things like borrowing histories, collateral, formal financial records and income statements. Without reliable data to understand an applicant's capacity to pay, and without joint liability groups to self-select high-potential borrowers and encourage repayment through social pressure, individual borrowers have little with which to prove their creditworthiness.

Further, as part of the Indian central bank regulations post the Andhra Pradesh crisis of 2009, the Indian government placed interest rate caps for non-deposit taking MFIs at 26 percent. And while in many cases this protects borrowers from predatory loan pricing, it also makes it more difficult to serve low-income individual borrowers, as the costs associated with credit review and collections in this segment are significantly higher. Because of the lack of reliable credit data and high costs of screening and servicing, many MFIs have shied away from individual lending, and opted for lower risk and lower return group facilities.

An emerging leader in Indian microfinance

Established in 2003 to serve the needs of India's under-banked, Janalakshmi Financial Services (JFS) has quickly grown into a

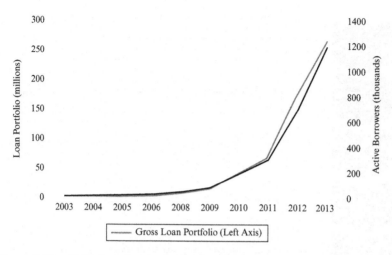

*Figure 8.13   JFS' decade of growth, data from Mixmarket.org
(Mixmarket, n.d., MFI)*

premier Indian Microfinance Institution. Today, JFS boasts more than
300 million dollars in assets and more than a million active borrowers
across 154 branches in 85 cities and 14 states (Janalakshmi, n.d.), making
it one of the top five largest MFIs in all of India (Mix Market, n.d.,
MFI) (Figure 8.13).

**JFS' market-based approach to financial inclusion is defined by three
distinct characteristics:**

1.   Sole focus on servicing the urban poor
2.   Tailored customer centric approach to financial products and services
     design and development
3.   Central role of technology and processes for efficiency and scalability.

JFS has pioneered models to graduate the urban under-served up the
ladder into individual lending products, and is one of the only MFIs that
has been able to successfully carry out graduation model lending in parallel
with its typical group microfinance lending.

Like any new lender of individual loans, JFS has faced difficulty in
overcoming the challenges of information scarcity to understand a customer's eligibility. JFS' individual lending has more than doubled each
year for the last three years, but without quantifiable data to measure
risk among prospective borrowers JFS has been forced to rely on time

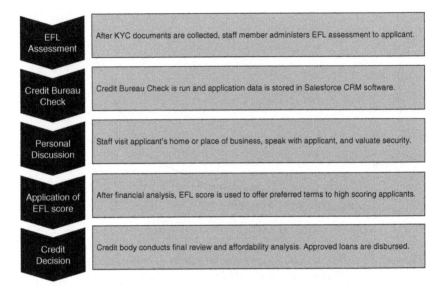

Figure 8.14   JFS' processes for JanaOne and EFS

and resource intensive measures to extend its individual lending portfolio. This has meant high screening costs and long turnaround times (TAT) for applicants.

Project Overview

Integrating EFL

JFS engaged EFL in April of 2013 to determine the feasibility of using EFL's credit scoring methodology to expand individual loan portfolios while controlling risk in the Indian microfinance market. In April 2013, JFS began using the EFL Survey to assess all new and returning customers applying for JFS's individual loan products, JanaOne and EFS (Figure 8.14).

JFS integrated EFL into its existing application processes, administering the EFL survey alongside other application materials. For the first year of the engagement, JFS did not use the EFL score for direct loan decision-making, rather it used the score to identify the highest potential candidates that it could fast track through the credit review process and offer preferential terms. By administering the survey to all individual loan applicants and tracking their performance over time, JFS was able to test the predictive power of EFL's scoring technology in the Indian market.

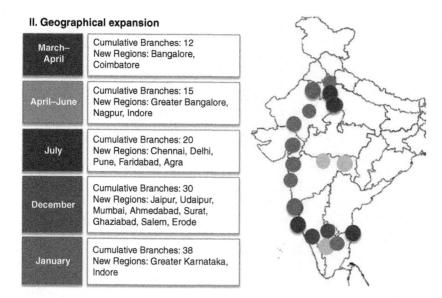

Figure 8.15   EFL rollout

Rolling Out EFL

Over the course of the first year, JFS scaled the EFL tool across 40 branches, training 120 JFS staff members to administer EFL surveys (Figure 8.15).

Deploying a combination of field testing on netbooks and branch testing using desktop computers, JFS administered more than 7,000 EFL surveys and disbursed more than 4,000 loans in the first 12 months (Figure 8.16).

Results

EFL's predictive power

The quality of any creditscoring tool lies in its ability to differentiate risk. Those who receive higher scores should perform better, that is, default less often, than those who score lower. The stronger the credit score, the better it can differentiate between good and bad clients, and the more it can help lenders control risk in their loan portfolios. By tracking the loan performance of JFS applicants who took the EFL survey and received EFS or JanaOne loans, we can evaluate how effective EFL's credit methodology was in measuring risk. In this case, EFL's model performance was

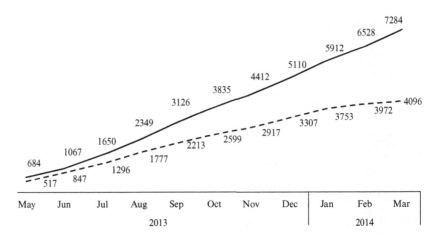

Figure 8.16   EFL applications and disbursements

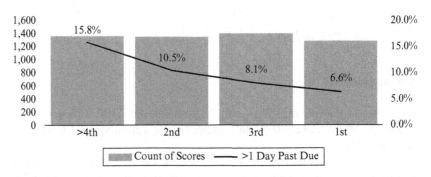

Figure 8.17   Bad rate by score bucket

measured against applicants who have fallen more than one day past due on their loan repayments.

Figure 8.17 divides JFS's applicant population into four groups of nearly equal size, or quartiles, based on applicants' EFL scores. Those who scored in the bottom fourth of the population are grouped into the column on the far left, and vice versa. The height of each column indicates the size of the total borrowing population. Borrowers that have fallen more than one day past due are characterized as "bad." The bad rate is the ratio of these borrowers in arrears to the total borrowing population in that quartile, and is illustrated by the downward sloping line.

Figure 8.17 demonstrates that EFL's psychometric credit model was able to accurately differentiate credit risk in JFS's Indian borrowing population.

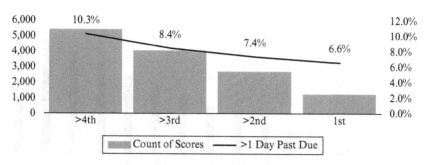

Figure 8.18   Cumulative bad rate by quartile

Borrowers who received lower scores defaulted more often than those who received higher scores. Specifically, the *borrowers in the bottom quartile were nearly 2.5 times more likely to fall behind on their payments as customers in the top quartile*. Figure 8.17 also illustrates the potential to control risk within a borrowing population. By screening out more applicants, a lender can reduce default rates in the resulting loan portfolio. Had JFS chosen to reject the bottom quartile, for example, *it would have removed a subset of the borrowers that fell behind on payments 50 percent more often than the rest of the population*.

Figure 8.18 further conveys the opportunity for portfolio segmentation by showing cumulative portfolio performance. Now, rather than seeing each quartile independently, we see them stacked as a running total. The column on the far right shows just the first quartile, the column to its left shows the first and second quartiles, and so on. Similarly, the line now shows the percentage of "bad" borrowers to the cumulative populations.

Had JFS chosen to lend only to the top 75 percent, using the EFL score as a pre-filter to drop the lowest quartile of applicants, *it would have seen a nearly 25 percent reduction in late repayment rates across its portfolio*. As the bank chooses to lend to a bigger population it deliberately chooses to take on higher levels of risk, enabling greater value captured through risk-based pricing and loan size adjustments. By increasing the interest rate or reducing the size of loans offered between the third and fourth quartiles, for example, a lender could mitigate the increased risk of the borrowing population.

Moving Forward

Over the course of the one-year engagement, EFL's credit scoring methodology proved the ability to accurately differentiate credit risk among JFS' individual borrower population. JFS extended the engagement to include an additional two years.

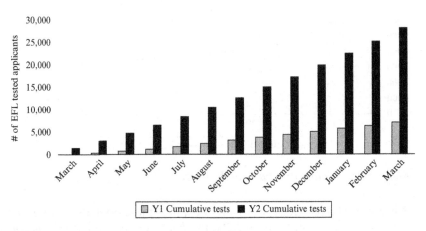

Figure 8.19 EFL survey volume projections

JFS has ambitious expansion plans for both EFS and JanaOne products over the next year and will maintain the EFL testing mandate for all new applicants. As a result, applicant test volumes are projected to grow four fold in year two of the partnership (Figure 8.19).

As the EFL–JFS partnership grows and EFL's credit scoring methodology continues to demonstrate its risk-sorting power, JFS will look to apply the EFL score to directly inform loan decision-making for its individual loan products. Doing so will allow JFS to grow lending and improve control over risk in the Indian market, as well as increase operational efficiency by cutting down on the costly and time intensive components of the existing credit application process. JFS may also start using EFL scores to lend to new, "thin-file" Janalakshmi applicants, reducing minimum criteria to expand access to finance and bring new borrowers into the formal financial sector.

By increasing efficiency and reducing risk within JFS's individual lending portfolio, the partnership between EFL and JFS will dramatically improve JFS' ability to lend to a large portfolio of individual microborrowers. Most importantly, the partnership has the potential to change the way that Indian MFIs approach individual lending, a segment that to date has remained largely out of reach.

WHAT'S NEXT?

EFL has grown quickly in recent years, working with leading financial institutions across Africa, Asia and Latin America. Today, an EFL application is administered somewhere in the world every five minutes, enabling hundreds of millions of dollars in loans to tens of thousands of borrowers, many of whom would otherwise would have been locked out of formal financial services. In the coming years EFL has ambitious plans to expand the use of its psychometric credit scoring technology to new customers, new segments, and new channels. By working with innovative financial institutions committed to expanding financial access at the base of the pyramid, EFL will continue to unlock the entrepreneurial potential of the world's emerging markets.

REFERENCES

BanBif (n.d.). Environmental and Social Management Report. *IDB*. Retrieved in March 2015 from http://idbdocs.iadb.org/wsdocs/getdocument. aspx?docnum=3743682.

Durgadevi Saraf (n.d.). Sarita microfinance in India: a comprehensive analysis of the growth. *Durgadevi Saraf Institute of Management Studies*. Retrieved in January 2015 from www.dsims.org.in/web/popular_media/Sarita_Microfinance_ in_IndiaA_Comprehensive_Analysis_of_the_Growth.pdf.

Economist Intelligence Unit (EIU) (2013). *Global Microscope on the Microfinance Business Environment 2013*. Retrieved in January 2015 from www.citigroup.com/ citi/citizen/community/data/EIU_Microfinance_2013_Proof_08.pdf.

Janalakshmi (n.d.). Retrieved in January 2015 from www.janalakshmi.com/.

Mix Market (n.d.). India market profile. Data retrieved in April 2015 from http:// mixmarket.org/mfi/country/India.

Mix Market (n.d.). MFI report: Janalakshmi Financial Services Pvt Ltd. Retrieved in April 2015 from http://mixmarket.org/mfi/jfspl.

Mix Market (n.d.). Peru market profile. Data retrieved in April 2015 from http:// maps.mixmarket.org/peru/.

Moneycontrol (2013, June 9). Default rate improves to 1% for MFI loans: Equifax. Retrieved in January 2015 from www.moneycontrol.com/news/business/default- rate-improves-to-1-for-mfi-loans-equifax_901649.html.

Stein, P., Goland, T., and Schiff, R. (2010). Two trillion and counting: assessing the credit gap for micro, small, and medium-sized enterprises in the develop- ing world. Washington, DC: *World Bank*. Retrieved in May 2015 from http:// documents.worldbank.org/curated/en/2010/10/16528328/two-trillion-counting- assessing-credit-gap-micro-small-medium-size-enterprises-developing-world.

World Bank (n.d.). Global Findex (Global Financial Inclusion Database). *World DataBank*. Retrieved in March 2015 from http://databank.worldbank.org/Data/ Views/VariableSelection/SelectVariables.aspx?source=1228#.

World Bank (n.d.). Private Credit Bureau Coverage (% of Adults). *World DataBank*. Retrieved in March 2015 from http://data.worldbank.org/indicator/ IC.CRD.PRVT.ZS.

9. Building a scalable training solution for necessity entrepreneurs in the missing middle

Jeff Brownlow

INTRODUCTION

I first met Jeremi Brewer in 2010 on a dusty street in Puebla, Mexico. As a young PhD student at Texas A&M studying entrepreneurship and micro-enterprise education, Jeremi had been hired to build and run a business academy in Mexico City. At the time, I was working as a management consultant at Bain & Company in Texas and had been invited to speak to the first group of students in Puebla and expose them to some of the analytical and strategic tools used by global companies. Upon meeting a group of 30 or so farmers and landscapers in an old church building, I was skeptical that they would get much out of our training, let alone be capable of building sustainable businesses. I spent the next week working day and night to help the students evaluate ideas, write business plans, and build rudimentary financial models. To my amazement, they demonstrated a hunger to learn and a passion for business that I hadn't seen anywhere else in the world. I watched with admiration as Dr. Brewer taught them to turn a blade of grass into cash and frustration into a powerful conviction that they could succeed.

After spending the past four years conducting rigorous research and interviewing thousands of microenterprise operators around the world, as well as spending countless hours scouring the globe for institutions dedicated to training "necessity entrepreneurs," I am more convinced than ever regarding the need for this book and am delighted to contribute to it. The institutions covered in this book have been identified as game-changers.

My relationship to the editors of the first volume of this series began in 2008 when I first met Mr. Gibson. At the time I was studying Finance at Brigham Young University and concurrently working as a consultant to several Hispanic social entrepreneurs who had founded an entrepreneurship and business center in Salt Lake City, Utah. Mr. Gibson was associated with the founder of the center and we became acquainted through a series of board meetings. During our conversations, he explained that he had built the Academy for Creating Enterprise[1] (the Academy) in Cebu, the Philippines in 1999 and that he was seeking to replicate his program in Mexico.

In 2010, Mr. Gibson hired Dr. Brewer to execute the launch in Mexico.[2] As Dr. Brewer was preparing to relocate his family to Mexico, Mr. Gibson had remembered my passion and desire to improve the world through entrepreneurship and finance education and he suggested that I join Dr. Brewer for pilot trainings they were conducting in Mexico. They knew that I had a love for the Latin people and that I believed in the power of helping others realize their potential.

However, despite my passion for working with entrepreneurs, I had become disenchanted with the world of "development work." Or, perhaps more specifically, I had become dissatisfied with the countless not-for-profits, NGOs, government-aid, international aid, and charities that cluttered the space of economic development. Furthermore, I had become disheartened with the entire microcredit/microfinance movement on many dimensions. Thus, while I was hesitant to formally interact with the Academy (an NGO) I did believe in their mission to "not give a man a fish" and to not "teach him how to fish" but, "to teach him how to sell the fish."[3] That was an idea (and mission) I was interested in learning more about. I was particularly intrigued with the Academy as I had spent two years serving as a missionary for the LDS church and had developed many friendships with individuals who were the target students of the Academy.

Not long after, I received a phone call from Dr. Brewer inviting me to join him for a training session in Puebla. To this day I fondly remember how I felt the first time I spoke with him. Within a matter of minutes I knew that he was either (1) significantly sheltered, naïve, and/or ignorant about how markets in developing countries function, or (2) he had acutely identified a pain in the market, as well as a *realistic* process of how to disrupt traditional "development work" in a positive and significant way. Candidly, I was inclined to believe that he had fallen so deeply in love with his own theories that he was ignoring many critical facts of development. Nevertheless, I could not deny his passion—it was contagious.

In my defense, Dr. Brewer was inexperienced, full of ideas, and spoke a mile a minute. His assertions and assumptions were primarily theoretical. But, there was something about his commitment, vision, and general willingness to wear his heart on his sleeve and be an agent of action that I deeply respected.

During our first conversation he cited some of the following information:

1. There were tens of millions (if not billions) of people who were pushed and/or compelled to provide for their families by starting a small business. They were, as he defined them, "necessity entrepreneurs."
2. The vast majority of these necessity entrepreneurs had little (and in most cases zero) formal business management training.
3. The best approach to training necessity entrepreneurs was to develop a culture-specific and culture-shifting curriculum.
4. There were no institutions currently addressing this problem around the globe.
5. He had empirical data (with a small sample size from graduates of Steve Gibson's Academy in the Philippines) demonstrating how necessity entrepreneurs from the base of the pyramid had been successfully trained to start and/or grow healthier businesses; specifically that the training could (a) increase gross revenues, (b) produce higher net profits, (c) provide higher personal incomes, (d) create more jobs for others and (e) obtain a solid foundation of business management through financial literacy.

His positions appeared empirically sound and he was persuasive. However, I had encountered a significant challenge as we discussed his theories. For example, when I searched for the terms "necessity entrepreneurs" and "missing middle" I found almost no sources that could support (nor deny) his claims. Certainly, there were infinite amounts of articles about microfinance and microcredit loans, but the information regarding business management or entrepreneurship training programs was scarce.

As the phone conversation continued with Dr. Brewer, I found myself questioning why Mr. Gibson—a highly respected entrepreneur, a retired professional professor from the Marriott School of Management at BYU, and a man I admired greatly for his achievements—had hired Dr. Brewer to build his Academy in Mexico. I simply could not understand why Mr. Gibson had hired an *academic* to build and manage such an entrepreneurial endeavor.

I ultimately decided to accept the invitation to Mexico because I was intrigued with the idea and because I love the country. To be clear, I decided to participate in the pilot program for several reasons. First, I am deeply motivated to create sustainable and scalable solutions for economic development. Second, I am passionate about leadership and business education. Third, I have always desired to dedicate my life to helping others realize their full potential. Finally, in the event that what I had heard from Dr. Brewer was, in fact, true—I realized it could have the power to change the world.

Prior to attending the training with Dr. Brewer in Mexico I had a major question that I hoped my trip would answer: *Are developing nations truly filled with "necessity entrepreneurs"?*

1. If not, then I will still be happy with the service I provided for a few people.
2. If yes, then, I want to know:
    - a.   What are the greatest needs they have?
    - b.   Who is already solving these needs?
    - c.   Can these needs be addressed at a global scale?

After a few days in Mexico I sat at a lunch table filled with entrepreneurs who inspired and motivated me. I could see their hunger and profound desire to learn. They inspired me because I could see in their dark faces how hard they have been working in their small businesses over the years. They inspired me because they were riveted by what they were being taught. This was a starkly different environment from the casual classrooms I had grown accustomed to in my life. In fact, instead of seeing the students sleeping, talking to one another or texting on their phones—as I expected would be the case and as I normally saw with my peers in the US—these students were sitting at the edges of their seats, asking insightful questions, taking copious notes and drawing parallels just as well as my associates at the top consulting firms and business schools.

Much to my surprise, these great people were not attending this seminar because they were seeking a "free meal" or a "free handout." These men and women were not attending the course in pursuit of a loan or investment, as they all knew upon signing up for the seminar that neither of these would be given. Instead, these people were attending this seminar because they recognized that they were "stuck" in their businesses and they recognized that they had not been able to make their small businesses grow over the course of many years (sometimes decades). Thus, instead of seeking the proverbial "free lunch" or "free handout" these necessity entrepreneurs were seeking knowledge with a drive that I have seen in few places before or since.

I returned to my office in Dallas feeling humbled. None of my new friends in Mexico had ever heard of Bain or the companies I was consulting for. Moreover, many of the students did not recognize the names Harvard, Stanford, Wharton or Thunderbird. It took me only a few minutes to realize that I had spent a week in a different world than the one I had grown accustomed to over the past decade and that these students were motivated by a deep source of hope. As one student said, "If I don't change . . . and if I don't learn how to improve my business . . . my children will live the same nightmare that I live . . . and I don't want that for them."[4] Thus, these students did not attend the Academy to get a piece of paper to hang on their wall, but rather, they recognized the need for change and they realized that the responsibility to forge a more prosperous future for themselves and their families rested squarely upon their shoulders.

Perhaps what touched me most was the deep feeling of empathy that I experienced with these simple yet powerful entrepreneurs. During the trip, I showed a few pictures of my family on the overhead projector. Each time I did this, I saw the physical countenance of the students change: they were deeply motivated to see that, like them, I was married, had children, and that my primary motivation was the exact same as theirs: to forge a more prosperous future for my family and posterity.

The desire to improve was palpable. The determination I had witnessed to learn the basics of business was strikingly different from the haphazard desire that I had seen for so many years as a student in college. The willingness to listen, take notes, and put what they were learning into practice immediately was contagious, and I vowed then to dedicate my life to living and working with this type of conviction, and to help as many people as possible do the same.

To this day I often reflect on my interactions with the first group of necessity entrepreneurs that I met in Puebla. I think about sitting with them and working on simple business models and I am grateful for the goodness it has brought into my life. The experience also opened my eyes to a few market insights: (1) I was building financial models on laptop computers that were owned by the students, which meant that these people had sufficient funds to own a computer; (2) the financial models I was building for these small businesses brought clarity to the business owners, which meant that they had financial literacy and an understanding of business; and (3) what I was doing could be scaled, as it was not my elite education or resumé that allowed me to create impact.

For the remainder of this chapter I will list a few of the most frequent questions I asked the students as we worked on different models for their businesses. The questions are in bold and the different answers I received are written beneath each question. After each question and answer segment, I include a "Notes and Observations" section wherein I provide the conclusions I reached after listening to the various answers provided by the students.

I am including these conversations here in an effort to demonstrate the diverse challenges and palpable realities that I faced as I have worked with small business owners enrolled in this course. In most of the cases mentioned below, I had such scarce information from their respective businesses that it was essentially impossible for me to provide constructive ideas for how they could grow their businesses: they had no written records of their sales, they lacked a control over their inventory, they were unaware of their financial status, and they did not practice as separate entities, financially. While their realities were overwhelming at first, I quickly took advantage of the situation and realized that it provided me with an opportunity to inquire about their (1) motivation in starting their companies, (2) financial literacy, (3) management practices and proficiencies and (4) critical thinking—all of which are outlined below.

MOTIVATION

Question: Why did you start this business?
Answers:

- [Student age 42] My job didn't pay me enough so I had to start something on the side to earn more money. Then, I started focusing on my side business because I could make more money.
- [Student age 37] When I lost my job I needed to do something to make money.
- [Student age 53] I have no education and getting a good-paying job is out of the question for me. This is why I had to start something.
- [Student age 30] My father taught me how to do this [agriculture]. This is all I know how to do.
- [Student age 37] I knew that I either needed to pay a coyote to take me to the USA so I could send money to my family, but I didn't want to leave, and I don't have a good job opportunity, so I started this business.
- [Student age 44] What else could I do? Starting a business was my only option. I had to do it.
- [Student age 38] I never went to school and so I always knew I had to have my own business to survive.

Question: What level of education do you have?
Answers:

- [Tomato Farmer] I have a college degree in electrical engineering.
- [Brick Manufacturer] I finished high school.
- [Greenhouse Builder] I finished high school.
- [Tomato Farmer] I have a business management degree.
- [Tomato Farmer] I have two business degrees.
- [Furniture Cleaner] I have a degree in accounting.
- [Steel Manufacturer] I finished the fifth grade.
- [Real Estate Firm] I finished high school and have a license to sell homes.

- [Photocopy Shop] I finished my college degree in human development.
- [Laundry Shop] I only finished half of my college degree in engineering.
- [Graphic Design Firm] I never went to college. Just high school.
- [Transportation Firm] I'm the first high school graduate in my family.

Question: Where did you get the idea to start your business?
Answers:

- I saw our neighbors down the street had a business doing this.
- This has been a family business for three generations.
- I was invited by a family member who was already doing this.
- I was approached by a friend who owned the business and he invited me to be his partner.
- My family owns the land and we have always farmed.
- I read books like *Rich Dad Poor Dad* and got the idea.
- I used to be employed doing [this same thing] and so I started on my own.
- I like computers and there was no Internet café in my town.
- I saw this same business in another city and so I started one in my town.

Notes and Observations

1. *Necessity* was the driving motivation behind the launch of the small businesses owned and operated by these students.
2. Individuals with college educations still end up starting some type of small business and my perception is that they have relatively the same questions as those without college degrees.
3. Innovation consists primarily of seeing what others do and copying.

FINANCIAL LITERACY

Question: What were your gross sales last month?
Answers:

- I'm not sure. What are "gross sales?"
- I don't know.
- Probably something like $10,000 pesos?
- I will have to check. I don't know.

- I usually sell about $15,000 pesos a month.
- I don't know. My accountant does that.
- I don't think I sold more than $20,000 pesos.
- $30,000 pesos more or less.
- Maybe $6,000 pesos?

Question: What was your net profit last month?
Answers:

- I'm not sure. What are 'gross sales?'
- I don't know.
- What do you mean?
- Probably something like $2,000 pesos? I think. [from he who said, "$10,000"].
- I will have to check. I don't know.
- $10,000 pesos approximately [from he who said, "$15,000 pesos"].
- I don't know. My accountant does that. I don't really know.
- $30,000 pesos more or less. It's the same as before. Right?
- Probably $10,000 pesos [from she who said "Maybe $6,000 pesos?"].

Question: Do you pay yourself a salary each week or month?
Answers:

- Not really. I usually take for myself what we need for the day.
- No, not a set amount.
- No. I don't. Should I?
- What do you mean? Like, pay myself a specific amount each week? Is that the way to do it? I don't do that.
- Sometimes. I usually pay myself what we need.

Question: What assets does your business own?
Answers:

- What is an "asset?"—[I then explain what an asset is].
- Well, my family owns the asset. My business just manages it.
- I own all the assets. My business doesn't own anything.
- My house and car and inventory, I think. Right?
- I use all my own property in the business. I don't separate the assets, they all belong to me.
- I don't have any assets. My business doesn't have any assets. I don't think. Do they? What do you mean?

Question: Do you use separate bank accounts for your home funds and your business funds?
Answers:

- No.
- I don't use a bank. I just keep my money hidden in different places.
- I do not.
- All my money is in one account for my family. Should I change that?
- Yes. I have a bank account for my business. And, I use a different account for my family funds. Otherwise it's too messy.
- I don't think so. I think it's just one account. I would have to check with my accountant, he would know.

Question: Do you know which product or service has the highest profit margin?
Answers:

- What do you mean?
- I don't understand.
- What is a profit margin?
- How would I know that?
- I only sell tomatoes and so that would be the product.
- Probably the candy I sell to the kids in my copy-shop; I sell that the most.
- I don't know. Sorry!
- My accountant will probably have that answer.
- Yes, it is my furniture washing.

Notes and Observations

1. Nearly all students were confused by the terms I used: gross revenue, net profit, gross margin/profit margin, assets, and so on.
2. ~90 percent of the individuals I worked with (35 of 40) did not know how much inventory they were selling each week/month; meaning, they didn't know how much they were selling (gross) each week/month.
3. ~95 percent of the students do not separate business and personal money; nor do they pay themselves a salary.

MANAGEMENT

Question: How many clients do you have on average each week/month?
Answers:

- I don't know.
- I have never checked.
- I only have, probably, 30 clients. I'm not 100 percent certain.
- It would be too hard for me to know that, there are too many.
- I have two clients. They buy my entire inventory each week.

Question: Which day of the week is the most popular?
Answers:

- I don't know.
- They are all about the same.
- I sell my product on Saturdays at the market. That's the only day I sell.
- Probably Fridays and Saturdays. That's when we are the busiest.
- I have never checked that. I couldn't say.

Question: Do you have an operations manual for your business?
Answers:

- No.
- I don't. Should I make one?
- Not really.
- No. I just do it all.
- No. I don't because I don't want someone to take all my plans and ideas and copy me.

Question: Do you have specific goals for how much you want to sell next month?
Answers:

- [From he who did not know how much he sold last month.] More than last month!
- [From she who didn't know how much she sold last month.] I'd like to sell two times as much so I can grow my business.
- I have a dream (hope), but I don't have it written down.
- I just want to sell enough to get more inventory so I can sell more.
- Not totally. I need to sell more so that I can pay my debts off.

Question: How many employees do you have?
Answers:

- I am the only who works in the business; my children help when I need it.
- I have three employees that work with me, but sometimes I only have two.
- I have six employees, but only four are full-time.
- My wife and I work in the business together. Do children count as employees?
- I work most of the time alone, but with big projects I hire temporary employees, sometimes ten or twenty people. It just depends on the size of the project.

Notes and Observations

1. The vast majority (~90 percent or more) of the students do not understand their current customer base, including: purchasing patterns, demographics and total quantity.
2. ~85 percent of the students do not use written systems or processes in their businesses.
3. Employment relationships appear weak and spotty.

TRAINING

Question: What type of business training did you receive prior to (or since) opening your business?
Answers:

- None. That is why I am here. I don't think there are trainings for this type of learning available in my area unless you go to the university.
- "Los golpes de la vida" (Hard knocks of life).
- My dad tutored me on how to grow the crops and who to sell them to.
- I went to college, but they never taught me how to register a company; they never taught me how to pay my taxes; nor did I learn how to market for a small business.
- I have never been trained on anything. This is my first course.
- I went to a course offered by my church, but the people training us didn't have any experience with business.

- Before I opened, I talked with other business owners and they gave me some ideas.
- I was an employee making [this product] and I figured I could do it better and make more money on my own.

Notes and Observations

1. Most of the students do not understand their current customer base, including: purchasing patterns, demographics, current quantity, potential customer base, and so on.
2. ~85 percent of the students do not use written systems or processes in their businesses.
3. Employment relationships appear weak, informal and spotty.

CRITICAL THINKING

Question: What do you think you need most to improve your business?
Answers:

- I need money. If you don't have money here, you can't start anything.
- Capital and training and someone who can help me sell more and/or make contacts for me.
- Somebody who will invest in me and my company so that I can make it grow.
- I need you to help me find somebody who would be interested in being a partner in my business with me. If they will invest the money, I will do all the work.
- I need to sell my business to someone so that I can start all over again.
- I need to learn organization.
- Probably having this training because I have never been taught how to run my business.

Notes and Observations

1. Most students believe that receiving more money is their greatest need.
2. Most students appear to be searching for a partner, mentor or confidant with whom they can interact for support.

ADDITIONAL THOUGHTS

On my flight home from Puebla, I reflected on the lessons I had learned and pulled out my computer to review the questions I hoped to answer during my trip.

For convenience to the reader, I provide a review of the questions here, as well as my answers to the questions: *Are developing nations truly filled with "necessity entrepreneurs"?*

1. If no, then I will still be happy with the service I provided for a few people.
2. If yes, then, I want to know:
    - a.   What are the greatest needs they have?
    - b.   Who is already solving this need?
    - c.   How can (if at all possible) the pain be solved at scale?

Question One: Are Developing Nations Truly Inundated By "Necessity Entrepreneurs"?

Answer: Provided the sample size (N=50) of those who participated in the training in Puebla was minimal, I knew it would be unwise to draw a final conclusion based on such a small amount of people. However, I also could not ignore the reality that nearly every business owner I was consulting during the course had started their business out of necessity. It was at this moment that I was persuaded to believe that the notion of necessity entrepreneurship had some merit. In other words: I was persuaded to believe in necessity entrepreneurship and I was motivated to more fully understand if this group of *Poblano*-business owners represented the broader population of Mexico, or if it merely reflected the reality of the people who lived in Puebla—one of Mexico's poorest states.

Question Two: What Are The Greatest Needs That Necessity Entrepreneurs Have?

Answer: In trying to find a constructive answer to this question I concluded that the most logical approach would be (1) to review the notes that I made during my conversations with each student and (2) reflect upon my impressions during those conversations. These notes and impressions organically evolved into the categories, notes and observations I mentioned earlier in this chapter.

As I reviewed my notes and reflected upon my impressions from the meetings I had throughout the week, I became somewhat perplexed. To begin with, the majority of the necessity entrepreneurs in the training felt trapped and/or "stuck" by their current circumstances. They were fully aware that their primary motivation in starting their livelihood businesses was necessity. They also recognized that they lacked the social, familial and financial capital to succeed, which led me to begin searching for an answer to my next question.

Question Three: Who Is Currently Solving This Need?

Answer: Because these necessity entrepreneurs had never received any type of formal business management or entrepreneurship training, they knew that they did not have the necessary skills to succeed with their businesses—which explains why they so desperately were seeking an external source with whom they could "partner."

Dr. Brewer and I have spent hundreds of hours discussing the questions I've discussed in this chapter over the past five years. We have searched for empirically reliable data to help explain to what degree necessity entrepreneurship exists in and impacts Mexico's economy. Since that first trip to Mexico, we have conducted a rigorous due-diligence process searching for organizations of all types—NGOs, government programs, MFIs, banks, technical schools, and so on—that were currently trying to solve this problem. Ultimately, our efforts—though valiant—provided us with very few examples of organizations that are effectively training necessity entrepreneurs. In this search we have found numerable articles and opinions on microfinance and microcredit organizations, but the amount of information regarding *training* these necessity entrepreneurs has been nearly obsolete. As such, I have found myself circling back to my original question again and again: Are developing nations (such as Mexico) truly filled with "necessity entrepreneurs"?

Believing that the answer to this question was a resounding yes, I did not know what to make of the apparent gap in the market. Whereas we found hundreds of *Wall Street Journal* and academic articles covering the microcredit and microfinance industry, along with Mohammad Yunus' receiving the Nobel Peace Prize for the "silver bullet," there were tens of billions of dollars invested in microfinance and microcredit. Indeed, the premise of micro-lending was promising: give women a loan so that they can start a business and feed their families. Yet, almost none of these institutions focused on training their recipients how to assume their debt responsibly. And, why should they? After all, Yunus had explained that, "[while] not all training is bad . . . we see absolutely no need for formal [business] training" (Yunus, 1999).

I was dumbfounded. No, I was incredulous. Certainly, I thought, there had to be an explanation for what appeared so illogical. The more I researched the more I realized that it was true: there were hundreds of millions of people around the globe borrowing tens of billions of dollars to start and/or grow a small business. Additionally, there were scores of articles supporting or praising the practice of lending money to individuals so that they could start a business, but these lending institutions were *not* instructing or requiring them to learn *how* to start, grow, and/or manage their businesses.

Question Four: How Can (If At All Possible) The Pain Be Solved At Scale? How Can I Solve This Question At Scale?

Answer: To answer this final question, both Dr. Brewer and I decided to prepare ourselves by focusing on the polar opposite sides of the equation. He focused on becoming a master content creator and trainer, and I focused on understanding markets of developing countries at the macro level. Together, we would discuss what we were learning. Together, we continued to search for answers to our four questions—a process that has proven beneficial on many levels and a process that has brought us to this very moment in time.

Through his postdoctoral research conducted in the Ballard Center for Economic Self-Reliance in the Marriott School of Management at Brigham Young University (BYU), Dr. Brewer has scoured the globe to map the institution involved in training microenterprise operators. His research has placed him in front of some of the most senior public officials in many countries and in offices consulting some of the world's most elite businessmen on how to address this pressing issue. His research has also placed him in the homes and businesses of some of the most humble necessity entrepreneurs. Furthermore, his research has allowed him to highlight those organizations focused on training necessity entrepreneurs, which are included in this book.

To date, the number of institutions dedicated to training necessity entrepreneurs at scale remains nominal. In fact, our research would indicate that the demand for training has steadily increased over the past four years while the supply of organizations dedicated to training necessity entrepreneurs has remained stagnant. Thus, we both felt that something had to be done to address this issue.

In 2012, upon seeing the need for a scalable solution to training necessity entrepreneurs, Dr. Brewer and I launched the Microenterprise Education Initiative (MEI) at BYU. We have enlisted the help of hundreds of interns from many of the world's leading universities. We have assembled a team of thought leaders from around the globe and asked them to share their opinions (based on research) about the need for offering necessity entrepreneurs skills in how to start and/or grow their small businesses. And, while our model is not yet perfected, we have made significant advancements to reach a large population of necessity entrepreneurs in 20 countries, using eight different languages, and we firmly believe that we are on the path to offering the industry a scalable solution to equipping necessity entrepreneurs with the hard business skills that they desperately need to compete and win in local and global markets.

CONCLUDING REMARKS

I wish to re-emphasize *why* I have taken the time to articulate the conversations I had with the people I met in Puebla in 2010. First, the experience has had a profound impact on how I view the world. In the midst of a completely foreign environment, I found myself surrounded by incredibly motivated people who sought answers to their businesses problems and found few solutions to address them. Second, I believe that by conveying their feelings and thoughts I am giving them a voice; it is my meager attempt to share with those who read this book just how desperately necessity entrepreneurs *want* to learn how to improve their businesses. In a way, by giving them a voice, I feel that I am able to silence the cultural relativists and amplify the desires of those who are often unheard. Finally, I have taken the time to write the words of these people as a way to remind myself of the *reason* that I have chosen to dedicate my professional career to this industry.

NOTES

1. The Academy for Creating Enterprise is a 501(c)3 formally registered as the "Called2Serve Foundation." Their original focus was to train members of the Church of Jesus Christ of Latter-day Saints how to start and/or grow a small business. In 1999, the sole focus of the Academy was to train men and women who had provided full-time missionary service. They have since expanded their reach to serve the general population of men and women of the LDS Church.
2. See Volume I or Chapter 7 of this book for detailed information re the Academy.
3. Personal conversation with Jeremi Brewer.
4. This was stated by one of the students in the classroom.

REFERENCE

Yunus, M. (1999). *Banker to the Poor*. New York: PublicAffairs.

10. SEBRAE: Serviço Brasileiro de Apoio às Micro e Pequenas Empresas

Jeff Roberts and Nathalia Myrrha

OVERVIEW

Brazil

Today, Brazil is the seventh wealthiest economy in the world, with a GDP of US$2.253 trillion. The country has achieved impressive results on poverty reduction, moving from 21 percent of the population living under the poverty line in 2003, to 11 percent in 2009. Realizing the importance of micro-businesses to its growth and economic development, the country incorporated in its constitution of 1988 differential treatment for small and medium businesses. It took into consideration the size disadvantages and other barriers to entry micro-businesses faced.

In 2003, a constitutional amendment was announced, changing the whole national system. It created a law that would regulate a simplified tax collection system for micro and small companies. As a support and instigator, SEBRAE released a report suggesting the creation of a complementary law ("General Law") that would regulate the differential treatment at a national, state and city level. SEBRAE also promoted several sessions directing the discussion of the topic (Histórico da Lei Geral, n.d.).

In 2006, the "General Law" (Lei Complementar no. 123) was released, establishing reduction of the tax load, simplified tax calculations, reduction in time taken to open a new business, installment of existing debt, simplified work relations and exemption of certain taxes for small and micro companies. By this law, micro-businesses were established as those having an annual gross revenue of less or equal to R$360,000 (~US$153,000) and small businesses were established with annual gross revenue greater than R$360,000 and less than R$3,600,000 (~US$1,530,000) (Santos and Souza, 2005).

However, the law imposed so many restrictions on what was classified as micro-business that its main purpose became corrupted. Article 17 of Section II establishes those limitations, which include any service providers of intellectual, technical, scientific, recreational, artistic or cultural activities, including instructors, brokers and dispatchers. It also excludes alcoholic and soft drinks producers, as well as transportation and allocation of workers services (Diário Oficial, 2009).

Micro-businesses and microentrepreneurs excluded by the law are charged the same taxes as regular businesses, which can reach 68.3 percent, making it nearly impossible to compete against big companies and service providers (Harpaz, 2013). As a consequence many entrepreneurs still choose to remain informal.

Another problem faced by micro-businesses is the high failure rates for new businesses. The failure rate for micro and small companies in Brazil with less than four years of existence was 59.9 percent in 2000 and 35.9 percent in 2005 (Martinho, Trierweiller, and Weise, n.d.). Although challenges exist with staying in business, the statistics show the country has made a lot of progress across the years. SEBRAE attributed this change to two factors: improvement of the economic environment and betterment of companies' quality.

SEBRAE

In 1964, the Brazilian National Bank of Economic Development (BNDE) started two national funding programs aimed at helping small and medium businesses. Realizing the problems caused by bad management and financial defaults the bank saw a need for management assistance and consulting for companies. In 1972, CEBRAE (Brazilian Center of General Management Assistance for Small Companies) was created by the BNDE and the State Special Operations Department (SEBRAE, n.d., *História*).

The institution changed around the years, becoming in 1982 affiliated with political actions. CEBRAE became the facilitator between government and small and medium companies. However, in the period from 1985 to 1990, during the corrupt governments of Fernando Collor and Jose Sarney, CEBRAE went through a period of tribulation, reducing its personnel and demanding change (SEBRAE, n.d., *História*).

In 1990, under a new law, CEBRAE changed to SEBRAE (Brazilian Service of Support to Micro and Small Companies), a not-for-profit organization, with an unlinked administration from the government, but still of public interest. Its mission was "to promote the competitiveness and sustainable development of Micro and Small Business in Brazil" (SEBRAE, n.d., *História*).

Although SEBRAE is not a microfinance institution and does not lend money, it sets the bridge between small businesses and the private sector. It acts as a provider and stimulator of training and sustainability all around Brazil.

SEBRAE has branches in all 26 states and the federal district. Those units follow national guidelines but are able to focus on local demands and prioritize according to regional needs. One can accredit SEBRAE's successes to its comprehensiveness and inclusion (SEBRAE, n.d., *Um Compromisso*).

Goals

In order to fully accomplish its mission and values, in 2013 SEBRAE created a strategic plan for the period from 2013 to 2022. The plan divided strategic goals into five areas of action: (1) mission compliance, (2) vision compliance, (3) interested parties, (4) processes and (5) resources (SEBRAE, 2012) (Table 10.1). By closely measuring the established goals SEBRAE hopes to continue to improve their performance and delivery of their products and services to the micro and small business owners of Brazil.

Success by the Numbers

SEBRAE has been continually expanding its programs and reach since it was founded in 1964. In 2013, SEBRAE reached 4.9 million participants through four key online programs, and nearly 10.8 million participants through four key face-to-face programs as shown below (Costa, N., personal communication, March 13, 2014) (Table 10.2).

Challenges

Although many of SEBRAE's courses are offered for free, there are also several courses that must be paid for. Prices vary according to region, number of hours and subject taught. The 15 hour courses are usually around R$120 (~US$50). The longer duration classes, above 70 hours, can be more than R$1000 (~US$425) (SEBRAE, 2014). For some low-income entrepreneurs trying to establish themselves in the formal economy, it can be hard to invest in training. Therefore, one of the obstacles faced by SEBRAE is how to attend to the lower-class masses, if they have no condition to pay for the services they wish to receive.

Another problem faced by SEBRAE is a common challenge at all levels in Brazil—corruption. A recent case happened in Sao Paulo, in 2013. The director Bruno Caetano dismissed more than one hundred technicians, going against the organizations' regulations, to hire others based on political criteria. According to the accusations they were all somehow related to

Table 10.1   SEBRAE's goals

Goal Category	Goal	Measurement
Mission Compliance	Promote competitiveness and sustainable development of small businesses and support entrepreneurship to strengthen the national economy.	Contribution rate for opening of small businesses, and the assistance to small businesses rate.
Vision Compliance	Reach excellence in developing small businesses, contributing to build a fair, competitive, and sustainable country.	SEBRAE's image among assisted small businesses (excellency/ effectiveness).
Interested Parties	Be a benchmark for promotion of small businesses competitiveness.	SEBRAE's image among assisted small businesses (competitiveness), applicability rates of products and services, and final results rates.
	Contribute with national development through strengthening small businesses.	SEBRAE's image among society.
Process	Reach excellence in service, focusing on the result for the client.	Client's satisfaction rate, number of small companies assisted.
	Create a favorable environment for development of small businesses.	SEBRAE's image among assisted small businesses (favorable environment), number of cities that implemented the "General Law", number of registrations for the premium "SEBRAE Perfect Entrepreneur".
	Promote entrepreneur culture and education.	Number of possible entrepreneurs assisted.
	Provide knowledge about and for small businesses.	Applicability of products and knowledge index.
	Articulate and strengthen strategic partners.	Rate of customers assisted with help from strategic partners, values of resources applied by partners relative to total resources.

Table 10.1   (continued)

Goal Category	Goal	Measurement
	Reach excellence in development of products, services and communication means adequate to client's needs.	Product's portfolio usage rate, percentage of available services offered by portfolio adequate to client's needs.
	Ensure effectiveness and transparency in resource usage and result reports.	Percentage of resources used for assistance, and communication effectiveness index.
Resources	Develop and retain committed, motivated, innovative, and result driven human capital.	Index of organization's environment, total hours of training.
	Expand and strengthen net of suppliers.	Index of suppliers' satisfaction, readiness index.
	Have the best technological and infrastructure solutions for SEBRAE's management and client assistance.	Client's satisfaction index.

the presidential candidate Jose Serra (Helena, 2014). Another example of corruption happened in 2011, in Porto Velho, Rondônia. One of the directors and four other employees of the state's (Rondônia) SEBRAE branch were arrested on charges of evasion of public funds. They used SEBRAE and phantom enterprises to rig public auctions and 20 percent of the R$39 million budgeted was suspect to being associated with those illegal operations (Mataresio, 2013).

ORGANIZATION STRUCTURE

The administration of SEBRAE is divided in three different departments. The first has the same responsibilities as a board of directors and is called the State Deliberative Council (CDE). They serve in non-remunerated positions and are indicated by associates. Their responsibilities include: electing and revoking directors and councils, approving the internal regiment of the organization and establishing norms (SEBRAE, 2009).

Table 10.2   SEBRAE program participation (2013)

	Online Participation	Face-to-face Participation
Consulting	64,096	2,042,604
Classes	867,301	1,042,176
Technical Training	3,974,912	4,748,785
Lectures, Workshops, Seminars	535	2,946,012

The second department is the executive directory, responsible for administrative and technical management. It is composed by professional employees in charge of meeting SEBRAE's goals, following its rules and policies, and establishing priorities for their action. Although they have autonomy to take most of the administrative decisions they are still subject to the State Deliberative Council (SEBRAE, 2009).

The third and last department is the Fiscal Council. This council is in charge of SEBRAE's finances and advises the CDE with accounting obligations (SEBRAE, 2009) (Figure 10.1).

Leadership

SEBRAE is composed of the following divisions and employees (SEBRAE, n.d., *Estrutura*) (Figure 10.1).

Branches

SEBRAE is located in every state including the Federal District in Brazil. One of SEBRAE's logos is "Where there is Brazil there is SEBRAE", reflecting its extensive reach. Besides the headquarters located in Brasilia, SEBRAE has almost 700 units around Brazil, 382 owned by the organization and 312 through partnerships. Each state headquarter has autonomy to set priorities and launch regional programs, always in accordance with national guidelines (SEBRAE, n.d., *Um Compromisso*).

ORGANIZATION SERVICES

SEBRAE provides many different services to its clients. Its main focus is to help small businesses grow and improve. SEBRAE accomplishes its mission through five different areas: education training, business consulting, technical information, promotion and access to markets, and access

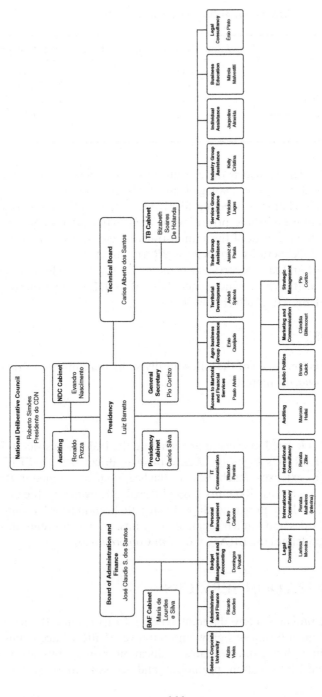

Figure 10.1 SEBRAE structural organization

to financial services (SEBRAE, n.d., *Conheça as Formas*). Besides those areas, SEBRAE launches several projects in furtherance of stimulating knowledge among Brazilians. A great example is the "College Student Entrepreneur Challenge," a national competition that instigates entrepreneur skills among college students (Desafio, n.d.).

Educational Training

One of SEBRAE's main focuses is helping people through training and education. To accomplish this goal, SEBRAE offers classes, lectures and workshops. Many classes are offered for free, but others are charged a subsidized price. Courses and events in the classroom vary from region to region, according to the local demand, while the Internet courses are available for people all over the country. The training is divided into three categories: (1) businesses in the process of being opened, (2) businesses with less than two years of experience, and (3) businesses with more than two years of experience (SEBRAE, n.d., *Matriz*).

For businesses in the process of being opened, classes include:

1. **Learning how to become an entrepreneur**. Focuses on skills and actions, market structure and research, cash flows, and management of small businesses.
2. **Starting a small business with big aspirations**. Teaches market and financial analysis, how to create a business plan, the entrepreneur profile and product and services concept.
3. **Women entrepreneurs**. Tackles strengthening feminine identity, self-esteem and entrepreneurship related to women's potential.
4. **Knowing how to become an entrepreneur**. Focuses on the ability to identify characteristics and behaviors that strengthen a company. Addresses issues such as who is the entrepreneur? Entrepreneur in action, and result orientation.
5. **Together we are strong**. Concentrates on expending economic activities through collective enterprises. Focuses on the importance of cooperation nets, partnerships and collective administration.
6. **Market analysis**. Prepares the entrepreneur to identify commercial viability, learning about competition, producers and consumers, quantitative and qualitative market research, importance of information and field research.
7. **Choosing the right franchise**. Teaches how to choose the franchise that fits the student's profile, interests and needs. It addresses strategic

planning, juridical aspects, relation between risk and return and how to become a successful franchise entrepreneur.

For businesses with less than two years of existence, the classes include:

1. **Rural revival**. Focuses on rural businesses and their everyday routine. Exposes students to situations that involve planning, plantation, growing, buying, selling and payment of expenses.
2. **Customer service**. Addresses professional profile, essential abilities, and the seven sins of customer service, client loyalty and how to professionally deal with complaints.
3. **Selling techniques**. Geared towards developing selling strategies, reflecting about the seller's role in the company and for the clients. Teaches the seller's function and professional attitudes, search of clients, negotiations and post-sale approach.
4. **Negotiation techniques**. Focuses on efficient tools for negotiation, strategies, communication and negotiation ethic.
5. **How to sell more and better**. Divided in two modules, this class is aimed at entrepreneurs and managers of small companies. Concentrates on recognizing business opportunities, market tools and planning a management model.
6. **An eye on quality**. Teaches the 5S methodology on how to organize a workspace, minimizing waste of resources and promoting physical, mental and social well-being of employees.
7. **Establishing associations**. Reviews existing practices in collective companies and stimulates cooperation among small and micro-businesses.
8. **Financial controls**. Teaches about accounting, cash flows, how to determine working capital and how to measure results.
9. **Financial planning and analysis**. Covers how to analyze and understand company's results through financial information. Teaches financial administration, cash flow protection, establishment of financial goals and feasibility of business.
10. **Establishing prices**. Focuses on how to set the correct price of the product, taking into consideration demand, competitors, costs, taxes and profit.
11. **Practical accountancy**. Concentrates on accounting principles and functions, financial statements, accounting results and financial-economic indicators.
12. **Personnel management**. Aimed to teach entrepreneurs and managers, it tackles labor market scenarios, hiring and firing of workers, recruitment and selection procedures, interviewing, performance

evaluation, ethics, positions and wages, work safety and personnel retention.

13. **Developing teams**. Addresses interpersonal relations, communication problems, ethics, motivation, formation and development of teams and emotional knowledge.

14. **Production management and techniques**. Covers planning, production cost control, quality control and performance indicators.

15. **Enterprising determination**. Works with self-steam and performance of the entrepreneur, covering his responsibilities, personal achievements and talents, and individual goals.

16. **Credit unions management**. Focuses on how to effectively run a credit union, teaching about credit unions' evolution, manager role and financial structure.

The third category is for businesses with more than two years of experience, and offers the following courses:

1. **Empretec**. Focuses on developing and stimulating the entrepreneur's personal characteristics. Teaching ten behavioral achiever's trades to promote competitiveness and longevity of the company in the market.

2. **Leadership**. Addresses the role of a leader in transformation of society, life strategies and leader's behaviors.

3. **Citizen leader**. Aimed for potential community leaders, discusses leadership related to citizenship roles, community meetings and development and negotiation of community projects.

4. **Excellency in leadership**. Aims to expand entrepreneurs, community leaders and institution leaders' influence, in order to consolidate a favorable environment for sustainable growth in the country.

5. **Project development for resource capture**. Teaches project development for use of public funds, for the sake of overcoming local problems.

6. **Rural empowerment**. Teaches rural entrepreneurs how to reach efficiency, efficacy of productivity through social organization, financial management, and rural administration and commercialization.

7. **Rural quality**. Focuses on how to apply quality principles to rural production in order to reduce costs, increase productivity and earnings, and improve quality of life.

8. **Quality management—excellency fundamentals**. Diagnoses companies' situations related to Excellency, defines and helps implementing indicators of companies' performance and helps improving management model of companies.

9. **Quality management—efficient partnerships**. Discusses business leadership posture, organization of work environment, social–environmental responsibilities, supply–demand relationships, relationship with the customer and establishment of fidelity.
10. **Quality management—processes**. Focuses on process management models, identification and analysis of processes improvement and standardization.
11. **Quality management—strategic vision**. Highlights the importance of strategic vision and performance measurements and teaches how to analyze basic elements to define and develop a strategic plan.
12. **Quality management—internal auditing**. Teaches about planning methodology and enforcement of internal audits of quality management.
13. **Quality management—ISO 9001 requirements**. Focuses on concepts, principles and fundamentals of quality management in order to meet the requirements of NBR ISO 9001:2000.
14. **Environmental management**. Aimed for footwear-leather micro and small companies, teaches about alternative tools of environmental management, helping to reduce costs and follow legislation.
15. **How to sell more and better (module 3)**. Instructs about market perception and alternatives identification for company's growth. Talks about competitive marketing, development of new products, new technologies, investment and partnerships.
16. **Logistics**. Focuses on logistic chain, logistic costs, administration and stocks, logistic processes, cost–benefit relations and work plan, in order to raise profitability.
17. **Energetic efficiency in micro, small and medium businesses**. Teaches about competitiveness, efficient use of energy, advantages and benefits of energy saving, energy waste, change processes, management and administration of energy, and technological development.
18. **Security management—best practices of food services**. Aimed for owners and managers of small restaurants and bars, focuses on best practices, dangers of contaminated food, personal health and hygiene, installations, waste management, plague control and water supply.

Business Consulting

In addition to entrepreneurial training, SEBRAE provides business-consulting services.

SEBRAE's consulting system intends to reach the necessities of different sizes of businesses from different parts of the country. Although some localities and specific needs are harder to assist, SEBRAE does its best at trying to include all types of demands. SEBRAE Itinerant is a great example of this effort to focus on demand. The Itinerant program's purpose is to go to remote localities that usually do not have access to the institution's services. The local population's needs are identified beforehand in a partnership with local governments and individual assistance is given where the event takes place. In 2007, about 399,720 entrepreneurs were helped through SEBRAE Itinerant, in 900 different localities (SEBRAE, n.d., *Você Sabe*).

One of SEBRAE's most important instruments of face-to-face assistance is "Business to Business." The program was created in 2009 and helped more than one million people in less than two years. The business being helped receives at least three consulting visits from entrepreneurial orientation agents, who analyze management, financial and operational processes, and elaborate a work plan that points to areas that need improvement. The agents can refer the client to courses and other SEBRAE services that would help with the needed changes. The agent is also responsible for a follow-up with the clients, measuring the client's progress and success. This program is free, which makes it very accessible to the interested public (SEBRAE, n.d., *Negócio*).

SEBRAE offers many other consulting services depending on the need of the client. "SEBRAE Plus," for example, focuses on companies with more than two years of existence, who already successfully maneuvered the start-up phase. There are also more specific programs, like "Sebratec," focused on technological solutions, or "Agroecological Integrated and Sustainable Practices," focused on organic agriculture (SEBRAE, n.d., *Consultorias*).

Technical Information

Over the years SEBRAE has compiled a large and accessible amount of information related to micro and small businesses. Those sources can be found at their centers, but a vast amount of the information is made available online on their website. SEBRAE has an online interactive library where anybody can find information on how to open a business, hot markets to be in, norms and legislation for microenterprises, studies and research, and just about anything related to micro and small businesses (SEBRAE, n.d., *Informação*).

SEBRAE also has a partnership with ABIMAQ that gives small and micro-businesses information about machinery producers and mechanical equipment. This partnership's goal is to make it easy for companies to find standardized and quality technology (SEBRAE, n.d., *Informação*).

Promotion and Access to Markets

SEBRAE offers many programs that intend to draw small businesses and markets closer.

It provides a collection of market studies and previsions for the near future that empower companies to make the best decisions relative to the market. The organization also offers online tools and orchestrates events that facilitate the connection between suppliers, companies and clients.

A great example of a tool offered online is the "SEBRAE compass." It presents thematic maps and geo-market analyses and reports, to give companies an idea of the market environment they will be facing (SEBRAE, n.d., *Aumente Seu*).

Another example is a "Marketing Online Plan," which allows companies to create their own market plan, based on examples and with online help from a tutor. These tools are useful not only to connect businesses to the market but also to make them marketable. The program "Micro and Small Company Internationalization," another one of SEBRAE's tools, exists to evaluate and give specific recommendations to small companies on how to participate more actively in the international market. "Brazil Trade" focuses on identifying new opportunities in the national market level, helping businesses to establish partners and promote their products at specific events. All of these tools are available online (SEBRAE, n.d. *Aumente Seu*).

Access to Financial Services

As mentioned previously, SEBRAE does not lend money; nonetheless it helps its clients to find qualified financial institutions that do. In 2012, SEBRAE launched a project called "Fostering Good Practices with Credit Unions." The purpose is to facilitate the connection between client and financial institution, connecting them at a regional level. The project aims to have institutions adopt the directives given in order to reach autonomy to develop products, services and policies adequate to SEBRAE's clients. Right now the project involves 17 states, but the goal is to expand the number of institutions and the volume of credit moved (SEBRAE, 2013).

ORGANIZATION FITNESS

SEBRAE's revenue comes mainly from social contributions, established by law for the organization's support. Other major sources of revenue are investments, partnerships and benefiting companies. In the past five years, SEBRAE's total revenue increased from about US$985 million in 2009 to nearly US$1.7 billion in 2013 (Table 10.3). This change is mostly attributed to an increase in social contributions as well as investments having doubled in size (Vieira, 2014).

With the exception of 2010, the organization has had average surpluses of US$125 million in the past five years. This is an indicator of good financial planning and financial efficiency. SEBRAE's major expenses are divided among employees and benefits, professional services hired, operational expenses and transfers. The organization's personnel expenditures account for roughly 60 percent of all expenses (Vieira, 2014), demonstrating consistency with the 50–70 percent personnel average expenditure for non-profit organizations in the United States.

ORGANIZATION RELATIONSHIPS

SEBRAE establishes partnerships with all types of organizations. It works with the federal, state and city governments, as well as with community representatives. In the private sector SEBRAE works with banks and private companies for long and short-term cooperation. In 2011, for example, SEBRAE and Google started a program called "Connect your business" that has helped more than 60,000 entrepreneurs create their website for free (Empreendedor, 2013). This case is a sample of many others that make evident the value and effectiveness of successful partnerships. SEBRAE also works with other non-profit organizations, helping them to achieve their missions.

Federal Government

In 1990, SEBRAE was granted autonomy, and became a social oriented institution, not politically entailed. However, in the last five years, 78 to 87 percent of their current revenue originated from social contributions. The social contributions are taxes imposed on medium and large companies. Hence, although SEBRAE is a separate institution from the government, it is mainly funded by public money (Bruno, 2001).

Another facet of SEBRAE's relationship with the government is represented by SEBRAE's program Fomenta. The program focuses on evaluating and recommending small businesses as possible suppliers for governmental needs. In 2013, the participation of micro and small businesses in public purchases grew 33 percent compared to 2012, accounting

Table 10.3 *SEBRAE revenues and expenditures FY 2009–2013*

SEBRAE FY 2009–2013 Revenues and Expenditures	2009	2010	2011	2012	2013
Current Revenue					
Social Contribution	$827,003,849	$961,993,568	$1,126,911,442	$1,427,400,000	$1,450,873,500
Financial Applications	$65,930,244	$78,169,769	$114,550,695	$109,855,000	$106,285,500
Partnerships	$40,968,468	$37,038,603	$30,938,968	$25,196,000	$29,355,000
Benefiting Companies	$35,872,355	$40,331,943	$41,983,018	$54,784,000	$60,164,000
Other	$15,548,318	$19,347,785	$127,744,460	$14,825,500	$13,228,500
Total Current Revenue	$985,323,233	$1,136,881,667	$1,442,128,582	$1,632,060,500	$1,659,906,500
Credit Operations	$0	$37,634,936	$723,168	$10,812,000	$31,366,500
Total Capital Revenue	$0	$37,634,936	$723,168	$10,812,000	$31,366,500
Total Revenue	$985,323,233	$1,174,516,603	$1,442,851,750	$1,642,872,500	$1,691,273,000
Current Expenditures	$240,455,266	$275,508,901	$321,237,857	$389,632,500	$450,240,000
Employees and Benefits					
Professional Services	$291,273,395	$361,894,609	$370,127,747	$464,102,000	$553,251,500
Operational Expenses	$187,422,725	$213,769,414	$221,280,418	$266,795,000	$291,940,000
Other	$29,451,155	$33,813,206	$44,782,181	$47,056,500	$63,156,000
Transfers	$83,277,650	$212,569,807	$209,149,922	$283,420,500	$140,875,500
Capital Expenditures					
Investments / Other	$31,085,445	$93,134,626	$80,164,594	$95,020,000	$107,278,500
Total Expenditures	$862,965,633	$1,190,690,562	$1,246,742,717	$1,546,026,500	$1,606,741,500
Total Deficit/Surplus	$122,357,600	–$16,173,959	$196,109,033	$96,846,000	$84,531,500

Note:
* Numbers expressed as USD using exchange rate of $1USD/R$2.

for 30 percent of all goods and services purchased by the government (Ministério do Planejamento, 2013).

SEBRAE also works in partnership with the Ministries of Science, Technology and Innovation; Agricultural Development; Social Development and Hunger Combat; Industry Development and International Trade; Finance; Planning; Tourism; and the Ministry of Sport. The partnership with each government department is connected to a specific project, which helps micro-businesses grow and expand their access to government programs (Costa, N., personal communication, March 13, 2014).

Financial Institutions

"National Bank of Economic Development and Social Development" (BNDES): SEBRAE plays an important role as an information disseminator for BNDES programs. The bank has several projects turned to helping micro and small businesses, and facilitating the borrowing process (Finame/Derem, 2000). One of them, Brasil Empreendedor, in partnership with SEBRAE and the federal government, aims to create three million new jobs through access to credit and educational training. In 2007, BNDES and SEBRAE established a contract to select ten collective projects, making available R$10.5 million (US$4.47 million) to help regional development. The two institutions are always working together in new projects and seminars and helping each other with their individual missions.

Other Banks: SEBRAE establishes agreements and partnerships with the main public and private financial institutions. The goal with these relations is to create technical cooperation, work together in studies and promote products and services that will serve micro and small businesses' interests. SEBRAE is in charge of the training, project planning and technical assistance. The banks' role is to facilitate access to capital, offering simplified and not bureaucratic solutions, and adapting credit lines to different regions. The main banks SEBRAE works with are: Banco do Brasil, Caixa Economica Federal, Banco do Nordeste do Brasil, Banco da Amazonia, Bradesco, HSBC, Santander and Itau (Costa, N., personal communication, March 13, 2014). Partnerships are established nationally and locally, in order to meet client's needs and expectations. In the state of Rio Grande do Sul, SEBRAE and Banco do Brasil established that clients would only get access to credit after they had taken certain classes offered by SEBRAE. This type of agreement is beneficial for both sides, seeing that it expands their number of clients and it increases the probability loans will be paid in time.

Credit Unions: One in every four credit unions (approximately

300 institutions) in Brazil work in partnership with SEBRAE. Because Credit Unions usually offer simpler guarantees and assist not only small and micro companies but also individual entrepreneurs and rural producers, the association is beneficial for both parties. The main Credit Unions that work with SEBRAE are: SICOOB, SICREDI, UNICRED, CECRED, CONFESOL and UNIPRIME (Portal do Cooperativismo, 2012).

ORGANIZATION FUTURE

In 2012, SEBRAE launched a strategic plan for the period 2013–2022. Developing the plan was a process that included reevaluation of previous strategic plans, macroeconomic prevision and analysis for the following years, reexamination of mission, values and organization's positioning, objectives and their indicators and lines of action. For that process SEBRAE relied on clients, managers, employees and technicians that contributed with insights and valuable opinions (see Table 10.1). By following their plan SEBRAE hopes to continue to offer high quality products and services to its clients and help promote micro and small businesses throughout Brazil.

REFERENCES

All websites were accessed in March 2014.

Bruno, G.M. (2001, July 24). Contribuição ao SEBRAE. Retrieved from www. legiscenter.com.br/materias/materias.cfm?ident_materias=25.

Desafio Universitário Empreendedor (n.d.). Retrieved from http://desafiouniversi tarioempreendedor.sebrae.com.br/plataforma/index.xhtml.

Diário Oficial da União. (2009) Lei Complementar no. 123. Retrieved from www. receita.fazenda.gov.br/Legislacao/LeisComplementares/2006/leicp123.html.

Empreendedor (2013, April 10). Parceria Entre SEBRAE e Google traz soluções on line para empresários. Retrieved from http://empreendedor.com.br/artigo/serie-de-videos-parceria- entre-sebrae-e-google-traz-solucoes-line-para-empresarios.

Finame/Derem (2000). Apoio do Sistema BNDES às Micro, Pequenas e Médias Empresas. Retrieved from www.bndes.gov.br/SiteBNDES/export/sites/default/ bndes_pt/Galerias/Arquivos/ conhecimento/especial/pme.pdf.

Harpaz, J. (2013, December 17). Brazil ranked most time-consuming tax regime in the world. *Forbes*. Retrieved from www.forbes.com/sites/joeharpaz/2013/12/17/ brazil-ranked-most- time-consuming-tax-regime-in-the-world/.

Helena (2014, January 2). Aecio Aparelha SEBRAE-MG Com o Cunhado. *Blogspot*. Retrieved from http://osamigosdopresidentelula.blogspot.com/2014/01/aecio-aparelha-sebrae-mg-com-o-cunhado.html.

Histórico da Lei Geral (n.d). Retrieved from www.leigeral.com.br/portal/main.jsp? lumPageId=FF8081812658D379012665B59A B31CE5.

Martinho, L.C., Trierweiller A.C., and Weise, A.D. (n.d.). Satisfação dos Clientes Empresariais da Consultoria SEBRAE—Agência Tubarão. *Convibra Administração*. Retrieved from www.convibra.com.br/upload/paper/adm/adm_1572.pdf.

Mataresio, L. (2013, December 12). Superintendente e Diretor do SEBRAE Estão Envolvidos em Fraudes, Diz MP. Retrieved from http://m.g1.globo.com/ro/ron donia/noticia/2013/12/superintendente-e-diretor-do-sebrae-estao-envolvidos-em-fraudes-diz-mpe.html.

Ministério do Planejamento (2013). Fomenta. Retrieved from www.planejamento. gov.br/conteudo.asp?p=noticia&ler=10979.

Portal do Cooperativismo de Crédito (2012). Dados Consolidades dos Sistemas Cooperativos. Retrieved from http://cooperativismodecredito.coop.br/cenario-brasileiro/dados- consolidados-dos-sistemas-cooperativos/.

Santos, R.C., and Souza, A.A. (2005). Planejamento Tributário: o Impacto dos Programas Governamentais Simples e Simples Geral nas Micro e Pequenas Empresas, 80. *Contabilidade Vista e Revista*. Retrieved from http://web.face.ufmg.br/face/revista/index.php/contabilidadevistaerevista/article/view/27 1/264.

SEBRAE (2009). *Resolução CDN No195/2009*, (5-15). Retrieved from www. sebrae.com.br/customizado/transparencia/Res.%20CDN%20-%20No%20195-2009.%20Estatuto%20Social%20do%20SEBRAE%20-%20Altera%20e.pdf.

SEBRAE (2012). Sistema SEBRAE Direcionamento Estratégico 2013–2022 (17–20). Retrieved from www.sebrae.com.br/customizado/sebrae/institucional/estrategia/html- estrategia/direcionamento-estrategico-2022.pdf.

SEBRAE (2013, November). Conhecer Cooperativa de Crédito. Retrieved from www.sebrae.com.br/customizado/uasf/noticias/revista-conhecer-sebrae-cooperativas-de-credito.pdf.

SEBRAE (2014). Agenda de Cursos SEBRAE/ES. Retrieved from http://vix. sebraees.com.br/cursos/.

SEBRAE (n.d.). Aumente Seu Relacionamento com o Mercado e Venda Mais. Retrieved from www.sebrae.com.br/momento/o-que-o-sebrae-pode-fazer-por-mim/como- atendemos/promocao-e-acesso-a-mercado.

SEBRAE (n.d.). Conheça as Formas de Atendimento SEBRAE. Retrieved from www.sebrae.com.br/momento/o-que-o-sebrae-pode-fazer-por-mim.

SEBRAE (n.d.). Consultorias e Diagnósticos Ajudam Empreendedores. Retrieved from www.sebrae.com.br/momento/o-que-o-sebrae-pode-fazer-por-mim/como-atendemos/consultoria.

SEBRAE (n.d.). Estrutura Organizacional. Retrieved from www.sebrae.com.br/customizado/transparencia/Organograma.pdf.

SEBRAE (n.d.). História do SEBRAE. Retrieved from www.sebrae.com.br/customizado/sebrae/institucional/quem-somos/historico.

SEBRAE (n.d.). Informação Para a Gestão de Seu Negocio. Retrieved from www. sebrae.com.br/momento/o-que-o-sebrae-pode-fazer-por-mim/como-atendemos/informacao-tecnica.

SEBRAE (n.d.). Matriz Educacional. Retrieved from www.sebrae.com.br/customizado/sebrae/institucional/como-trabalhamos/produtos-e-servicos/folder_matriz_educacional.pdf.

SEBRAE (n.d.). Negócio a Negócio. Retrieved from www.sebrae.com.br/momento/quero- melhorar-minha-empresa/acesse/negocio-a-negocio/.

SEBRAE (n.d.). Um Compromisso do Tamanho do Brasil. Retrieved from www. sebrae.com.br/atendimento.

SEBRAE (n.d.). Você Sabe o Que é o **SEBRAE** Intinerante? Retrieved from www. sebrae.com.br/atender/momento/quero-melhorar-minha-empresa/utilize-as- ferr amentas/atendimento-ao-cliente/bia-1388-1/BIA_1388.

Vieira, L.A.C. (2014, March 13). Previsão do PPA (Pessoas e Empreendimentos) e Orçamentária (Instrumento) do SGE. *SIACWEB*.

11. Self-reliance through self-employment: an approach by The Church of Jesus Christ of Latter-day Saints

Geoffrey K. Davis and Andrew Maxfield

INTRODUCTION

This chapter sheds light on two main factors driving the founding process of the new Self-Reliance through Self-Employment: An Approach by the Church of Jesus Christ of Latter-day Saints.

Since its founding in the Northeastern United States in 1830, The Church of Jesus Christ of Latter-day Saints has espoused the Christian doctrine of seeking after and ministering to the poor as a central institutional priority. This has led to the creation of various systems and initiatives to assist its own as well as the world's poor generally.

However, the Church's growth in recent decades—resulting in a diverse global membership of over 15 million—has necessitated new approaches suited to a new reality: the need to help millions rather than thousands in a cost-effective, scalable and results-oriented framework.

In the following pages we outline blueprints of the Church's current and most comprehensive poverty-alleviation effort. These are evolving even as we write, and they will continue to evolve as they are implemented around the world over the coming years. Our aim is to provide an overview of current plans; this may be followed later with an update based on results.

SELF-RELIANCE: A BRIEF HISTORY

Among its members, the Church has always taught the ideal of building local communities that are "of one heart and one mind" with "no poor among them" (*Pearl of Great Price*, n.d., Moses 7:18). The path to this communal outcome, paradoxically, is self-reliance: a defining characteristic of individuals who demonstrate the "ability, commitment, and effort to provide the spiritual and temporal necessities of life for self and family" (The Church of Jesus Christ of Latter-day Saints, n.d., Welfare Principles).

Beginning in the mid-nineteenth century, the Church's efforts have focused on helping members to become self-reliant while simultaneously encouraging them to serve and help one another. However, self-reliance-focused programs have changed over time.

Sharpened by the Great Depression of the 1930s, Church welfare programs, such as networks of food storehouses and Church-owned farms, grew to meet the short-term relief needs of Church members—the majority of whom, at the time, lived in the United States. The Church successfully coordinated the donation of relief supplies and foodstuffs to European members post-World War II, but this far-reaching aid was an exception for a system that functioned best at home.

Church growth through the middle of the twentieth century, still primarily in North America, catalyzed new evolutions in welfare programs. To serve a larger number of Church members with a greater variety of needs, the Church complemented its short-term relief programs with new initiatives meant to help individuals with longer-term self-reliance needs: job training programs, social services and employment services.

Although the Church's new programs and initiatives enabled it to serve record numbers of people, the systems depended on assumptions that would be challenged by the Church's international growth through the 1980s, 1990s and early 2000s. This was growth of a different kind: faster, international growth where Church infrastructure was less developed and, frequently, among the world's poor. By 1997, the majority of members lived outside the United States. Spanish became the new dominant language of the Church, but it would be just one of 170 languages spoken by Church members. By 2014, of the Church's 15 million members, 3.7 million live in South America, 1.3 million in Mexico, and nearly 700,000 in the Philippines. In addition, nearly another million members live in the developing nations of Africa, Asia and Oceania (The Church of Jesus Christ of Latter-day Saints, n.d., Facts and Statistics).

In the last 20 years, the Church sought to meet new demands on its welfare programs and anticipate future needs, launching international aid storehouses and employment workshops; an array of global humanitarian initiatives and partnerships; and in 2001, its flagship Perpetual Education Fund (PEF), a self-replenishing educational loan program for needy Church members aged 18–30 outside of the US. The significant improvements achieved by each of these advances—such as the PEF's success in helping 60,000 individuals in 57 countries to obtain education and vocational training—revealed the potential impact of the Church's efforts. At the same time, these successes, coupled with the growing breadth and diversity of needs indicated a need for fundamental, rather than incremental, innovations.

Further, recent advances in microenterprise development throughout the world—especially in economies with rampant unemployment and burgeoning Church membership—pointed to self-employment, or necessity entrepreneurship, as a viable, if not essential, path to self-reliance for many Church members and a previously missing component of the Church's global relief strategy.

DESIGN PRINCIPLES AND CONSTRAINTS

These waves of growth, stress, experimentation and innovation gradually exposed the following design constraints and principles, which provided the rationale and foundation for developing the new, multifaceted approach to ministering to the poor and needy globally: PEF Self-Reliance Services. In designing the new approach, we needed an architecture that would allow us to:

- Help at least 1.5 million Church members become economically self-reliant within three to five years.
- Address a variety of needs among a wide gamut of poor Church members.
- Address pervasive cultural barriers to becoming self-reliant.
- Balance the needs of providing the poor with short-term relief while also building their long-term self-reliance capacity.
- Be built on a streamlined, scalable, flexible, cost-effective administrative platform that functions in geographies where the Church has limited infrastructure, using volunteers and minimal paid staff, and adapting local activities to local resources.
- Shift from activity measures (for example, counting the number of educational loans issued) to outcomes (for example, the number of individuals and families that permanently exit a condition of poverty and become self-reliant because of the program).
- Leverage best practices and advances in fields such as microenterprise development and microfinance—adapted to the context of the Church's resources, structure and delivery channels.

Although PEF Self-Reliance Services, as it launched in mid-2014, comprised three major categories of effort—Employment, Education and Self-Employment—this chapter focuses only on the third and newest: Self-Employment.[1]

A guiding principle of these self-reliance initiatives is the Church's teaching that the spiritual and the temporal are two sides of the same coin. Because of this, the program is infused with religious principles and teachings, and scriptures are often used to illustrate key concepts. However, due to the nature of this publication, we focus this chapter on the programmatic aspects of the strategy instead of the religious aspects.[2]

SELF-EMPLOYMENT SYSTEM OVERVIEW

> A self-reliance group meeting uses a council model and is different from most Church classes, lessons, or workshops. There are no teachers or trainers. Instead, a group facilitator, called by local leaders, assists members as they counsel together, learn together, mentor each other, commit to act on what they are learning, and hold each other accountable for commitments. This group mentoring and counseling process, together with the workbooks and videos, creates a dynamic learning environment that strengthens each member in their development of a self-reliant life. (Self-Reliance Leader Guide, 2014, p. 2)

We began the design process by assembling a team comprised of Church division leadership and a cadre of consultants and advisors.[3] We initiated collaborations with a variety of NGOs and other organizations and started a wide review of best practices in microenterprise training. We also conducted a study of best practices in mentoring models, from individual one-to-one mentoring to group based, from paid mentors to volunteers to remote mentors. We then began a cycle of generating hypotheses, testing them in pilots, and iterating based on results. We went through three broad iteration cycles with multiple mini-cycles. This led to a new microenterprise development system, which emphasizes process over content and action over pure knowledge. The group-based system focuses simultaneously on helping necessity entrepreneurs to (1) build successful businesses and (2) turn specific actions which drive increasing business profitability into habits that lead to durable family prosperity—that is, self-reliance.

Prior to designing the Church's self-reliance program, several members of our design team collaborated on an extended program design process with an NGO called Cause for Hope at a location in Oaxaca, Mexico. We were studying poverty through a behavioral lens and wanted to discover which behaviors, if enacted routinely, might lead a program participant out of poverty. Based on our first-hand observations and a review of a variety of other poverty alleviation programs, we identified a small handful of "vital" behaviors which distinguished individuals who made steady progress out of poverty from those who remained stuck.

These essential behaviors were attending self-reliance group meetings (see descriptions below); saving money every week, even in "token" increments; keeping up-to-date, separate records for personal and business finances; and making and keeping weekly commitments related to improving business profitability. Participants in our pilot who regularly did these behaviors saw steady increases in income and assets (including savings), making a steady trajectory toward and past the threshold of self-reliance (see subsection "Assessment, Measurement, and Choosing 'My Path'"), while those who didn't engage in these behaviors did not progress similarly.

From an influence[4] perspective then, our task was to create a system that would motivate and enable participants to do these disproportionately important behaviors regularly, and ultimately, habitually.

The following subsections describe the Self-Employment system from a design vantage point, and for illustrative purposes, the progress of Emil and Maria, hypothetical participants,[5] as they make their journeys from poverty, through the Self-Employment program, to self-reliance.

Recruiting and Intake

Throughout the world, lay leaders of local Church congregations (called "wards" or "branches") review the spiritual and temporal needs of their members in monthly welfare meetings. Members with exceptional needs receive special attention. Local leaders may allocate relief funds to help members with short-term needs and refer members to Church self-reliance programs for long-term capacity building. Members may also choose to self-enroll in self-reliance programs. (Assistance is also available to interested nonmembers.)

At the level of the stake (diocese) or region, the Church hosts "fireside" presentations to advertise self-reliance programs and encourage enrollment. In areas where the Church has sufficient infrastructure, the intake process, including one-on-one consultations and program administration, may take place in designated "Self-Reliance Centers" staffed by paid staff, local volunteers or missionaries. In 2014, there were nearly one thousand such centers worldwide.

Emil, a mechanic and handyman, has been out of work for seven months, and his family is suffering. Knowing of Emil's plight, Emil's bishop (pastor) sends him to learn about Self-Reliance programs at a monthly fireside meeting, as well as providing Emil short-term aid.

Maria is a single mother. She desperately wants to increase her income. She hears about the Self-Reliance programs from a friend and decides to learn more by enquiring at the Self-Reliance Center.

Table 11.1   Excerpted self-reliance capacity assessment questions

My Self-Reliance (You and Your Immediate Family)
Mark "X" to Show Where You Are Now. Be Honest.

We provide our family three meals a day.	Never	Sometimes	Often	Always
We provide clean water to drink and wash.	Never	Sometimes	Often	Always
We are protected and safe in our home.	Never	Sometimes	Often	Always
We spend less than we earn. We save money.	Never	Sometimes	Often	Always
We can get medical care when we need it.	Never	Sometimes	Often	Always
We have clean, modest clothes.	Never	Sometimes	Often	Always
We have enough to give our children an education.	Never	Sometimes	Often	Always
We have fuel, transportation, and sanitary facilities.	Never	Sometimes	Often	Always
We are free of consumer debt.	Never	Sometimes	Often	Always
We sacrifice to serve others.	Never	Sometimes	Often	Always

Assessment, Measurement and Choosing "My Path"

Having arrived at an informational fireside or consultation, participants are invited to complete an assessment (with assistance as necessary). The assessment helps members identify (1) gaps between their current and desired levels of self-reliance (Tables 11.1 and 11.2), (2) opportunities and strengths that may form platforms upon which to build self-reliant lives and inform decision-making, and (3) which of the three Self-Reliance paths to pursue. In addition to completing pre and post-program assessments, participants repeat these "gap" assessments at weeks six and twelve to monitor their own process, as well as tracking their income at weekly and monthly intervals.

These intake assessments provide one basis for measuring members' progress through the self-reliance system, though the Church also monitors a variety of indirect measures to determine whether members are progressing and at what rate.

At the fireside, Emil sits with a number of other interested people. After hearing about the idea of Self-Reliance and the options available to him, Emil opens a booklet called "My Path to Self-Reliance." With assistance as needed, Emil works his way through five short sections:

Table 11.2   Income gap assessment tool

TOTAL INCOME NOW *What do you spend and earn now—* *each month?*	TOTAL INCOME GOAL *What would you need to spend and* *earn to answer "Always" to each of the* *questions above—each month?*
Expenses	**Expenses**
Tithing, offerings	Tithing, offerings
Savings	Savings
Rent	Rent
Food	Food
Transportation	Transportation
Water	Water
Electricity, Heat	Electricity, Heat
Phone	Phone
Medical, Doctors	Medical, Doctors
School Costs	School Costs
Clothing	Clothing
Debt Payments	Debt Payments
Other	Other
TOTAL EXPENSES	**TOTAL EXPENSES**
Income	**Income**
Wages	Wages
Other Income	Other Income
TOTAL INCOME	**TOTAL INCOME**

Note: Total Income GOAL – Total Income NOW = Income GAP.

- How self-reliant am I? (An income-gap and personal capacity assessment)
- What skills do I have?
- What work could give me the income I need?
- What is my path to self-reliance?
- What self-reliance group should I join?

Emil already knows his family is suffering, but he begins to see in greater detail the gap in his family's present income and capacity and the self-reliance threshold. This clarifies his understanding and orients his thinking. He concludes, at least tentatively, that his strengths and opportunities point toward the possibility of opening a motorcycle repair business. He joins a "Starting and Growing My Business" group, which meets weekly in his town, and commits to participating in a 12-week cycle of learning and taking action.

Maria meets with a Self-Reliance specialist to review her options. She too completes the intake assessment. Although she is mostly self-reliant by definition of the assessment tools, she sees opportunity for improvement and growth, given her strengths. At least tentatively, she concludes that she would simply like to position herself to get a better job, so she joins the "Accelerated Job Search" group, which meets weekly in her town.

Group Process: A Scalable Vehicle for Training, Mentoring and Accountability

Now that participants have chosen a path, they begin meeting with their self-reliance groups—cohorts of peers hoping to make similar progress down a common path. This peer-group process—derived from such models as Alcoholics Anonymous; other 12-step, group-based addiction recovery programs; Delancey Street Foundation; the Saddleback Church "Small Group" community model; and others—provides the social backbone and organizing rhythm for the entire self-reliance system. It emphasizes action: translating new ideas (that is, training content) into lasting skills and habits that "overdetermine" a participant's chances of escaping poverty permanently. The process is also designed to take advantage of the mentoring power we discovered in our study mentioned earlier. The group process is architected to help the group members provide each other (1) support and encouragement, (2) accountability for commitments made and (3) problem-solving support.

Participants enter with the expectation of participating for about 12 weeks and also with the understanding that they may repeat the process as many times as they wish in order to accomplish their growth goals. Further, participants are notified that when they have progressed through the system, they may have the opportunity to serve as facilitators of future groups.

Self-reliance groups follow a standard format during each weekly meeting. Although each two-hour meeting allows an hour for learning new content, which is packaged in the "Starting and Growing My Business" curriculum, the process focuses largely on leveraging the group-mentoring dynamic to promote group problem-solving, mutual encouragement and accountability for taking action. The group-based mentoring design, which we imported from our experiments in Mexico, is further enhanced by the Action Partner system, in which each participant is paired with an individual "action partner" from the group for mid-week accountability, coaching and encouragement.

While the program is designed to be trainer independent, in most cases a "facilitator" will be pulled from the ranks of the local congregation to help the group process thrive. These facilitators—usually lightly trained and always volunteers—may often include "graduates" of past self-reliance groups, which increases their credibility and empathy with group members.

Facilitators prepare for the meeting by contacting group members, preparing the meeting place and reviewing the meeting content and format.

Table 11.3 details the meeting process and Table 11.4 shows the list of topics for the Self-Employment self-reliance group process.

Participants depart from a group meeting with new knowledge, bolstered morale, group support, a plan to improve, and a written and verbal commitment to take action on that plan prior to the next group meeting. During the intervening week, assigned action partners check in with each other to provide help and encouragement and to make sure each person is following through with his or her commitments. Then the process repeats.

After 12 weeks, all participants receive Certificates of Completion, and qualifying participants receive Certificates in Small Business Entrepreneurship from LDS Business College.[6] Although the certificates mark an end to one group process cycle, participants are encouraged to continue participating in the cycle of making and keeping commitments and providing peer support for as long as their goals require.

This bias toward action stems from a training philosophy that emphasizes learning by doing. Instead of building a business *plan*, participants literally build businesses, repeatedly forming and testing hypotheses. Instead of focusing on the classroom, this model annexes the world of implementation. In fact, this training model presupposes that participants learn new business skills primarily in service of the greater purpose of increasing their self-efficacy, or their belief—as reinforced through many successful actions—in their ability to accomplish goals and steadily improve their condition through their own volition.

The training model also accommodates varying degrees of literacy among group members, anticipating that a participant with a fourth-grade reading competency can navigate all written materials. However, because the curriculum revolves around video and illustrated examples and group discussion, participants with limited literacy skills can still benefit from the curriculum, though they may choose to ask a family member or friend for help.

As the fundamental, cellular unit of the self-reliance system, these peer-mentoring groups are organized locally, based on local demand. Because groups rely either on volunteer facilitators from local congregations or on self-facilitation by group members, they scale easily and without major incremental resource commitments. Further, groups can divide (as membership grows), recombine, and morph to meet the needs of their members.

Emil attends his first few "Starting and Growing My Business" group meetings with ten other participants from his town. By the second week he has interviewed ten business owners and customers and chosen to start his motorcycle

Table 11.3   Weekly peer-mentoring group meeting format

20 Minutes: My Foundations	Participants begin with a lesson from a booklet entitled "My Foundation: Principles, Skills, Habits." Each lesson consists of a one-page discussion guide with a related video. These lessons address overcoming underlying cultural barriers to self-reliance. Topics include time and money management, problem-solving and communication, among others.
20 Minutes: Report	Participants report individually on their success in keeping the commitments that they made the previous week. Commitments relate to each week's content and focus on improving the profitability of the participants' businesses. Group members help each other identify and overcome barriers that keep them from keeping commitments.
60 Minutes: Learn	In truth, most of the participants' learning happens *outside* of the formal group meeting. Because this Learn segment is just an hour long, we focus on teaching just enough to then send participants out on a path of weekly action, where the real hands-on, experiential learning takes place.
	Nevertheless, the Learn section does introduce participants to new content. Following the prompts in the integrated curriculum materials (Read, Watch, Discuss, Practice), participants learn new ideas and skills related to starting and growing a profitable business. The topics range from choosing a product or service to sell, determining pricing structures, separating personal and business finances, marketing, sales tactics and more.
	Throughout the process, they discuss one another's business needs and concerns, and provide constant peer mentoring. They generate ideas, diagnose and solve problems and provide coaching and cheerleading. They engage in role-playing activities to practice new skills.
10 Minutes: Ponder	During a short period of reflective practice, participants consider what they've learned in the context of their needs and goals. They also consider their experiences from the past week and the ideas and impressions they've had. Not only do they jot down notes to formalize what they learn, but they also prepare a personalized Weekly Business Goal based on their conclusions.
10 Minutes: Commit	Finally, participants make commitments—or promises to act—for the upcoming week. The commitments include the personalized Weekly Business Goal in addition to assigned commitments that stem from the content of the Learn section, such as conducting market research or making and testing a marketing plan. Participants formalize—or ritualize—their commitment to action by committing to the group, generally, and to an action partner, specifically.

Table 11.4   Starting and growing my business topics

Starting	How do I start or improve my business?
	What do people want to buy?
	How do I buy my product and set the sales price?
	How do I know if my business is making a profit?
	How do I separate my business and family money?
	How is my business progressing?
Growing	How will I grow my business?
	Can I afford to invest to grow my business?
	How do I know if I should use a loan to grow my business?
	How will I attract customers and close sales?
	How will I increase my profits?
	How do I continue to improve my business?

repair business. His cohort members decide on other businesses to start or improve. Emil helps a group member repair a delivery truck, and that member helps Emil advertise. Emil begins to keep separate records for his new business and his family finances. He identifies ways to be more disciplined with his resources and ways to increase his business revenue.

With the help of his group members, Emil enters into a contract with a company to do regular maintenance on a fleet of motorcycles, which further improves his business revenue. Each week, Emil's action partner calls him to ask about his commitments and to provide encouragement and accountability. Emil responds in kind. Some weeks he hits unexpected obstacles or discovers that his commitments need modifying. But, with the help of his group, he keeps pushing forward.

After three weeks in the "Accelerated Job Search" track, Maria begins to wonder if self-employment might be the path for her instead. She obtains permission to join the "Starting and Growing My Business" group off-cycle and works with group members to catch up. Because of her existing skill set and work experience, she had already been hatching a business idea: a specialty fabric store. She shares it with her group members, and they provide feedback about her proposed location and pricing structure, which challenges her thinking.

Instead of investing in the business immediately, she decides to test her idea more thoroughly. After a few weeks of making and keeping commitments, she starts her business and develops a plan to acquire productive business assets, which requires that she pay herself a lower wage than she would have liked. Over time, however, her business grows to the point that she hires two employees and can afford to increase her own wages. As she continues to develop her business model, Maria begins to sell custom children's apparel. After six months in the group process as a participant, Maria volunteers to be a facilitator for newly forming groups in her town.

Table 11.5   The Four Rights

Right Reason
  Am I borrowing for a productive (not personal) business reason?
  Is a loan better than cash to grow my business?
  Will the things I buy with the loan make me money immediately?
  Do I know everything that could go wrong?

Right Time
  Have I been in business long enough to know my business well?
  Is this part of a plan that I have to grow my business?
  Can I demonstrate customers will buy everything I want to sell?
  If I buy something for my business, will it last longer than my loan?

Right Terms
  Can I list 3–5 good lenders?
  Do I know the true cost of the loan?
  Can I explain all of the terms of the loan?
  Can I explain why one lender is better than another?

Right Amount
  Have I made a six-month cash flow projection?
  Can I make a payment and still make money?
  If I don't have extra sales, can I still make the payment?

Financing

The Church recognizes that mentoring and training are necessary but insufficient when a necessity entrepreneur simply lacks access to capital. However, because of the wide variety of qualified lenders in the market, the Church doesn't provide financing itself. Instead, it focuses on helping participants identify the proper uses for borrowed capital and introduces them to vetted lenders as appropriate.

First, before participants consider borrowing money, they study the true costs of using borrowed funds, the stark differences between consumer debt and productive business debt, and the Four Rights for borrowing: the Right Reason, the Right Time, the Right Terms, and the Right Amount (see Table 11.5). Armed with this knowledge, participants are then encouraged to visit a variety of lenders and, as a group, discuss, analyze, and compare competitive offers. Finally, if appropriate, participants may make the individual decision to obtain debt financing for promising business projects.

Next, to help participants locate qualified lenders, the Church has developed a lender evaluation system, already in use in Self-Reliance pilot areas.

First, from PEF Self-Reliance Services headquarters in the US, a team of 30 multilingual interns evaluate lenders via phone interviews and standardized questionnaires based on a modification of the global standard SMART Campaign from Accion International. Second, on-the-ground staff, volunteers or missionaries visit the same lenders and ask an additional set of questions. The combined responses factor into a lender rating database, to which participants and administrators refer.

Emil's engine repair business has grown steadily since he began the self-reliance group process two months ago. Like many people in his position, he has been intrigued by loan offers. He has dreamed up a number of uses for borrowed money—a new truck, a new refrigerator, new marketing materials. However, the group process forces him to tame his enthusiasm as he learns about planning for debt by using the Four Rights and making a multi-month cash flow projection that includes the debt repayment expense.

With some sobering feedback from his group members, Emil begins to see that he hasn't been thinking of using debt for the right reasons. Especially after visiting lenders and comparing their offers with his group, he concludes that he should avoid debt for the time being and focus, instead, on self-funding his business growth.

Maria's fabric store and custom children's apparel business has been a hit: she sells out of her inventory by midday every day. However, her business has stopped growing—and she thinks she knows why. She and her employees all use the same few sewing machines to produce the custom clothes they sell. She discusses the problem with her group, and they suggest that her business needs more machines. She begins to realize that with additional machines, she would immediately be able to increase sales, to a point that her business could comfortably afford the loan payment necessary to obtain the machines.

With her group members, Maria obtains and analyzes competitive offers from various lenders. Finally, she decides to borrow funds—and comes well-prepared to the lender of her choice.

FROM PILOT PROJECTS TO GLOBAL ROLLOUT

The LDS Church initiated the design phases of the new PEF Self-Reliance Services programs in early 2013 by convening working groups of industry professionals, academics and consultants, drawing heavily on the peer-group models developed by Cause for Hope and Influencer Institute in Oaxaca, Mexico, in 2012–2013. Following several months of design, we began testing and iterating various aspects of the program—recruiting, intake, assessment, group formation, facilitation, group process, foundational skills training, path-specific training, and so on—at sites in Ghana and Guatemala.

Simultaneously, we have been creating a measurement and evaluation system. In 140 product development sites throughout the world, our self-reliance group facilitators will receive additional training as program evaluators. They will provide qualitative and quantitative feedback about process, content and behavioral and financial outcomes. Facilitators and staff will track participants' commitments (both for understanding compliance and lessons related to growing businesses in local settings), income and savings growth, and progress against intake assessment measures. Further, we are implementing focus groups with facilitators, participants, local church leaders and PEF Self-Reliance Services staff, volunteers and missionaries to study the integration and optimization of the new programs in the context of existing Church programs. In-field global product and program development coordinators will interface with program staff at US headquarters.

To date, results from the field have come primarily in the form of program development feedback. As our program rollout continues and our pool of data grows, we will correlate our program inputs and activities to self-reliance outcomes and adjust our program design and delivery accordingly. Our preliminary observations—based on focus groups and surveying at sites in Ghana, Guatemala and the Dominican Republic— have included the following:

- 75 percent of pilot participants reported being able to demonstrate improvements to their income during the 12-week self-reliance process if asked to show their daily financial records. These improvements ranged from modest gains, to growth by 200 to 400 percent.
- 75 percent of pilot participants reported saving money each week, having never done so previously.
- 100 percent of participants who remained engaged through the 12-week cycle reported having improved their businesses by developing new skills and habits, such as record keeping, marketing, and so on.
- 90 percent of pilot participants kept weekly self-directed business improvement commitments and 70 percent kept assigned commitments.
- 50 percent of pilot participants contacted their action partners during the week to motivate and help each other to take action.
- 80 percent of pilot participants taught the My Foundations principles (designed to address cultural barriers to escaping poverty) to their family members on a weekly basis.

Because our pilot project outcomes already complement other Church welfare programs, and because of the ever-increasing demand for self-reliance services, we intend to roll out the program globally in phases over the next several years, knowing that we will release new versions of the program at regular intervals based on results from implementation.

We aim to help at least 375,000 church members become self-reliant by 2018. We estimate that 60 to 70 percent of these members will fall into the necessity entrepreneur category, implying that about 250,000 new self-employment jobs will need to be created. PEF Self-Reliance Services has already helped members create about 8,000 new self-employment jobs in 2013. We expect this number to increase dramatically as the initiative rolls out worldwide.

Additionally, PEF Self-Reliance has overhauled its flagship educational loan program. Loans are now available to members through age 60, borrowers are now paired with mentors to guide them through the process to ensure the education leads to employment, and they can qualify for a graduated loan forgiveness program based on repayment and performance incentives.

ANOTHER STEP FORWARD

These recent innovations at PEF Self-Reliance Services build on a 184-year history of The Church of Jesus Christ of Latter-day Saints striving to effectively follow the example of Jesus in seeking after and caring for the poor and needy. Early indications from the pilots indicate that we may be on to something profound, but we still have far to go—and the stress-testing of broad implementation will reveal the weaknesses and flaws in the model.

Among other things, we already know that our "Starting and Growing My Business" curriculum is basic, by necessity of our target audience. At some point, we will need to either partner with providers of more advanced training or develop our own. We also know that many of the most needy are in remote areas where regular in-person group meetings are not practical. We will continue to adapt and evolve the approach as we learn more and as the context changes.

However, provided that our assumptions about the scalability and power of peer-mentoring groups hold, we will be able to serve and lift record numbers of individuals and families in developing areas. And if our hypotheses about influencing human behavior hold, we'll witness hundreds of thousands, perhaps millions, of God's children making steady strides out of poverty through these efforts. We appreciate your interest in our efforts, systems, curricula and ideas as we pursue that mission.[7]

NOTES

1. For information regarding PEF Self-Reliance Services Employment or Education programs, see srs.lds.org.
2. In our pilot programs, the most successful participants, in terms of temporal gains, were also those who also espoused the spiritual belief that God wants them to become self-reliant and would help them get there. For more information about our views regarding the connection between the motivating force of personal beliefs and behavior change, as well as the connection between faith and action, please contact the authors.
3. PEF Self-Reliance Services is chaired by Robert C. Gay, a senior Church leader, former CEO of Huntsman Gay Global Capital, former managing director of Bain Capital, and co-founder of Unitus, a global microcredit company. The vice chair is Mike Murray, former chairman of Unitus. The program director is Geoff Davis, former CEO of Unitus. Rex Allen, PhD, an expert in instructional design and training, played a lead role in the design process. Consultants and designers included representatives from Interweave Solutions, VitalSmarts, Influencer Institute, The Academy for Creating Enterprise, Brigham Young University's Ballard Center for Economic Self-Reliance, BYU Idaho Pathway, LDS Business College, as well as many others.
4. We followed the "Influencer Model" as set forth in *Influencer: The New Science of Leading Change* (McGraw-Hill, 2nd edition, 2013). The model posits that influencing behavior begins by identifying a bundle of "vital behaviors" which, at "crucial moments," lead individuals invariably toward the results they seek. These behaviors are often discovered by examining positive deviant populations. Then, the influencer's task is to motivate and enable individuals to do the vital behaviors through a robust, multifaceted influence strategy, including personal, social, and structural components.
5. While fictional, these accounts represent a composite of experiences we've observed among participants in our pilot programs.
6. LDS Business College is a Church-owned, two-year college in Salt Lake City, Utah focused on training students in business and industry.
7. To receive complimentary electronic copies of our Self-Reliance materials, please contact the authors.

REFERENCES

The Church of Jesus Christ of Latter-day Saints. (LDS) (n.d.). Facts and Statistics. Retrieved on February 19, 2016 from www.mormonnewsroom.org/facts-and-statistics.

The Church of Jesus Christ of Latter-day Saints. (LDS) (n.d.). Welfare Principles and Leadership. Handbook 2: Administering the Church. Retrieved on February 19, 2016 from www.lds.org/handbook/handbook-2-administering-the-church/welfare-principles-and-leadership.

The Pearl of Great Price: A Selection from the Revelations, Translations, and Narrations of Joseph Smith First Prophet, Seer, and Revelator to The Church of Jesus Christ of Latter-day Saints. (n.d.). Retrieved on February 19, 2016 from www.lds.org/scriptures/pgp?lang=eng.

Self-Reliance Leader Guide. (2014). Salt Lake City, UT: The Church of Jesus Christ of Latter-day Saints.

12. Microfranchising: a solution to necessity entrepreneurship

Philip Webb and Jason Fairbourne

INTRODUCTION

A rising percentage of people around the world operate in the informal sector. In sub-Saharan Africa, for example, the number reached nearly 80 percent in 2002. By 2009, estimates exceeded 90 percent. Nine out of ten workers operate microenterprises within a growing *informal* economy (ILO, 2002).[1] Unfortunately, this increase in activity does not equate to an increase in income levels.

Microfinance served as a Nobel prize-worthy vehicle to capitalize the businesses of would-be entrepreneurs. However, microfinance has little regard for how the capital should be utilized. Microfranchising, on the other hand, picks up where microfinance falls short. Since the majority of these workers or forced entrepreneurs in developing nations assume this role—the role of entrepreneur—out of necessity, they have a glaring need for a clear-cut, turnkey business system to implement.

In recent years, microfranchising has emerged as a compelling solution to the entrepreneurial burden. It is an innovative, market-based approach for development practitioners, NGOs, aid administrators, microfinance institutions and especially necessity entrepreneurs to consider. At its core, microfranchising is a development tool that leverages the basic concepts of traditional franchising, but it is principally focused on creating opportunities for the world's poor to own and manage their own businesses, and to restore their self-reliance and human dignity.

Microfranchising serves as a better alternative than the traditional micro-lending or other microenterprise building efforts. The necessity entrepreneurs at the bottom of the pyramid have limited education, limited experience and limited ideas for new products or service. Yet well-meaning programs assume that "necessity is the mother of invention," and participants in remote villages are able to create, launch and grow successful new enterprises. The fallacy of the entrepreneur directs their assumptions. Their programs are built on the false hope that the world's poor wish to be entrepreneurs, but are only held back by lack of capital. In reality, necessity is not the mother of invention and capital does not an entrepreneur make.

In this chapter we pinpoint the entrepreneurial burden by first, identifying the fallacy of the entrepreneur and second, by exploring the nature of the necessity entrepreneur. To address this dilemma that necessity entrepreneurs face, we review the inherent risks and rewards associated with microfranchising. We demonstrate that above any other development tool or poverty-alleviating solution, the microfranchising model is more suited for the necessity entrepreneur and more completely addresses the fallacy of the entrepreneur.

The implementation of microfranchises in developing countries promises to help alleviate more individuals and families from poverty, enhance economic self-reliance, and stimulate individual, community and country economic development.

THE FALLACY OF THE ENTREPRENEUR

> Entrepreneurs are innovators who use a process of shattering the status quo of the existing products and services, to set up new products, new services. (Joseph Schumpeter)

> An entrepreneur searches for change, responds to it and exploits opportunities. Innovation is a specific tool of an entrepreneur hence an effective entrepreneur converts a source into a resource. (Peter Drucker, 1985)

Twenty-five years ago, W.B. Gartner (1990) asked in the *Journal of Business Venturing* a seemingly simple question: "What are we talking about when we talk about entrepreneurship?" At the time, entrepreneurship was by no means a nascent field of academic study, but was beginning to gain ground as a viable focus for both management theorists and business practitioners. Peter Drucker, Joseph Schumpeter, and even as early as Jean-Baptiste Say, had built a solid foundation of scholarship. Gartner hoped to augment the discussion by identifying the defining characteristics of entrepreneurship. Ultimately, he concluded what entrepreneurs already know from their own experience: entrepreneurship is extremely difficult and highly complex.

Given this complexity, Gartner could only narrow a list to eight recurring themes or characteristics of entrepreneurship (1990).[2] These labels do little to answer his own question or to encapsulate the essence of the entrepreneur. Today we know that entrepreneurship is not so easily catalogued. In fact, these eight traits serve merely as the building blocks for any number of combinations (Robinson, 1991). Gartner's list, while hardly conclusive, illustrates just how few of us can truly identify with the label "entrepreneur." Indeed, it only reinforces that the call to be an entrepreneur is not for everyone. Moreover, if entrepreneurship was as nuanced and complex then, imagine how it has evolved in the celebrated Age of Information and burgeoning global economy.

Today Gartner's list is anachronistic because it assumes that all are entrepreneurs of opportunity, *not* of necessity. (To his credit, Gartner was writing during a decade of business boom and the economy was not nearly as globalized as it is today.) But do those same traits apply to the woman selling produce from a roadside stand in Chennai, India or the man selling woodcarvings in Phnom Penh, Cambodia? Surely these and *billions* of others in similar circumstances could be considered entrepreneurs, by even the most rudimentary standards.

This is the *fallacy of the entrepreneur*—the erroneous assumption that anyone can simply *be* an entrepreneur. In fact, few people in the world are naturally entrepreneurial. Yet, incredibly, in developing countries where infant mortality rates sometimes exceed business survival rates, by some measures as many as 80 percent to 85 percent of laborers can be considered entrepreneurs. This is by default, not by choice. For the four billion people living on less than $4 a day, *necessity is the only choice*. There is simply no other option. Even in the United States those who think they are entrepreneurial have little chance of success. After all, it is common business school fodder to cite the ominous warning: eight out of ten businesses fail in the first five years (if they last that long). Coupled with the fact that most people at the bottom of the pyramid have few options other than to go down this risky road, they start at a disadvantage. From there, the difficulties swell.

The fallacy of the entrepreneur should come as no surprise. Not everyone can be, let alone wants to be, an entrepreneur. This is just as true in the United States as it is in developing nations. The skilled laborers of those emerging economies are just as varied as they are here at home. Only, in a developing country, the odds are far from favorable. Few people would identify themselves as entrepreneurial. In the United States, for example, that number is, at most, one out of ten. To be a true entrepreneur requires you to be creative, innovative, have a high risk tolerance, capable of "converting a source into a resource" as Drucker (1985) demands; and perhaps most important for the necessity entrepreneur, capable of absorbing the shocks and setbacks that commonly occur in a start-up. It is a challenging journey fraught with inherent risks. *This* is the *entrepreneurial burden*.

THE NECESSITY ENTREPRENEUR

Michael Gerber's seminal work, *The E-myth*, reinforces this notion that labeling every business owner or manager an "entrepreneur" is simply unsound (Gerber, 1985). He highlights the fallacy of the entrepreneur by outlining three business personalities: the Technician, the Manager, and the Entrepreneur. A successful entrepreneur must carefully navigate through these disparate, inner voices and somehow foster their coexistence. It is split personality disorder with the added pressure of making payroll! One thinks of the necessity entrepreneur—the farmer or the baker who must suddenly harvest and sell their wares in a marketplace. To success-fully compete against other bakers, all making the same fried bread, the necessity entrepreneur (Technician) must awaken and channel the other two personalities.[3]

Delving deeper, Robinson discovered a marked difference between an entrepreneur and a business owner/manager (Robinson et al., 1991). At first glance, the two terms seem connotative; in reality they are *not* interchangeable. This discrepancy lies largely in the difference between having an "entrepreneurial mindset" and "entrepreneurial skillset." In other words, though one may have the *skills* necessary to undertake an entrepreneurial role, it is likely he or she lacks a key ingredient, namely the *mindset* of an entrepreneur. This mindset means the mental makeup, or psychological bent to tolerate the risk and rigors and thrills that come with a startup. This is the spirit of entrepreneurship. (Robinson calls this spirit "achievement motivation.") Above all else, when predicting entrepreneur-ial capability the mindset or "attitude approach" serves as the best baseline for success (Robinson et al., 1991).[4] In addition, assuming one has the pro-pensity (mindset) to be an entrepreneur, education (to acquire the skillset) dramatically increases a chance for success.[5] Thus, the complexity is ampli-fied because not only must the necessity entrepreneur have the attitude and appetite for the entrepreneurial lifestyle, a specific skillset is required, enhanced by extensive and targeted education.[6] These factors—attitude (mindset), education (skillset)—must be aggregated for success as an entre-preneur. Rarely do you find someone who has developed both the mindset *and* skillset necessary to successfully start an innovative business. This is poignantly apparent in the informal sector where the billions at the bottom of the pyramid have such little success with their cottage industries, due in large part to the nature of the informal economies in which they operate.

Operating in an Informal Economy: The Necessity Entrepreneur's Burden

Unfortunately in developing countries, even if the necessity entrepreneur has the keen entrepreneurial mindset to take the leap of faith and start a microenterprise, her education, infrastructure and capital markets are grossly limited. Success is highly unlikely. The inevitable setbacks that entrepreneurs are expected to endure can be crippling to the technician or laborer at the bottom of the pyramid, living hand to mouth or, at best, paycheck to unsteady paycheck. It is a self-defeating cycle, only compounded by these negative factors.

For this reason, Zoltan Acs identified people who are:

> Self-employed because they have no better option *necessity entrepreneurs*. Unlike *opportunity entrepreneurs*, who enter the market because they identify and want to exploit new opportunities, necessity entrepreneurs usually prefer to deploy, manage, and grow someone else's business idea or to work directly for someone else [emphasis added]. (Christensen, Lehr, and Fairbourne, 2010, p. 46)

And sadly, even if necessity entrepreneurs initially succeed, they rarely have capacity to grow their microenterprise. Furthermore, those skilled laborers do not enjoy the "ecosystems of support" that entrepreneurs have in a developed economy (Christensen, Lehr, and Fairbourne, 2010). This includes well-established financial systems that boast transparency, supply ready capital and reward the risk-taker. Formal social and capital networks connect the entrepreneur with the funder, generating new ideas and businesses. Meanwhile, in developing countries, that ecosystem is nonexistent. The technicians of informal markets operate without the same safety-nets or structures in place. In these markets, particularly rural areas, few businesses exist that even offer jobs, let alone inspire the necessity entrepreneur to envision a new way to create value for the consumer. To generate a business idea that creates value and creates jobs seems beyond feasibility. Worse still, by merely copying an existing business, these necessity entrepreneurs inadvertently create competition for other low-skilled business owners, reducing profits for everyone. It is not uncommon, then, for necessity entrepreneurs to resort to this option: copy a neighbor's business. International travelers have surely experienced walking through a market and passing identical shops with identical merchandise, the would-be shopkeeper offering little to no innovative products or services.

Consider another common occurrence: a commuter train pulls up to the station and 20 different women press the passengers, each hoping to sell their inventory of fried bread. All 20 women are necessity entrepreneurs. They saw a market need—hungry passengers—and each one attempted to meet this need with the exact same product at the exact same price. What they cannot foresee is the unintended consequences: when they copy each other, they produce more supply than the local demand, and ultimately the women end up diluting profits and wasting food. While this would be difficult in a developed country, the situation is even more dire for the necessity entrepreneur, who operates with no savings and certainly no emergency funds. A single misstep would be devastating.

Gartner's legacy is a list of what he considers defining characteristics.

Robinson expanded this theme to show that there is more to being an entrepreneur than teachable skills. The mindset must be a part of the equation. However, assuming that just anyone can be an entrepreneur by simply starting a business is a fallacy indeed. When considering the global economy and the rising tide of informal markets that the forced entrepreneur must operate in, both Gartner's list and Robinson's insights are patently flawed because they fail to address what is now considered the entrepreneur's most common characteristic on the planet: necessity.

What resources, then, are available to the necessity entrepreneur? What solutions have been posited by the international development communities? If these are the fickle straits necessity entrepreneurs find themselves in—forced to play the role of multiple business personalities while yet an unskilled, untrained laborer—what models can they count on? Surely the billions of aid dollars poured into their informal markets have yielded promising results.

MICROFINANCE AND ITS LIMITS

> No discussion of market approaches to poverty alleviation would be complete without some mention of microfinance. (David Lehr[7])

For some time, microfinance or microcredit has been hailed as a viable and innovative solution for mitigating the needs of the necessity entrepreneur and hopefully eradicating global poverty. Certainly this model, for which microfinance pioneer Muhammad Yunus justly won the Nobel Prize in 2006, has done more good than many well-meaning aid attempts. At its core, microfinance grants the world's poor access to capital in the form of small or micro-loans. For the first time the world's poor have access to formal financial institutions. This has allowed nearly 150 million people to start microenterprises with the hope of increased earnings, clearly a commendable effort.

Even proponents of microfinance, however, recognize the model has limitations. One fundamental challenge is the *position it places the borrower*. In essence, borrowing a micro-loan keeps the necessity entrepreneur confined in that role (forced entrepreneurship); once she has taken out a loan, she must employ that capital into a microenterprise of some kind to earn a return for sustenance *and* loan repayment. Microfinance institutions (MFIs) do well to get capital to the remote reaches of the developing world—and millions of the world's necessity entrepreneurs have benefited by this effort. Indeed they have provided a key variable in the poverty-solving equation, namely *access* to capital at the bottom of the pyramid.

Remarkably, the MFIs that administer these loans have created a much-needed infrastructure that penetrates the most remote villages of developing countries. After all, prior to the introduction of these small loans, the poor had limited ability to start and grow microenterprises. But beyond capital and credit, microfinance does not consider *how* the capital can most productively be deployed.

Isolated as a stand-alone solution, microfinance's poverty-solving equation includes three interrelated elements:

1. Microfinance institution (infrastructure): facilitates or administers the micro-loans.
2. Micro-loan (access to capital): necessitates the creation of a microenterprise.
3. Microenterprise: typically the only option available to the necessity entrepreneur.

As noted, given the circumstances the borrower finds herself in, chances are good that she will have little choice but to copy the same microenterprise that other loan recipients in the village started, creating the same dilemma the 20 women at the train station tolerate. Moreover, while affording millions the opportunity to climb the economic-development ladder, microenterprises tend to plateau early and usually remain very small, often because of the very fallacy of the entrepreneur discussed above. Namely, those who operate in the informal economy do not have the basic knowledge or training on how to start and grow new business, let alone the disposition to undertake such a risky venture. To place the necessity entrepreneur in that position is unfair to all parties involved. The weak link in this chain is the microenterprise—too often a limited, struggling cottage industry that fails to scale or provide adequate income for loan repayment. A conspicuous gap in the equation begs consideration.

Imagine you live in rural Kenya and a microfinance institution approaches your village with the opportunity to take out a micro-loan. After the excitement and celebration dissipates and the loans have been administered, now what? How would you use the new-found capital most productively? Are you ready to go into debt and risk all your resources for a roadside mango stand, one that is conveniently situated right next to your neighbor's mango stand? Herein lies the power of the micro*franchising* model as a tool for alleviating poverty and eliminating the burden necessity entrepreneurs must carry. By offering a business package—a system she can plug into her local market—microfranchising alleviates the need to do it all on her own.[8]

MICROFRANCHISING

> Giving people ownership of their businesses, as well as the tools, relationships, and systems to help their business thrive, transforms [owners] into a powerful force for change. (Charles Hart, in Flannery, 2007, p. 70)

In recent years, microfranchising has emerged as a promising component and a logical complement to microfinance. Though still a relatively new concept, microfranchising is a compelling market-based solution to address the gap in the equation, particularly in light of the limitations the necessity entrepreneur faces. By providing the necessity entrepreneur with a sound business blueprint to follow, microfranchising takes the concept of enterprise development a step further than microcredit. Indeed, when talking about the poor moving up the economic-development ladder, microcredit provides access to the ladder; microfranchising strengthens the rungs.

Moreover, microfranchising works well when partnered with the MFI. Theirs is a mutually beneficial relationship. The microfranchisee often needs start-up capital to establish her microfranchise and the MFI provides timely access to the working capital required. Conversely, the microfranchise is beneficial to the MFI because the provision of a loan to a proven, successful business that has ties to a larger organization greatly reduces the risk of loan default due to business failure.

Microfranchising serves as a better alternative than the traditional micro-lending or other microenterprise building efforts. The necessity entrepreneurs at the bottom of the pyramid have limited education, limited experience and limited ideas for new products or services. Yet well-meaning programs assume that "necessity is the mother of invention" and participants in remote villages are able to create, launch, and grow successful new enterprises. Again, the fallacy of the entrepreneur directs their assumptions. Their programs are built on the false hope that the world's poor wish to be entrepreneurs, but are only held back by lack of capital. In reality, necessity is *not* the mother of invention and capital does not an entrepreneur make.

Microfranchising Defined

The term "franchise" often brings to mind successful fast food chains, such as, McDonald's, Wendy's and Taco Bell. What makes these familiar franchises so successful?[9] Surely it cannot just be menus of burgers and burritos. Rather, the secret to their success is the *systematization of their operations*. A franchised business model is systematized so that an operator can open the "business-in-a-box" to train franchisees and then replicate the system—a textbook turnkey operation.[10] Above any other development tool or poverty-alleviating solution, the microfranchising model more completely addresses the fallacy of the entrepreneur and is more suited for the necessity entrepreneur.

As defined in earlier works, "*micro*franchising is the replication of business systems at the grassroots. It assumes the principles of franchising only on a smaller scale and with the intent to benefit those at the bottom of the pyramid" (Fairbourne, Gibson, and Dyer, 2007, p. 2). Microfranchising subscribes to the same precepts of franchising, with one overarching difference: while built from a for-profit perspective, the model leans heavily on the developmental benefits and social impact a strong, sustainable microenterprise affords the microfranchisee and her community. At its fundamental level microfranchising is a method of poverty elimination, job creation, and private sector development. And it addresses three core problems that prevent many necessity entrepreneurs from becoming economically self-reliant: the lack of skills needed to grow a successful business, the lack of jobs in developing countries, and the lack of goods and services available, particularly those that meet market demands.

The term microfranchising carries multiple meanings, all equally significant. Franchising, of course, suggests the full-service, prepackaged business system that that necessity entrepreneur can replicate and manage in her own market. But the prefix "micro" has raised some eyebrows. "Micro" should call to mind the success of microfinance—a revolutionary approach to poverty alleviation—particularly its guiding emphasis on the social aspects of development. Additionally, the "micro" should not imply that the businesses are not fully developed. Rather, microfranchises are fully developed, well-functioning enterprises; far more appropriate and sustainable than the default "copied" businesses that the women at the train station resign themselves to when trying to sell fried bread. "Micro" also signifies the low-income customers these enterprises serve and the relatively little capital required to replicate them (see Lehr, 2008).

The key then, is the business model. Whereas before the necessity entrepreneur had little choice but to buck the entrepreneurial burden by assessing her technical skills (baking fried bread), looking for a unique market opportunity (crowded train station), finding a competitive niche and innovating some product or service to fill the customers' need (none, she joins 19 other women attempting the exact same thing), then tragically *taking the risk* to use what scant resources she can muster to throw into her fragile "business." Conversely, the business model a microfranchise offers has been thoroughly tested and proven. The start-up costs are low, which reduces barriers to entry. The risks have been mitigated, reducing exposure to those already in poverty. And because it is a system that can be replicated many times over, it maximizes economies of scale. These attributes alone help the necessity entrepreneur "sidestep many of the pitfalls of existing development interventions" (Christensen, Lehr, and Fairbourne, 2010, p. 47).

> The billions of people who live on less than $2 per day need easy-to-implement, low-risk, likely-to-scale ways to earn more income. They need options that don't entail creating copycat businesses or self-employment out of desperation rather than preference. And they need opportunities to build their management potential and business acumen.
>
> Yet many of the most popular development initiatives—that is, those that help people start new businesses—assume that what holds people back is simply lack of education or lack of capital. When implemented in isolation, many of these initiatives require considerable creativity, risk taking, and capital to establish and grow. Because creativity, an appetite for risk, and capital are often wanting in the world's poorest places, entrepreneurship programs may not serve the world's most vulnerable people.
>
> In contrast, microfranchising holds much promise for enriching people at the bottom and even middle of the economic pyramid. Microfranchises introduce new ideas and business practices to areas that lack formal markets or differentiated products. They lower risk for new business owners, while offering them the potential for a steady and predictable income. They allow local people to bring new and welcome products and services to the community. Sometimes, they also help corporations and organizations penetrate new markets. (Christensen, Lehr, and Fairbourne, 2010, p. 49)

Microfranchising is not just another interesting or appealing approach to be considered. Given the alternative (forced entrepreneurship), the need for microfranchising might be greater than ever. An Economist *Times* article declared "Micro-franchising: the next big thing" (Aiyar, 2007), which certainly added gravitas to the model. Especially when we acknowledge that the following dilemma, as described by Tina Rosenberg in the *New York Times*, is all too common:

> What if every time people came up with a new product, they also had to devise a completely new way to sell it? Imagine that we had no Amazons, eBays, Targets or Walmarts—no distribution chain at all, and no stores near potential buyers. Nor is there a way for potential customers to learn about the product. Oh, and they can't afford it anyway—they can't afford much of anything.
>
> Many of the world's poor occupy this alternate universe. Every week someone comes up with an ingenious new water filter, vitamin packet, solar lamp, efficient cookstove, fortified food, new medicine. But these great ideas often fail, or simply don't reach many people—for want of a business model.
>
> Franchises support one in eight jobs in America, and they are very successful. Most new businesses fail, but franchises do well. It's not hard to see why. A franchise is a business that has been tested over and over. It has an assured supply chain, low-cost inputs (because the franchiser can buy in bulk), training for managers, and a trusted brand.

Micro-franchisees get the same things on a smaller scale—and they need them even more. Microcredit in its classic form considers lack of credit to be the only obstacle to business creation. It isn't. Most people aren't entrepreneurs.

It's much more realistic and simple to train someone to be a manager than an entrepreneur. Microfranchising is the provision of the full business package. *The franchisee just has to follow the steps.* (Rosenberg, 2012; emphasis added)

The benefits this model offers make it a significant contribution to the economic development discussion. Microfranchising improves survival rates among business start-ups, enhances job creation and establishes asset ownership among the poor by moving informal microenterprises out of obscurity and toward formal banking relationships. Though microfranchising can provide scale, profits and access to the bottom of the pyramid markets for corporations, it is fundamentally a poverty alleviation tool.

Microfranchising and the Entrepreneurial Burden

Microfranchising is based on the assumption that the world's poor are burdened enough already. Taking out a micro-loan only creates unwelcome exposure for the necessity entrepreneur. Instead, by offering a low-risk, ready-made job opportunity for those who want to join the formal economy, but do not want to carry the inherent risks of starting a business from scratch, microfranchising reduces that exposure. By doing so, the microfranchisee builds her own business while acquiring practical skills and assets. The microfranchisor, meanwhile, establishes additional sources of revenue and distribution.

With microfranchising, the necessity entrepreneur can play the role of the business owner or manager, which is something different altogether than the entrepreneur that must display the mindset and skillset so rarely developed in either informal or formal markets. A business owner, on the other hand, can manage a proven model and established system (Christensen, Parsons, and Fairbourne, 2010). The risks have been mitigated, the concept has been proven, the customers and the market have been identified, the model has already succeeded many times over (see Table 12.1).

Implementation

Field experts and practitioners are constantly learning and adapting best practices with microfranchising (Lehr, 2008).[11] So the following components by no means suggest an exhaustive list, but they do provide key considerations to increase successful implementation of microfranchises.

Table 12.1   Entrepreneur, necessity entrepreneur and microfranchisee comparison

	Entrepreneur	Necessity Entrepreneur	Microfranchisee
Risk	High Risk "High Risk, High Return"	Magnified Risk "High Risk, Low Return"	Mitigated Risk "Low Risk, High Return"
Skillset	High degree of expertise, Advanced skillset	Limited education, Limited experience, Limited ideas for new products/ services	Minimal skillset required Simple, specialized training
Mindset	Requires high risk tolerance to weather setbacks of a start-up	Entrepreneurial Burden: Necessity is the only choice	Structured tolerance, risk is mitigated
Economic Sector	Formal economy, developed infrastructure	Informal economy, limited infrastructure	Informal economy, MF model mitigates lack of infrastructure
Competition	Differentiates business from competition	Creates competition by copying businesses, low barrier to entry	Creates barriers to entry for competition
Market	Seeks niche market, blue ocean opportunities	Restricted market, resorts to limited copycat microenterprise	Market and customer already identified, likely to scale
Business Model	Innovative, creative business models	Homogenous business models	Tested and proven business model, turnkey system
Socio-economic Benefits	Enjoys potential upside, "being own boss"	Isolated, survival mode "self-employment desperation"	Self-reliance and dignity through successful partnership
Financing	Sophisticated capital to seed or grow business	Micro-loan leads to forced entrepreneurship	Microfranchise fosters business owners/manager

For the microfranchisor to provide a proven business model to the microfranchisee, there will likely be some initial hand-holding and training of basic business principles. Finance and branding, marketing and sales, delivery and distribution, leadership and management should all be clearly established and easily absorbed for the novice necessity entrepreneur. The microfranchisor must be patient, flexible and willing to provide the necessary training and comprehensive understanding of the market to afford the microfranchisee her greatest opportunity for success.

On a whole, a successful microfranchise offers:

1. A small business that can be easily replicated by following proven marketing and operational concepts.
2. A cooperative mentoring and symbiotic relationship between microfranchisor and microfranchisee that benefits both.
3. A proven business system that works and provides a blueprint for success.
4. A business system that provides technical and managerial assistance from microfranchisors.
5. An established business that does not require microfranchisors to identify and start new enterprises (Fairbourne and Gibson, 2007).

These enterprises can start with as little as $25 and typically no more than $1,000 or US$1,500. They provide common business systems like an operations manual, written job descriptions, daily, weekly, monthly task lists, single entry bookkeeping system, approved suppliers with volume discounts in place and acceptable performance targets (Fairbourne and Gibson, 2007). But every successful microfranchise begins with a comprehensive understanding of the local market.

Understanding the Market

As mentioned, any tourist in a developing country can recall seeing rows upon rows of identical products when visiting the local markets. Each store seems to be selling the exact same items as the one right next door. This is one major challenge of entrepreneurial activities in the developing world: necessity entrepreneurs, wanting to start their own business, simply start one just like their neighbor's. This problem arises from a lack of understanding of the market in which they are operating. Failure to adhere to this consideration inevitably leads to a failed business. Indeed, many of the microenterprises undertaken in developing markets fail because the necessity entrepreneur ignored this fundamental consideration and did not accurately identify a veritable market opportunity. Microfranchises, on the other hand, provide their microfranchisees with the result of significant research and planning about the market in which they will be working (Alon et al., 2010).[12] Therefore, the microfranchises must meet local level needs, primarily serving as an appropriate and simple operation for the laborer with little formal training to manage.

As a caveat, for the microfranchisor to expand into new markets, including different cultures and geographies, and continue to meet local level needs, the model must often be modified to adapt to these local nuances. This may be as simple as allowing each microfranchisee the flexibility to adjust her model to the needs of her community, while keeping an eye toward quality control and consistency. Many times this benefits the microfranchisor. If the adaptation does well, they can incorporate the new products or services into its model and relay the innovation throughout its entire network.

Fairbourne Consulting developed a three-pronged approach to assessing and engaging a new local market.

1. Phase one begins with Research and Design, wherein a team utilizes a market safari method of boots on the ground to shadow the customer base, conduct focus groups, one-on-one interviews, and so on, to hone analysis of local knowledge and markets. This phase is primarily fact-finding. The process involves gaining knowledge, categorizing information, analyzing key findings, mapping market trends, redefining and refining the research and beginning to design a model that meets market demands. It is a fluid process, constantly adapting to fully understand the key findings that will most influence a microfranchise. Clearly, this in-depth approach goes well beyond academic and institutional research. But the most innovative and successful business models are often influenced more by direct observations of local market behavior, by what the consumers are actually doing than what desktop research predicts they will do.
2. The second phase involves a Live Market Test. Herein a prototype business model is introduced to the market for initial consumer feedback. Consumer preferences, pricing structures, and distribution systems are tested and retested. This way the operations can be fully systematized by the time the microfranchise is ready to roll out. As with the first phase of Research and Design, the Live Market Test requires substantial refining and modifying to ensure the process can be replicated.
3. Now that the microfranchise's various systems and operations have undergone such testing and scrutiny, the third phase involves Launching and Replicating. Once the successful processes are implemented, the microfranchisor can focus on strengthening the infrastructure, developing and implementing expansion plans, transitioning operations to a local management team and then increasing their core competencies.

It should be evident that the successful microfranchisor must devote considerable time, attention and resources to understanding the market *before* a microfranchise is launched. But with an established distribution chain, the microfranchisor enjoys added benefits that enhance the experience and success of the microfranchisee (Lehr, 2008).[13]

David Lehr (2008) suggests the following as traits of a successful microfranchisor:

- Has a comprehensive and ongoing training program
- Holds regular meetings at all levels
- Offers feedback system for franchisee input
- Openly communicates via newsletters, memos, emails and other means of information exchange
- Makes help services available
- Provides effective promotional advertising
- Offers financial and managerial reports that can be used to improve the microfranchise.

Training, Mentoring and Business Development

Microfranchises offer services that stand-alone microenterprises do not. They involve a mentoring relationship between the franchisor and franchisee. The underlying theory behind microfranchising is that management is a skill that can be learned by training. Being naturally entrepreneurial is not a requirement. Thus, microfranchisors are looking for people who can be trained to manage or maintain a business system. The microfranchisee operates under uniform standards and has a detailed operating system that is developed and enforced by the franchisor. Microfranchisors provide initial and ongoing training and mentoring. *The creative burden is borne by the microfranchisor, not the microfranchisee.*

It is not uncommon for a successful entrepreneur to want to become a "social entrepreneur," to reach out and encourage others in poverty to find similar success. For the social entrepreneur looking to have an impact in a developing country, microfranchising affords a viable method to not only establish a successful business, but to mentor and develop the necessity entrepreneur. Too often that encouragement is lost in an outdated approach to development. Instead:

> Microfranchising brings already successful social entrepreneurs together with people who are motivated to create their own small enterprises, but who often lack the skills and capital that can lead to success. Together, they can grow the overall impact of a business and create a local ownership and management opportunity. (Lehr, 2008, p. 4)[14]

In the case study below, a microfranchising effort called Living Goods illustrates in detail these benefits. Notice the targeted training, field experience, and resources available for business development.

Case study: Living Goods

> Living Goods began a joint venture with BRAC, the giant antipoverty organization [MFI] from Bangladesh. . . . About 600 of Living Goods' sales representatives are women from BRAC's microfinance groups recruited to work as health promoters—Living Goods provides financing and some operational help. (Another 250 reps are separate from BRAC, trained and managed by Living Goods.) The partnership allows Living Goods to extend its reach and BRAC to experiment with ways to make its network of community health promoters more sustainable.
>
> The women essentially become their village doctors. They get two weeks' training in basic health care—preventive measures, and also how to diagnose and cure the most common diseases: malaria, childhood pneumonia, diarrhea. They learn when to refer a patient to the health clinic. Then they spend two weeks in the field. They first follow a working sales representative. Then they go back to their communities and go door to door asking questions about each family's health—in the process introducing themselves and the Living Goods brand.
>
> The representatives get the blue T-shirt and other marketing materials for free and are loaned a bag of about $60 worth of merchandise. They pay back that loan over 48 weeks from their earnings—they get 15 to 20 percent of whatever they sell. After that, they pay cash for stock at the branch headquarters. Every month all the reps in a district—some 50 people—gather for a half day to update their training and share their victories and defeats. (Rosenberg, 2012)

Yes the microfranchisee has taken out a loan and is expected to work to pay that back, but the terms are manageable and the opportunity far more viable. How motivating to work with these business development opportunities rather than forced to create a microenterprise on your own.

Case study: HC Duraclean and the benefits of microfranchisee training
HC Duraclean, a cleaning company in Malaysia, has been growing rapidly in recent years. Expanding from providing commercial cleaning to their parent company in 1997, the company now provides to a wide range of commercial and residential cleaning services and is now providing airplane and airport cleaning.

HC Duraclean's fast growth can be attributed to the high quality of service they offer which is achieved through an extensive training program. Each HC Duraclean franchisee receives extensive training to ensure standardized high quality cleaning services. Franchisees are put through an orientation and training program that includes classroom training as well as on-the-job demonstrations and training. Franchisees are trained in business management as well as cleaning techniques. All franchisees are then certified and can begin their own HC Duraclean businesses.

To promote growth, franchisees are encouraged to start in the carpet and upholstery cleaning business and then, after they have established a customer base, to diversify into hard floor, duct and ultrasonic cleaning. By providing their franchisees with extensive training in business management, HC Duraclean has created an extremely successful microfranchise and is growing rapidly. The franchisees are better prepared to enter the cleaning market and understand, not only their product, but how to run a small business as well.

Hiring

Screening the right candidates for a microfranchise is often overlooked as a variable that can mean the difference between a mediocre and successful microfranchise. Managers, local operations teams, and microfranchisees all require careful screening and placement. When hiring it helps to consider their existing skills and attitudes, and even their reputation in the community. Though they will be trained, it helps to build off a foundation of basic skills and a positive attitude. Ultimately, when hiring, it helps to select microfranchisees who would make good managers themselves, not just employees. They have the initiative and energy to put behind the business. Not all low-income or necessity entrepreneurs fit this mold. As with many aspects of initiating a microfranchise, some handholding may be helpful. Quarterly business review meetings and field visits by a team leader can prove well worth the time it takes to stay connected to the microfranchisee. Naturally, the complexity of the screening process need only meet the complexity of the enterprise. But when creating a cohesive system for replication, screening for talent cannot be overlooked.

Branding

Branding is uniquely important when working in the developing world because customers have a very limited income and must choose what they spend their money on very wisely. This will lead customers to be extremely brand conscious because they cannot afford to purchase a product that might break or be ruined, as they cannot afford to buy a replacement. Microfranchising gives necessity entrepreneurs access to a proven brand. This allows the franchisee to start a business with a customer base already in place. Amul started as a dairy product, but because the Amul brand name is so strong, two elderly women were able to start an Amul pizza franchise and become wildly successful on the brand name of Amul alone (see Case Study: Amul Pizza).

Branding in the developing world requires good research and testing that can only be achieved by an organization with the resources to do so. For example, when Medicine Shoppe—a pharmacy chain in the slums in India—initially opened their stores they made sure they were very modern looking facilities that were clean with good lighting. To their surprise they found that the poor customers they were trying to serve would not come into the stores, assuming from their clean modern look that they would be too expensive for them to afford (Lehr, 2008).

Branding in microfranchising must also bring credibility to the microfranchisee. Many microfranchisees were formerly farmers, laborers, or worked in other unskilled, less-respected professions. For the customers to accept the microfranchisees' products they must also accept the microfranchisee as someone qualified to endorse and sell those products. VisionSpring encountered this difficulty when their customers had difficulty accepting eye care advice from their former neighbors. To overcome this obstacle, VisionSpring included a certification program and banner as part of their microfranchise model. The banner read "Authorized Vision Entrepreneur: Trained to Conduct Free Eye Screening." The microfranchise kit also included the certificate showing that the franchisee has been certified to carry out eye screenings (Lehr, 2008). The resulting trust dramatically increased VisionSpring's impact and reach.

Because developing markets lack the traditional marketing strategies such as television, radio, newspapers, magazines and even social media, microfranchises must look to other methods to establish their brand. The most common method is word of mouth. Many microfranchises are sending out local representatives who develop consistent relationships with target markets and constantly talk to and educate them about the brand (Kistruck et al., 2011). While this is an effective marketing technique, it is expensive and difficult in countries with poor transportation routes. Furthermore, word of mouth marketing is difficult to spread quickly, especially in rural areas.

Brand acceptance is also difficult in countries where cultural fragmentation is common. Language barriers and a wide variety of different cultural norms lead to difficulties in marketing. Long histories of violence, abuse, corruption and exploitation leave many of the markets where microfranchises operate distrustful of outsiders. Because of the difficulty in establishing a brand that can bridge cultural fragmentation, many microfranchisors must focus on finding microfranchisees who are tied to the local community. This allows them to build a local base to build their brand. Local branding builds loyalty to the product and helps the microfranchisor to develop brands that are accepted in many different areas (Kistruck et al., 2011).

Microfranchisors would do well to take more of a supportive approach to franchise standardization than a top-down approach. Because of the highly variable nature of the areas in which the microfranchisees are working, standardization is difficult to achieve. If the microfranchisor is more supportive of the microfranchisee in helping them to implement practices that will work in their area they will see greater success. One such example of doing this is setting up marketing as the primary responsibility of the microfranchisee while the franchisor focuses on business training, and support services.

Case study: Amul Pizza—strength of the brand

Jayalaxmi Srinivasan and Padma Sreenivasan longed to create an old-age home to honor the elderly. When Padma's husband died leaving her a young widow, her parents stepped in to care for her children while she went to work. She wanted to repay that debt. As she and Jayalaxmi looked for ways to fund their dream they came across an ad by dairy producer, Amul, asking for pizza franchisees. The women decided to take the opportunity. "We couldn't even spell the word pizza let alone make it," says Jayalaxmi, "but we went ahead to bag the coveted franchise as it was a means to an end." Despite their lack of knowledge about pizza, Padma and Jayalaxmi jumped on the chance to become franchisees of Amul. They invested 5,000 Rs (US$113) and started Pizza Haven in 2003.

Padma and Jayalaxmi enjoyed huge success from the very beginning. The Amul brand is extremely strong in India. The high quality ingredients from Amul and the reasonable price left the women hoping to keep up with demand. In order to meet their demand, Padma and Jayalaxmi hired women from the destitute home, Little Sisters, to help in the kitchen. In addition to their salaries, Padma and Jayalaxmi agreed to sponsor the women's children's education as well. Soon the women, now affectionately known as the Pizza Grannies, needed to expand. They approached the local MNC's and started renting counter space from them during teatime. Soon their demand from the MNC workers increased so much that they started introducing new varieties and flavors. Profits soared and the women were even able to delink from Amul and remain profitable. In June 2005, just two years after becoming pizza franchisees, the women were finally able to buy 22,000 square feet of land to start their project (Lal, 2005).

Benefits of Microfranchising

Microfranchising is attractive because it accomplishes dual purposes. First, it builds businesses and brings employment and enterprises to the community. Vodafone, the world's largest wireless phone company, uses a micro-franchise model throughout Africa. Their phone cards are sold through kiosks. In South Africa, there are 5,000 of these kiosks spread throughout the country. In addition to generating income for the microfranchisee who owns the kiosk, each kiosk generates, on average, jobs for five employees. Additionally, franchisees enjoy access to the networks, marketing options, and supply chains of their parent company or sponsoring NGO. This gives them a much greater chance of success and growth than a company unaffiliated with a larger parent organization. Microfranchising also links the franchisee into the formal economy with all of the benefits that come from operating in the formal sector. These include "access to training, formal market collateral, [and] legal protection" (Christensen, Parsons, and Fairbourne, 2010, p. 596).

Second, microfranchises create social good (Sireau, 2011).[15] Having a social impact on the triple bottom line (people, planet, profit) is no longer a hollow tagline but a legitimate and worthy pursuit. Whereas corporations are characterized by their singular focus on profit, social enterprises like micro-franchises seek to have a positive impact with not only profit, but the community and environment as well. Many microenterprises aspire to have this social impact, but too often fall short. Microfranchising increases the odds of attaining this impact. "When done well, microfranchising also enriches companies and communities" (Christensen, Parsons, and Fairbourne, 2010).

Microfranchising, just like traditional franchising, allows corporations to scale more quickly by overcoming the resource constraint problem and with increased scale comes increased profits. Especially in international markets, franchising has been increasing in popularity as a growth method (Alon et al., 2010, p. 160). The case of Amul in India is a classic case of a corporation using microfranchising as a model to reach scale and profitability.

Case study: Amul
Amul is perhaps the largest microfranchising company in existence. Amul was started in 1946 in India as a dairy cooperative to help farmers who were being abused financially by middlemen. The model was simple, let farmers continue to do what they do well—produce milk—but help them to do it more efficiently through technology innovations. Collection centers were built in each village and farmers deposited their milk twice a day. After collection the milk was taken to a union dairy plant to be tested

for quality and processed. Farmers are paid for their milk by weight and fat content (to discourage watering down of the milk). The milk is also tested for quality and if the quality is low the payment will also be lower, encouraging farmers to sell a high quality product. By simplifying the pick-up methods, farmers were able to waste less time trying to sell and deliver and instead were able to focus on producing more high quality milk.

Amul uses a coop model in which the farmers are the owners of the cooperative. But because it is such a large cooperative, management is brought in to manage the day to day operations of the now dairy giant. Amul grew from its beginnings in 1946 to a huge cooperative now that includes 2.79 million producer members in over 13,000 villages across India. Amul has been so successful at their mission that they have almost completely cut out middlemen in the dairy process which allows them to market their dairy product across India at lower prices. Amul's sales of dairy products in 2008–2009 were $1.5 billion. Amul has rapidly been diversifying their product offerings expanding into dry milk, baby milk, ice cream, condensed milk, butter and others. Their ice cream products are so popular that they captured 30 percent of India's ice cream market only four years after their introduction.

Amul has also started franchising at the other side of their operations as well—recruiting franchisees to sell other products they produce, such as the Amul Pizza grannies noted in this chapter.

Amul is a true success story in microfranchising. They have not only created a stable income sources for millions of farmer-producers, but by doing so have also created a dairy company capable of delivering high quality dairy products to millions of people at very reasonable prices. While doing all of this they are making a significant profit (Amul Case Study).

Distribution and Infrastructure

As discussed, on the individual level microfranchising provides those who do not possess an entrepreneurial skillset with a business blueprint that, if followed, will lead to greater individual economic success. For those who do not have entrepreneurial skills and would be better suited as an employee or technician microfranchises create these jobs. On a corporate level, microfranchising can be utilized as a delivery system, especially when paired up with a microfinance institution. Building off of the remarkable infrastructure that MFIs have been able to establish, microfranchising enhances the distribution of products and services to otherwise inaccessible areas of the world. After all, it is the MFI that administers these loans and thereby creates a much-needed delivery system that penetrates the most remote villages of developing countries (see Fairbourne, 2006).

Many multinational corporations see an unfulfilled demand for their goods and services, but they lack either an adequate distribution system or the deep knowledge of local markets to profitably deliver products and services (Lehr, 2008).[16] Due to the difficulty in reaching the poor, common goods and services come at a higher price. This is what Prahalad calls the "poverty penalty" (Prahalad and Hart, 2006). Resources are limited and sold in such small quantities. If they arrive at all, they cost much more than those in developed countries pay for the same good or service. Because there is a lack of delivery system, poverty is perpetuated. Microfranchising curbs the poverty penalty, beginning with enhanced economies of scale. "Compared with an individual entrepreneur, the franchisor often has better negotiating power with suppliers and is able to reach economies of scale in other areas (such as product design, use and development of new technologies, and supply chain development)" (Lehr 2008, p. 4). With microfranchising, organizations can increase their distribution networks and ultimately sell more products and services while maintaining a dignified relationship with their independent distributors from the bottom of the pyramid. Developing markets have been growing at a much higher rate than developed markets. According to the McKinsey Global Institute, Africa today is a $1.6 trillion economy with $860 billion in consumer spending. Those numbers are expected to swell to $2.6 trillion and $1.4 trillion by 2020. Similarly, India's GDP is over $3.5 trillion and is estimated to quadruple over the next decade (Roxburgh et al., 2010). Early entrants in these markets can leverage their first-mover advantage and establish brands that consumers will recognize and trust for decades.

Avon understood this early on. Many can remember their mother's yearly visit with a local Avon representative to buy make-up. But what they did not realize at the time was that the Avon business model was opening doors for Avon in markets all over the world.

Case study: Avon

Avon began their business in 1886 selling perfume door-to-door. In 1954 Avon created their international division and began doing business in Brazil in 1958. Avon's model of direct sales through independent contractors allows them to eliminate middlemen and cut costs so their beauty, fashion and home products can be sold at lower prices. Avon Brazil has allowed Avon huge access into the Brazilian beauty markets. In 2008 Brazil became the second largest market for perfume, hair and personal hygiene products in the world. This growth has come largely from the economic growth of the "C class", a group who previously would only use these products for special occasions and are now using them on a day-to-day basis.

Avon's unique microfranchising model allowed them to have unprecedented access to these "bottom of the pyramid markets" who are quite brand conscious and loyal to brands. Avon lowered their prices on basic products in order to market them more effectively to this growing group of consumers.

Avon Brazil's sales force is now their largest sales force worldwide with between 1.1 and 1.2 million women selling for the company as independent contractors. Brazil's make-up market grew 10.1 percent in 2008 up to $1.3 billion and is forecast to grow to $1.9 billion by 2013. Avon holds the largest share of Brazil's make-up market with 23.3 percent of the market. Avon's market saturation in Brazil is such that Avon sells one eyeliner in Brazil every two seconds.

Avon's use of microfranchising allows them to not only lower prices to a point where they can capture a significant portion of bottom of the pyramid markets, but also allows them to effectively sell in those markets through their network of local distributors (Avon Case Study).

Dignity

The poor don't need handouts; they need hand ups. They don't want to be treated as charity cases; they want to be treated as equals. It is only when we begin to understand how the roles of positive psychology and human dignity play into international development and foreign aid that we will start to see a dramatic shift in our ability to make a sustainable positive difference in the world. Poverty is a more complicated issue than purely economic growth or stagnation. It has perpetuated over centuries not only due to exploitation, corruption and lack of opportunity, but also in part due to these psychological and societal patterns and trends. As human development improves, measured by human dignity, nearly every aspect of the quality of life of a society will improve as well. This therefore, should play a major role in how we look at development and foreign aid in general.

Aid administrators and development practitioners, frantically spinning their wheels, sometimes forget that amid all the good and impact they're seeking to achieve a recipient stands at the other end of the line. What does it mean for the individual to receive charity? How does it feel to be almost entirely dependent on someone else for your basic necessities at times? Perhaps one of the most significant aspects of microfranchising is that it fosters dignity through partnership. Once the necessity entrepreneur is employed, wears a new uniform, has some change in her pocket, she can carry her head high because she is plugged into a system that breeds success. She enjoys a new sense of community and camaraderie. For many, this newfound dignity is beyond price.

Some question whether or not it is ethical to sell to the poor as opposed to a philanthropic approach. Exploitation of any group of people is wrong but going into business with someone does not mean that you are trying to exploit them. The idea of a symbiotic, mutually beneficial business relationship between those with means and those in poverty can make for a profitable outcome for both parties economically and psychologically.

A key to microfranchising is to treat people at the bottom of the pyramid as equal partners in every business model. Instead of the poor, it is crucial to see people with unrealized potential. Working in tandem, a microfranchise creates livelihood opportunities essential to sustain an adequate quality of life in developing markets. Ultimately everyone, especially those at the bottom of the pyramid, deserves human dignity. Doing business with the poor increases their dignity and self-respect. As equals, microfranchisor and microfranchisee have a symbiotic relationship where they can earn profit *with* the poor, not *off* the poor. The fundamental goal is to design innovative businesses that build self-confidence, increase self-reliance and increase personal dignity for all.

Case study: BonVi

Fati John—Ghanaian Necessity Entrepreneur—was earning $2 a day when we met in her small village called Zyguri, outside of Tamale, Ghana. She was one of four wives, timid, shy and illiterate. Even after becoming an APED microcredit borrower under a World Vision program, she worked 16 hours a day selling used clothes and yams trying to meet her debt obligations. And she was still unable to send her four children to school.

Becoming a BonVi microfranchisee changed her and her family's life. Paying an initial $85 to start her own business selling health products to surrounding villages, Fati increased her daily profits from $2 to $20. Due to the training, branding and continued support she received from her microfranchisor partner organization, she was set up to succeed regardless of her entrepreneurialism. Now she only works fewer hours a day and is taking charge of her life. She can afford to send her children to school and is more confident and self-reliant. She has even begun paying for herself to take English classes.

Rather than struggling to survive at the poverty level, Fati John is now a profitable business owner with a better future (BonVi Case Study).

Microfranchising Risks

Most start-ups fail. The risks are enormous and the margins for error are very small. These risks are only magnified when trying to start a business in a developing economy. A host of potential problems can cause the business to fail—problems that are almost nonexistent in the developed world: drought, loss of power and electricity for extended periods of time, a crucial delivery road being wiped out, government instability, bribes, and the list goes on. In addition, practitioners must not forget that a microfranchise is like any other business, and to be successful, must identify and address market failures. "Some of the common mistakes that would-be microfranchisors make are the same mistakes that many new businesspeople make" (Christensen, Parsons, and Fairbourne, 2010). These include not spending enough time on proper business development or failing to conduct extensive market analyses to achieve proof of concept. It must be acknowledged that starting a business is always risky and microfranchising is not immune to that risk.

However, microfranchising mitigates many of the risks a typical microenterprise encounters. Not only does microfranchising start with a proven business model so that the guess work is taken out of the equation for the franchisee, but it also provides a network of support to protect against the risks. The franchise network helps indemnify the franchisees against the risks. This allows them to invest and grow their businesses with confidence.

CONCLUSION

As a market-based solution, Microfranchising is successful because it recognizes the necessity entrepreneur for what she is and the position she must operate in at the bottom of the economic pyramid. As David Lehr posits: "Though very different from franchising in its size and scale, microfranchising can be as powerful an economic accelerator in the developing world as franchising currently is in the developed world" (Lehr, 2008, p. 4).

Yet, microfranchising is not meant to be a stand-alone solution for eradicating poverty (Lehr, 2008).[17] As suggested, the necessity entrepreneur greatly benefits from targeted training. Additionally, the model works best when implemented in concert with a microfinance institution. Even with these two powerful models at her disposal, the necessity entrepreneur is not absolved of failure. After all, with any venture, the risks are all too real. Hard work, patience and flexibility are often necessary ingredients. But the benefits are far more attainable. Compared to the conventional start-up, microfranchising poses far fewer risks and offers more immediate benefits for the necessity entrepreneur (Christensen, Parsons, and Fairbourne, 2010).

When done well, microfranchising promises to help alleviate more families from poverty, restore self-reliance and human dignity, and stimulate individual, community, and country economic development.

NOTES

1. See updated statistics detailing "worsening global economy picture" in a subsequent report: "The informal economy in Africa: Promoting transition to formality: Challenges and strategies," 2009. Retrieved on February 19, 2016 from http://www.ilo.org/wcmsp5/groups/public/---ed_emp/---emp_policy/documents/publication/wcms_127814.pdf.
2. Gartner's list of eight traits: personality traits, innovation, organization creation, creating value, profit or non-profit, growth, uniqueness, and the owner-manager (Gartner, 1990).
3. Gerber delineates the roles as follows: defining the business (entrepreneur), hands-on labor (technician), and bridging these two into a cohesive enterprise (manager). Each approaches core fundamentals—work, time, money—in different but necessary means. Overcoming the obstacles to create and sustain a successful business requires the symbiotic contributions of all three. Unfortunately, for the dozens of bakers in the small marketplace, fulfilling the role of all three personalities is far from realistic—to the detriment of the enterprise.
4. "There seems to be a clear relationship between entrepreneurship and achievement motivation" (Robinson et al., 1991, p. 4).
5. "Education has a strong positive influence on entrepreneurship in terms of . . . success" (Robinson, 1994, p. 141).
6. By ascribing education as a key component, we are not suggesting an MBA or even college degree. Even basic skills, such as bookkeeping or inventory-management skills often suffice. These acquired skills, however basic, only improve the Necessity Entrepreneur's chance of success.
7. Charles Hart, former president of HealthStore Foundation, as cited in Flannery, J. (2007, p. 70).
8. "Microfranchising may be especially beneficial in economies where educational options are limited and there is a weak business community. New business ideas and improvements typically emerge as entrepreneurs build on existing businesses and learn from their competitors. In economies where markets are less developed and little variation exists, new idea creation is more difficult" (Lehr, 2008, p. 5).
9. In 2007: Franchised businesses provided 9,125,700 jobs, or 6.2 percent of the US private workforce. There were 828,138 franchised business establishments in the United States. Franchised businesses supplied an annual payroll of $304.4 billion, or 4.2 percent of all private payrolls in the United States. Franchised businesses produced goods and services worth $802.2 billion, or 3.4 percent of private output in the United States. Franchised businesses contributed $468.5 billion to GDP, or 3.9 percent of all private nonfarm GDP in the United States (IFAEF, 2011).
10. As David Lehr describes, the "strength of franchising comes from its reliance on a business model that has been tested and proven to work" (Lehr, 2008, p. 4).
11. "Microfranchsing, still in its infancy, will see much iteration as models and practices are refined" (Lehr, 2008, p. 5).
12. Microenterprises, compared to corporate franchisers, lack the number of data points about their surrounding markets—about what is in demand and what will sell. By becoming a microfranchisee, the entrepreneur gains access to this data (Scheffler, 2010).
13. "Compared with an individual entrepreneur, the franchisor often has better negotiating power with suppliers and is able to reach economies of scale in other areas (such as product design, use and development of new technologies, and supply chain development). The franchisor is usually better equipped to focus on marketing and growth as

well. Furthermore, with the presence of a central franchisor, innovations developed by one franchisee can be quickly implemented throughout an entire network of franchisees" (Lehr, 2008, p. 4).

14. One microfranchising group illustrates the mentoring necessary for success: "We help them indirectly, not actually go out and hold a big [franchise brand] banner that says 'Come to us,' but in terms of mentoring, we try to mentor the franchisee and we discuss with them how to market their outlet. For example there might be a franchisee who is new to the kind of business that we have given to them, so they need to know how to get the clients in the outlet. Maybe they have never done community outreach activities. They need to know how to do a community outreach activity, which actually pulls the community to the outlet. So what we occasionally do is sit down with them if they need a topic of discussion with the community. We come up with the topic. Again it's what they have told us they want to talk to the community about. If they are jittery about it being the first time for community outreach event, then, you know, we would let them know we're coming and go out to them for their community outreach activity and we would give them the support in terms of showing them how to meet other" (Kistruck et al., p. 521).

15. "The goal of social franchising programmes is to use the commercial relationship of a franchise network to benefit provider members, and then to leverage those benefits into socially beneficial services; socially beneficial either because they are of higher quality than services previously available, or because they are less expensive, or because greater availability and awareness of availability leads to greater use of a good service" (Montagu, 2002, p. 123).

16. "Microfranchising also can benefit corporations, providing them an additional option for selling their products and service to base of the pyramid customers" (Lehr, 2008, p. 4).

17. "Certainly no one instrument is a 'cure-all' for the economic and social challenges in developing nations, but the initial signs of the benefits of microfranchising are highly encouraging" (Lehr, 2008, p. 5).

REFERENCES

Aiyar, S. (2007, January 17). Microfranchising: the next big thing. *The Economic Times*. Retrieved on February 19, 2016 from http://articles.economictimes.india-times.com/2007-01-17/news/28423007_1_spectacles-poor-women-rural-areas.

Alon, I., Mitchell, M., and Munoz, M. (2010). Microfranchising in less developed countries. In *Franchising Globally: Innovation, Learning, and Imitation*. Basingstoke: Palgrave Macmillan. Retrieved on February 19, 2016 from www.ebooks-bank.com/book/Franchising%20Globally.pdf#page=174.

Amul Case Study. *Fairbourne Consulting*.

Avon Case Study. *Fairbourne Consulting*.

BonVi Case Study. *Fairbourne Consulting*.

Christensen, L.J., Lehr, D., and Fairbourne, J. (2010). A good business for poor people. *Stanford Social Innovation Review*, 43–49.

Christensen, L.J., Parsons H., and Fairbourne, J. (2010). Building entrepreneurship in subsistence markets: microfranchising as an employment incubator. *Journal of Business Research*, 63(6), 595–601.

Drucker, P.F. (1985). The practice of innovation. *Innovation and Entrepreneurship Practice and Principles*, New York: Harper & Row.

Fairbourne, J. (summer 2006). Microfranchising: a new tool for creating economic self-reliance. *ESR Review*.

Fairbourne, J. and Gibson, S.W. (2007). *The Microfranchise Toolkit: How to Systematize and Replicate a Microfranchise*. Provo, UT: Brigham Young University.

Fairbourne, J., Gibson, S.W., and Dyer, W.G. (2007). *Microfranchising: Creating Wealth at the Bottom of the Pyramid*. Cheltenham, UK and Northampton, MA, USA: Edward Elgar Publishing.

Gartner, W.B. (1990). What are we talking about when we talk about entrepreneurship? *Journal of Business Venturing*, 5, 15–28.

Gerber, M.E. (1985). *The E Myth: Why Most Small Businesses Don't Work and What to Do about It*. New York: Harper Business.

Hart, C. (n.d.) as cited in Flannery, J. (2007). Micro-franchise against malaria: how for-profit clinics are healing and enriching the rural poor in Kenya. *Stanford Social Innovation Review*, 70.

HC Duraclean, www.hcduraclean.com.my/new/Default.php.

International Franchise Association Educational Foundation (IFAEF) (2011). Direct contributions to the US economy. In *Economic Impact of Franchised Businesses*, 3. Retrieved on October 12, 2012 from www.buildingopportunity. com/download/National%20Views.pdf.

International Labor Organization (ILO) (2002). The informal sector in sub-Saharan Africa, Working Paper. Retrieved on February 19, 2016 from www.ilo.org/ wcmsp5/groups/public/---ed_emp/documents/publication/wcms_122204.pdf.

Kistruck, G., Webb, J., Sutter, C., and Ireland, R.D. (May 2011). Microfranchising in base-of-the-pyramid markets: institutional challenges and adaptations to the franchise model. *Entrepreneurship: Theory & Practice*, 35(3), 29, 503–531.

Lal, N. (2005). India: pizza grannies. *Women's Feature Service*, New Delhi, July 11, 2005.

Lehr, D. (2008). *Microfranchising at the Base of the Pyramid*, Working Paper, August 2008. Retrieved on October 25, 2012 from www.acumenfund.org/ uploads/assets/documents/Microfranchising_Working%20Paper_XoYB6sZ5. pdf.

Montagu, D. (2002). Franchising of health services in developing countries. *Health Policy and Planning*, 17(2), 123.

Prahalad, C.K., and Hart, S.L. (2006). The fortune at the bottom of the pyramid. *Strategy+Business*, 26. Retrieved on February 19, 2016 from www.cs.berkeley. edu/brewer/ict4b/Fortune-BoP.pdf.

Robinson, P.B., and Sexton, E.A. (1994). The effect of education and experience on self-employment success. *Journal of Business Venturing*, 9, 141–156.

Robinson, P.B., Huefner, J.C., and Hunt, K.H. (April 1991). Entrepreneurial research on student subjects does not generalize to real world entrepreneurs. *Journal of Small Business Management*, 42–50.

Rosenberg, T. (2012, October 10). The 'Avon Ladies' of Africa, *New York Times*. Retrieved on October 12, 2012 from http://opinionator.blogs.nytimes. com/2012/10/10/the-avon-ladies-of-africa/.

Roxburgh, C., Dorr, N., Leke, A., Tazi-Riffi, A., van Wamelen, A., Lund, S., . . . Zeino-Mahmalat, T. (2010). *Lions on the Move: The Progress and Potential of African Economies*. McKinsey Global Institute. Retrieved on February 19, 2016 from www.mckinsey.com/~/media/mckinsey/dotcom/insights%20and%20pubs/ mgi/research/productivity%20competitiveness%20and%20growth/lions%20 on%20the%20move%20the%20progress%20of%20african%20economies/mgi_ lions_on_the_move_african_economies_full_report.ashx.

Scheffler, K. (2010). From access to finance to access to franchise. Retrieved on February 19, 2016 from www.microfinancegateway.org/gm/document-1.9.46208/Access%20to%20Franchise_August_2010%20v2.pdf.

Sireau, N. (2011). Microfranchising: how social entrepreneurs are building a new road to development. *Greenleaf Publishing*, 3. Retrieved on February 19, 2016 from www.greenleaf-publishing.com/content/pdfs/microfranchising_ch1.pdf?productid=3425 http://solar-aid.org/.

PART IV

The next step

Conclusion

This second volume on Necessity Entrepreneurship highlights the efforts currently being made by policymakers, non-profit founders, and for-profit institutions individually (and independently) to try to find ways to educate and empower necessity entrepreneurs. And, I believe that my words in the introduction of this volume are worth repeating here:

> This volume is dedicated to every single individual who is searching for answers to the complex problem of how to best train necessity entrepreneurs ... you may be a student of social entrepreneurship, international relations, economics, law, or education; or, you may be a professor, policymaker, entrepreneur, or some type of NGO practitioner. Whatever your trade and/or focus is, it is my sincere hope that you will find answers, ideas, and hope as you reading through the in-depth overviews of the programs highlighted in this book.

For the past decade, I have spent my professional career trying to find the best answer to this simple question: *Can we equip the hundreds of millions of necessity entrepreneurs around the world with the necessary tools for their businesses to grow?*

This question has been the impetus behind nearly every professional decision I have made. It influenced where I chose to conduct my internships as an undergraduate college student; it impacted the books that I read; it motivated the countries that I visited; it helped me decide where to conduct my graduate studies; and, it also pushed me to determine where I would live and raise my own family.

Trying to find a "legitimate" answer to this question has afforded me some of the most meaningful experiences in my life. And, by "legitimate" I specifically refer to the ability to provide an answer where policymakers, practitioners, entrepreneurs and investors all can agree will work.

The emotional underpinning of my question stems from a variety of factors. First, it is widely known that small business owners (whether formally or informally registered/operated) are collectively the economic engine that provides employment and propels commerce in nearly every nation. Second, the most basic unit of each society is the family unit. Third, we know that the most nations do not offer the macroeconomic stability to supply high enough paying jobs at the same rate universities and/or vocational schools are producing technicians. The combination of these basic realities ultimately *pushes* hundreds of millions of people into starting and/or operating their own businesses. They become *necessity entrepreneurs*.

In an effort to find satisfactory answers to my question, I first began digesting information from the most vocal—and most confusing—arena possible: government programs. Unfortunately, the more I poked and prodded the more I realized that the vast majority of programs lacked the right people, the right experience, and the right execution. Furthermore, trying to find current data on the various initiatives and projects that had been conducted was next to impossible. And, as is the case with most federally funded programs, I was discontent with how the bureaucracy stifled and negatively impacted the amount of applicable information that ended up in front of the consumer.

While searching the various government programs I also conducted a thorough due-diligence process in the non-governmental arena. Specifically, I investigated every program I could find in the NGO field because they were exactly that: *non-government* programs. From the outset, I had more hope that I would find more suitable answers and ideas about how to best train the necessity entrepreneurs around the world. I thought that I would find better answers because many of them were founded by successful businessmen and businesswomen, who usually had years of experience in building sustainable solutions for their respective markets. I simply assumed that their skills of building a business would directly transfer into training necessity entrepreneurs how to achieve the same results. Unfortunately, the more NGOs I evaluated and worked with the more I realized that most of the founders were more interested in measuring "outputs" (how many people they train) than "outcomes" (what actually happens to the person and their businesses). Moreover, I also learned that running an NGO meant you would spend most of your time using anecdotes to go and raise more money.

After several years of evaluating programs during my doctoral studies, I decided that I would dedicate my dissertation to research and support Stephen W. Gibson's "Academy for Creating Enterprise" (ACE). Until that point in time, ACE was the program that most represented what I thought would help necessity entrepreneurs improve their own lives and build better businesses. Without question, it was the most efficient organization (NGO) at *actually training* necessity entrepreneurs *how* to operate their lives and businesses more effectively. I spent more than six years with ACE and loved *almost* every minute of my work there. However, as with every other NGO, ACE had several limiting factors: (1) they had a restricted demographic (they only teach members of their church), (2) after two years of starting ACE in Mexico (a new country for the program) on a 3.7 acre campus, I had become the Executive Director (aka fundraiser) and that was not a position that allowed me to be with the people I most wanted to be around, (3) scaling ACE's training was nearly impossible, as everything they taught was done in-person, on big campuses, and with volunteers, and (4) I was limited on my upward mobility in the organization.

In addition to the government programs and the NGO programs I had researched, I concurrently scoured the globe in search of answers to my question among the private sector. Surprisingly, I realized that there were very few institutions dedicated to training necessity entrepreneurs around the globe. In part, this was a key finding. The more I searched the more motivated I became because I simply could not find more than a handful of programs in the private sector focusing on training entrepreneurs. In fact, this reality quickly shifted from a pleasant surprise to a concern: if I can't find enough programs to evaluate, how will I write a book about them? Nevertheless, as this volume demonstrates, there are a few key institutions dedicated to training entrepreneurs, as well as nascent programs from world-class researchers and tier one institutions like Harvard University, Stanford University, Brigham Young University, and Texas A&M University.

As I mentioned before, during my days as a doctoral student, I decided to dedicate my life to finding a scalable solution to the chronic, economic phenomenon known as necessity entrepreneurs. What I have discovered during this process is important:

1. Motivation (the reason for starting) is what differentiates a "necessity entrepreneur" from an "opportunity entrepreneur."
2. Necessity entrepreneurs have varying degrees of formal education.
3. Necessity entrepreneurs abound in developing nations and exist in developed nations.
4. In a longitudinal interview I conducted with 7,000 necessity entrepreneurs, only 17 percent have access to formal training for their business operations.
5. Necessity entrepreneurs recognize that they need basic business training so that they can improve their businesses.
6. Necessity entrepreneurs usually have small, family firms.
7. There is an answer to train millions of necessity entrepreneurs around the world.

Index

Academy for Creating Enterprise/
   Called2Serve Foundation (and)
   104–18, 228–9
   25 rules of thumb 113–16
   Academy Mexico 111–13
      campus 111
      current status of 112
      curriculum and handbooks
         112–13
      directorship, leadership and
         teachers 111–12
      history of 111
      teaching models 112
   alumni learning centers – 'chapters'
      117
   Church of Jesus Christ of Latter-day
      Saints 104 *see also subject entry*
   directors and teachers 108
      Fantone, J. 108
      Brewer, J. 111–12, 114, 144–6
      Brewer, R. 111–12
      Blas Pérez, G. 111–12
      Heyn, R. 112
   founders: Gibson, B.M. 104–10,
      113–14
      Gibson, S.W. 104–10, 113–14,
         116–17, 144–6, 203, 207, 228
   history 104
   in the Philippines 104–11
      2010 – institutional innovations
         and growth 111
      directorship and teachers 108
      'discovery learning' methodology
         109
      enrollment 107
      funding 105–6
      instruction and methodology
         108–9
      launch & learn 110
      location 106
      physical facilities 106
      student tuition fee 107–8
      teaching model 106
      teaching models 110–11
      Where There Are No Jobs
         curriculum 109
Acs, Z. 199
active labor market programs
   (ALMPs) 3, 17, 32
Aiyar, S. 204
Alon, I. 207, 214
American Insurance Group (AIG) 59
articles on microfinancing (*Economist
   Times* and *New York Times*) 204–5
Austria 4, 6, 9, 18, 20, 22, 24

Banco Financiero 127–34
   executive overview 127–8
   moving forward 134
   new EFL-enabled product offering
      130–32
      using the EFL score 131
      rolling out EFL 131–2
   partner overview 128–9
      Banco Financiero's ambitions in
         MSME space 129
      changing Peruvian market 128–9
   project overview: new product
      launch 129–30
   results 132–4
Banerjee, B. 57
banks
   Brazilian National Bank of
      Economic Development
      (BNDE) 161, 175 *see also*
      SEBRAE
   Inter-American Development Bank
      121, 124
   twelve large 86–7
   World Bank Group 93
Bates, P. 5
Baumgartner, H.J. 8

Bekker, S. 23
Belgium 4, 6, 9, 18, 20, 22, 24
Bennett, J.R. 24, 32
Benus, J.M. 3
Bharatiya Uiva Shakti Trust (and)
        57–74
    brief history of 58
    business proposals and services
        60–65
        entrepreneur support services 61
        mentoring, mentor model and
            mentors 61–3
    conclusion 72
    funding 63–5
        collateral free loan assistance 63
        internal income 64–5
        micro-equity growth fund 63–4
        partnership income 64
        source of BYST funds 64
    going forward (by) 71–2
        expanding domestic reach 71
        focusing on the 'missing middle'
            72
        going global 71
        increasing mentor pool 71
    the 'guru-sishya tradition' 59
    impact on entrepreneurs: their
        stories 68–70
        Arun Awatade, Iris Polymers
            69–70
        Godavari Satpute: Godavari
            Akashkandil 70
        and impact on the economy 70
        Sharad Tandale, Innovation
            Engineers and Contractors
            68
        Sonam Patil, Shree Group
            Designers and Manufacturers
            68–9
    Indian Corporate Connect: TATA
        Group; Escorts Ltd; Bajaj
        Group 66–7
    inspiration for 58
    institutional partnerships 65–6
        International Labour
            Organization (ILO) 66
        UN Development Program
            (UNDP) 65
        Youth Business International
            (YBI) 65

Lakshmi Venkatesan 57
    multinationals 67
    objectives of 60
    organization structure 60
Blanchflower, D. 19
Block, J. 3
Bögenhold, D. 4, 31
Boone, J. 25
Bosma, N. 3
Brazil 160–61 *see also* banks *and*
    SEBRAE
Brüderl, J. 21, 47
Bruno, G.M. 173
building a scalable training solution
    (and) 144–59
    additional thoughts – review of
        questions 156–9
    concluding remarks 159
    critical thinking: questions and
        answers 155
    financial literacy: questions and
        answers 150–52
    management: questions and answers
        153–4
    motivation: questions and answers
        149–50
    relationship to Brewer, J. *and*
        Gibson, S.W. 144–6
    training: questions and answers
        154–5
BYST *see* Bharatiya Uiva Shakti Trust

Caliendo, M. 3, 5, 8, 40, 47
Card, D. 24
Carling, K. 5, 7
case studies *see also* Banco Financiero
    and JFS
    Germany: Hierarchical
        Organization of Program
        Administration 17
    microfranchising (and)
        Amul 214–15
        branding: Amul Pizza 213
        dignity: BonVi 218
        distribution/infrastructure: Avon
            216–17
        HC Duraclean and benefits of
            microfranchisee training
            210–11
        Living Goods 210

Cause for Hope and Influencer
Institute peer-group models
(Mexico) 191
Christensen, C. 108
Christensen, L.J. 199, 204–5, 214,
219
Church of Jesus Christ of Latter-day
Saints 104 *see also* self-reliance
through self-employment
conclusion 227–9
and important discoveries 229
Corral, A. 3
Costa, N. 162, 175
Cowling, M. 5
Cueto, B. 5
Czech Republic 4, 7, 9, 18, 20, 22, 24,
29

Das Dores Guerreiro, M. 24, 32
Dencker, J.C. 5, 21, 40, 46–7
Désiage, L. 3
Disrupting the Classroom 108
Drucker, P. 196–7
Duggan, C. 8
Duhautois, R. 3
Dyer, W.G. 203

Economic Cooperation and
Development, Organization for 8,
21, 35
economies 6
Employment Outlook 9
Eisenhardt, K.M. 47
Ellegaard, C.E. 21
The E-myth 197
Entrepreneurship Finance Lab (and)
121–43
DiDonna, D.J. 124
the future 142–3
Khwaja, A. 121, 123–4
Klinger, B. 121, 123–4
mission of 121
organization background 121–5
organization structure (services and
relationships) 126–42 *see also*
Banco Financiero *and* JFS
impact 126–7
SMEs and financing gap 121–3
European Union (EU) 30
integration efforts of 6

Structural Funds 7
unemployment in (2013) 39
Europe/European
2020 Strategy 9, 34
Employment Strategy 8
Social Fund 8
Statistical Agency 39

Fairbourne, J. 199, 203–5, 207, 214–15,
219
Fairbourne Consulting: approach to
assessing and engaging new local
market 208–9
financial crises 44–6
of 2008 3, 39
global 46
Great Depression (1930s) 180
Flannery, J. 202, 220
France 3, 6–7, 9, 18, 20, 22–3, 28
and 'Aide au chômeur créant ou
reprenant une enterprise'
(ACCRE) 4, 23
Fritsch, M. 5

G-20 121, 124
Gartner, W.B. 196–7, 199–200, 220
Gerber, M. 197–8
Germany 4–5, 7–9, 17–20, 22, 24, 29
see also case studies
bridging allowance 6–7
government support programs in
Greece (and) 39–49 *see also*
Greece
future research/conclusion 46–8
comparisons across programs and
geographical areas 48
program outcomes 47–8
support mechanisms 47
generic program: OAED 'New
Freelancers' 41
Greek Manpower Employment
Organization (OAED)
40–42
Ministry of Development 43
program differences in the course of
the financial crisis 44–6
business premises 46
financial assistance 45
stronger emphasis on job creation
45

target group of unemployed
   individuals 44
specific categories and criteria 41–3
Support of Entrepreneurship of
   Unemployed Individuals and of
   Start-ups (2012) 43, 46
unemployment rate (2013) 39
Women Entrepreneurship (2013)
   43–4, 46
governmental support programs across
   Europe *see* unemployment to self-
   employment
Greece 4, 7, 9, 18, 20, 24, 39–49
Grubb, D. 21, 35
Gruber, M. 5, 21, 40, 46, 47
Guérin, I. 21
Gustafson, L. 5, 7

Hanhua Guarantee 75–90
   finances 84–6
      budget for last five years 84
      client relations 85
      expenses 85
      funding 84–5
   impact of 76
   major changes/challenges for 76
   mission/vision 75–6
   organization future 87–8
      challenges for 87–8
      plan for 87
   organization relationships 85–7
      corporate 86–7
      government 85
   organization services 79–84
      basic information for clients
         80–81
      business training 82–4
      debt (loans) 79
      equity (venture capital) 82
      interest 82
      materials 81–2
   organization structure 77–9
      branches 79
      leadership 77
      organization chart 77
      organizational service chart
         77–9
   program description 75
   program goals 76
Harpaz, J. 161

Harrison, L. 109
Hart, C. 202 *see also* Flannery, J.
Hart, S.L. 216
Heckl, E. 21
Heckman, J. 35
Horn, M. 108
Hungary 5

India(n) *see also* Bharatiya Yuva
   Shakti Trust
   Confederation of Indian Industry
      (CII) 58
   Foreign Contribution Regulation
      (Act) FCRA 67
   Income Tax Act 67
   International Finance Corporation
      (IFC) 63, 93, 121
Ireland, R.D. 212–13, 221
Isusi, I. 3

Jakobsen, L. 21
JFS 134–42
   characteristics of market-based
      approach to financial inclusion
      137–8
   moving forward 141–2
   partner overview 134–7
      as emerging leader in Indian
         microfinance 136–7
      graduating group customers to
         individual loans 136
      understanding Indian
         microfinance market 134–6
   project overview 138–9
      integrating EFL 138
      rolling out EFL 139
   results: EFL's predictive power
      139–41
Johnson, C. 108
Journal of Business Venturing 196

Kellard, K. 5, 19, 21, 34
Kentikelenis, A. 47
Kistruck, G. 212–13, 221
Kluve, J. 24, 32, 35
Kritikos, A. 3, 40, 47
Künn, S. 5, 40, 47

Lal, N. 213
Lalonde, R. 35

Lehr, D. 199–200, 203–5, 209, 212, 216, 219–21
López, M.R. 97, 99

Marich, M. 57, 66
Martin, J. 21, 35
Martinho, L.C. 161
Mataresio, L. 164
Mato, J. 5
Meager, N. 4–5
Metcalf, H. 8
microfranchising (and) 195–223
  benefits of 214–15 *see also* case
    studies
  branding 211–13 *see also* case studies
  conclusion 219–20
  defined 202–5
  dignity 217–18 *see also* case studies
  distribution and infrastructure
    215–17 *see also* case studies
  the entrepreneurial burden 205
  the fallacy of the entrepreneur 196–7
  hiring 211
  implementation 205–7
  microfinance and its limits 200–201
  the necessity entrepreneur 197–200
    operating in an informal economy
      198–200
  risks 218–19
  training, mentoring and business
    development 209–11 *see also*
    case studies
  understanding the market 207–9
Middleton, S. 5, 19, 21, 34
Montagu, D. 221

Narasimhan, T.E. 57
Netherlands 4, 6, 9, 18, 20, 23–4
Nolan, A. 5, 21, 24

O'Leary, C.J. 5
Oswald, A.J. 19

Parker, S.C. 5
Parsons, H. 205, 214, 219
Pecher, I. 21
Pete Suazo Business Center (PBSC)
  (and) 50–54
  Bennett, US Senator R. 51–2
  current status of 54

founders and history 50–51
  Gonzalez, Gladys 50–51
  Heyn, R. 52
  institutional financing/funding 52
  mentoring 53
  micro-loans 53–4
  minority focus 51
  Mundo Hispano newspaper 50
  personal finance training/workshops
    52–3
  Sheehan, T. 51, 53
  Suazo, P. 50–51
  technology assistance 53
  Utah Microenterprise Loan Fund 50
Pfeiffer, F. 8
Poland 4, 5, 7, 9, 18, 20, 29
Prahalad, C.K. 216
Preisendörfer, P. 21, 47
Premkumar, S. 64
Prospera: microenterprise among
  necessity entrepreneurs (and)
  91–103
  collaboration: Bysan and Prospera
    95–9
  del Refugio López, M. 96–9
  driver of Prospera and growth of
    microenterprises in Mexico
    102–3
  early stage 'pivots' 94–5
  founder: Enrigue, G. 92–3, 103
  further improving Mexican
    microenterprise (through)
    100–102
  Be Responsible and Prosper 100
  customer development stages –
    get, keep and grow 100–101
  distribution channels 101–2
  partnerships for sales 102
  product development 101
  'share and prosper' 102
  the future 103
  León, A. 96–9
  mission and innovation potential
    of 91
  mission and vision 93–4
  programs
    Be Responsible and Prosper 94–5,
      100
    Learn and Prosper 93–5, 100
    Save and Prosper 93–4

Share and Prosper 94–5, 102
Talentos responsables (responsible
    talents) 95–6
social change model 95, 103
as social enterprise in urban areas
    91–2

Rai, N. 57, 64
Rajendram, D. 57
Redor, D. 3
Reize, F. 8
research on
    influence of nonfinancial business
        support services 21
    nature and processes of firm
        creation 4–5
Robinson, P.B. 196, 198, 200, 220
Robson, P.J.A. 24, 32
Rodríguez-Planas, N. 5
Rosenberg, T. 204–5, 210
Roxburgh, C. 216

Sandner, P. 3
Santos, R.C. 160
Saraf, N. 57
Say, J.-B. 196
Scandinavia 22
Scheffler, K. 220
Schmidt, C.M. 24, 32, 35
Schoonhoven, C.B. 47
Schumpeter, J. 196
Schütz, G. 24, 32
SEBRAE (and) 160–78 *see also*
    banks
    Brazil 160–61
    challenges and corruption 162, 164
    goals 162–4
    organization fitness 172–3
    organization future 176
    organization relationships 173–6
        federal government 173–5
        financial institutions 175–6
    organization services 165–72
        access to financial services 172
        business consulting 170–71
        educational training categories
            and classes 167–70
        promotion and access to markets
            172
        technical information 171–2

organization structure: leadership
    and branches 164–5
release of 'General Law' 160–61
success by the numbers 162
self-employment support programs,
    evolution of 4–9
    continued refinement and recent
        developments of policy schemes
        7–9
    early policy-development initiatives
        6
    universal adoption and expansion of
        policy 6–7
self-employment support programs,
    overview of current 9–26
    centralized vs decentralized structure
        17
    governmental vs privatized provision
        of support 24
    grants vs loans 20
    influence of subjective assessments
        19
    key program dimensions – summary
        25–6
    mandatory vs voluntary
        participation 22–4
    nonfinancial business support
        services 21
    practices related to provision of
        financial support 19–20
    program eligibility and admission
        criteria 18
    program structure 17
    provision of fallback solution 20
    single payment vs recurring
        payments 20
    specific vs general programs 17–18
    types of business support service
        21–2
    viability-check of new business
        concepts 18–19
self-employment system overview
    182–91
    assessment, measurement and
        choosing 'my path' 184–6
    financing and the Four Rights
        190–91
    group process: scale vehicle for
        training, mentoring and
        accountability 186–9

recruiting and intake 183–4
self-reliance through self-employment:
    Church of Jesus Christ of Latter-
    day Saints (and) 179–94
another step forward 193–4
a brief history of self-reliance
    179–81
design principles and constraints
    181–2
PEF Self-Reliance Services 181–2,
    192–3
from pilot projects to global rollout
    191–3
self-employment system overview
    182–91 *see also subject entry*
Seth, M. 64
Shah, S.K. 5, 21, 40, 46–7
Shane, S. 19, 21
Sheikh, S. 21–2
Sireau, N. 214
Slovakia 22
SMART Campaign, Accion
    International 191
Smith, J. 35
Souza, A.A. 160
Spain 4–5, 9, 18, 20
and Unemployment Capitalization
    Benefit 6
Staber, U. 4, 31
Stack, J. 3
Steiber, N. 21
Storey, D. 5, 8
Sutter, C. 212–13, 221
Sweden 3–5, 7, 9, 18, 20, 23
Switzerland 4, 6, 9, 18–20, 24

Tata, J.R.D. 72
Thomas, K.-G. 24, 32
Trierweiller, A.C. 161

unemployment to self-employment
    (and) 3–38 *see also* government
    support programs in Greece
conclusion, outlook and future
    research 31–4
contrasting policy approaches 26–31
    1. low strictness of eligibility/
        medium–high levels of
        financial support 28–9
    2. high strictness of eligibility/
        high level of financial
        support 29
    3. low level of financial support
        29–30
    and key insights 30–31
introduction to 3–4
self-employment support
    programs, evolution of *see
    subject entry*
self-employment support programs,
    overview of current *see subject
    entry*
United Kingdom (UK)/Great Britain
    4–5, 9, 20, 24, 63
'business startup scheme in (1983)
    6
Business Support Simplification
    Programme (BSSP, 2009) 17
Diageo 67
revision of self-employment support
    programs (1990s) 8
Start-up Loans program (2012) 8
Youth Business International, UK
    58, 65
United Nations Development Program
    (UNDP) 65

Vallat, D. 21
Van Es, F. 21
van Ours, J.C. 35
Van Vuuren, D.J. 21
Venkatesan, L. 64
Veverková, S. 7
Vieira, L.A.C. 173

Wagner, M. 3
Webb, J. 212–13, 221
Weber, A. 24
Weise, A.D. 161
Wifuproject (and) 99
    Delavergne, S. 99
    Giraud, M. 99
    Sierakowski, R. 99
Wössmann, L. 24, 32

Yunus, M. 157, 200

Ziegler, R. 47